Architecture and Artifacts of the Pennsylvania Germans

Architecture and Artifacts of the Pennsylvania Germans

Constructing Identity in Early America

CYNTHIA G. FALK

The Pennsylvania State University Press
University Park, Pennsylvania

Library of Congress Cataloging-in-Publication Data

Falk, Cynthia G.
     Architecture and artifacts of the Pennsylvania Germans :
     constructing identity in early America / Cynthia G. Falk.
     p.   cm. — (Publications of the Pennsylvania German
     Society ; v. 42. Pennsylvania German history and culture
     series ; no. 9)
Includes bibliographical references and index.
ISBN 978-0-271-03338-9 (cloth : alk. paper)
1. German Americans—Pennsylvania—Ethnic identity.
2. German Americans—Pennsylvania—History.
3. German Americans—Dwellings—Pennsylvania.
4. Architecture, German—Pennsylvania—History.
5. Material culture—Pennsylvania—History.
I. Title.

F160.G3F35 2008
974.8'00431—dc22
2007038385

Printed in China by Everbest Printing Co. through Four Colour
Imports, Louisville, KY
Published by The Pennsylvania State University Press,
University Park, PA 16802-1003

Designed by StepUp Communications Inc.

The Pennsylvania State University Press is a member of the
Association of American University Presses.

It is the policy of The Pennsylvania State University Press to
use acid-free paper. Publications on uncoated stock satisfy
the minimum requirements of American National Standard for
Information Sciences—Permanence of Paper for Printed Library
Material, ANSI Z39.48—1992.

For Elizabeth and Isaac

Contents

Illustrations

Acknowledgments

The study of material culture is seldom a solitary endeavor. This book would not have been possible without the generosity of numerous people who allowed me to study their homes or provided access to the buildings and collections under their care. I am especially indebted to David Barquist at the Philadelphia Museum of Art; Wendy Cooper and Charles Hummel at Winterthur Museum; Wayne Eichfeld at Old Zion Church, Brickerville; Eugene Hoffman at Fort Zeller; Ken and Hope LeVan, formerly at Oley Forge Mansion; Morgan McMillan and Kim Praria at the Peter Wentz Farmstead; Rob Reynolds at the Hottenstein house; Michael Showalter at Ephrata Cloister; Mark Turdo at the Moravian Historical Society; and Jim Stokes, who shared his knowledge of historic buildings in Conestoga Township, Lancaster County.

I am grateful to Bernie Herman, Kjirsten Gustavson, Eric Kernfeld, Gabrielle Lanier, Sally McMurry, and Diane Wenger, who joined me in fieldwork as I examined many of the buildings that inform this project. Others, including Ed Chappell, Alan Keyser, Carl Lounsbury, Lisa Minardi, and Abigail Wenger, were willing to share their own field experiences in the form of observations, notes, drawings, and photographs. I would also like to thank all those who facilitated long-distance archival research, including Joel Alderfer at the Menonite Heritage Center; Josh Blay at the Berks County Historical Society; Rev. Carl Heinrich A. Schmutzler at Old/Alt Zion, Philadelphia; Rüdiger Kröger at the Moravian Archives, Herrnhut; Susan Newton, Jeanne Solensky, Heather Clewell, and Emily Guthrie at Winterthur; Paul Peucker at the Moravian Archives, Bethlehem; Becky Preiss and Lila Fourhman-Shaull at the York County Heritage Trust; Tom Ryan and Barry Rauhauser at the Lancaster County Historical Society; and Coxey Toogood at Independence National Historical Park.

The beginnings of this project can be traced to my years as a student in the Winterthur Program in Early American Culture and the American Civilization Program at the University of Delaware. Financial support during this research period was generously provided by a Louis F. McNeil Fellowship, a Winterthur Research Fellowship, and a McNeil Dissertation Fellowship, all of which allowed unparalleled access to knowledgeable staff and exemplary library, manuscript, and object collections at Winterthur Museum. A University Competitive Fellowship from the University of Delaware afforded me valuable time to start processing and writing about the information I had collected during a period of many personal transitions.

My time at the University of Delaware was filled with great intellectual support as well. I am most grateful to Bernard Herman, the director of both my master's thesis and my doctoral dissertation, for sticking with me as this project took shape. Bernie and fellow dissertation committee members Lu Ann De Cunzo, Ritchie Garrison, and Christine Heyrman often worked with a product and on a timeline that suited me better than it did them. I thank them for the guidance, insight, and great flexibility they provided. Many of the ideas in this book were influenced and improved by this group of dedicated mentors.

Fellow students at the University of Delaware offered a safe forum for testing new ideas. I began the American Civilization Program at Delaware with one other student, Diane Wenger. Diane, who has helped this project along by doing everything from arranging tours of buildings to taking photographs and reading chapters, has proved an ideal classmate and colleague. A cross-disciplinary group of students, including Anna Andrzejewski, Pat Keller, Ann Kirschner, Louis Nelson, and Tom Ryan, provided a regular outlet for chapter drafts and much-needed camaraderie during the research and writing process. I can only hope that I contributed to their projects as much as they did to mine.

As this project was transformed from dissertation to book, two scholarly meetings helped me rethink ideas and refocus my energies. The first was the 2004 annual meeting of the Vernacular Architecture Forum in Harrisburg, Pennsylvania. This conference, which included two days of tours of the Pennsylvania German landscape, provided the opportunity to visit or revisit some of the buildings discussed in this work and to confer with others about their interpretation. A second gathering occurred at Winterthur Museum in the spring of 2006. Funding from a National Endowment for the Humanities consultation grant brought together a group of scholars to facilitate initial planning for an exhibit on Pennsylvania furniture. The ensuing discussion raised many issues about the study and public presentation of ethnic and regional material culture that helped further refine my thoughts at a critical point in the revision process.

My interpretation of Pennsylvania German material culture has additionally been strengthened by those at the Pennsylvania German Society and Penn State Press who read my work. The insight of numerous readers approaching the material from a variety of vantage points proved exceptionally instructive. I am especially grateful to the anonymous readers at the Pennsylvania German Society and to Simon Bronner, editor of the Pennsylvania German History and Culture series, who provided detailed comments on multiple drafts of the manuscript. As a first-time author, I benefited greatly from Simon's guidance and gentle reminders, which ensured that the publication process went smoothly.

Also to be thanked are all those affiliated with the Cooperstown Graduate Program, a two-year museum studies master's program cosponsored by the State University of New York College at Oneonta and the New York State Historical Association, where I have made my academic home since leaving the University of Delaware. I am grateful to the students, faculty, and staff who provided intellectual and moral support during the final stages of writing and revision. I am especially indebted to JoAnn Van Vranken for facilitating interlibrary loan and research requests, to Rosemary Craig, Danelle Feddes, Brian Richards, Sara Schuyler, Peter Severud, Rebecca Slaughter, and Mark Turdo for reading portions of my manuscript, and to my chair, Gretchen Sorin, and colleague Chris Sterba for their encouragement and assistance. It should also be noted that monies from a State of New York/United University Professions Joint Labor-Management Individual Development Award, in addition to funds from the Pennsylvania German Society, helped secure the images from museum and archival collections that illustrate this work. Emily Taylor generously helped make one particularly problematic picture handsomely serviceable.

I would be remiss if I did not conclude by recognizing the role my family has played as I have researched and written this book. My parents, Jim and Betty Layton, have done everything from translating German date stones to photographing buildings, proofreading text, and providing a physically and emotionally comfortable place to stay during numerous research trips to Pennsylvania and Delaware. My brother, Tim Layton, not only taught me to use AutoCAD but also encouraged me to think further about landscape as an important element of material culture. My husband's sister, Derry Palmer, and her family, who conveniently live in Nazareth, were always willing to babysit or provide a meal when I traveled their way to do research or take pictures. My husband, Glenn, and our children have agreed to begin or end countless trips to Pennsylvania visiting buildings or museums or archives. It is safe to say that without the support of all these family members, this project would never have been completed.

This book is dedicated to my daughter and son, Elizabeth and Isaac. Although their contributions are not as tangible as those of some others, they are perhaps the most important. Not even born when I began working on this project, both have tolerated mom's being at the computer or in the library or off researching more often than not. As I balance my own identities as spouse, parent, author, and teacher, it is often they, and their father, who have not received the attention they should. Perhaps now, with this book complete, I will be able to spend a little more time studying my own house and its occupants rather than the buildings and people of long ago.

Introduction

In the late 1790s, while touring the Pennsylvania countryside, a French duke stopped to rest at Clements's Tavern on the border between Montgomery and Bucks counties, not far from Philadelphia (fig. 1). According to the duke's published narrative of his journey, the tavern keeper, Clements, was "of Dutch descent," his grandfather having left Holland to start a new life in America many years earlier. During the course of the duke's visit, Clements displayed what appeared to his aristocratic guest to be nothing more than an old andiron. To its owner, however, the fireplace implement was considerably more valuable than the antique metal from which it was made. The duke's host explained that the andiron had belonged to his great-grandfather and was brought by his grandfather to the New World. As the duke informed his readers, "Clements sees in this old piece of furniture, which is displayed in his kitchen, a family monument, which makes him trace two hundred years of his genealogy."[1]

Two conclusions can be drawn from the duke's brief account of his visit with Clements. The first is that people in the eighteenth century, as today, invested material goods with meaning. Objects served as symbols of otherwise intangible ideas, as the old andiron did of Clements's heritage.[2] The second is that the meaning attached to material culture was, and is, not fixed.[3] The traveling aristocrat learned about the personal symbolism of the andiron by talking with his host, discovering that the warmth of the burning logs it once held was exceeded by years of warm memories held by Clements. Without that oral history, the duke would have seen the andiron as simply an old but useful household item. Today, if Clements's andiron were to survive in a public or private collection, it would likely be given yet another interpretation, endowed with symbolism as an artifact of past technologies and lifestyles.

This project examines the meanings ascribed to buildings and belongings in late eighteenth-century Pennsylvania. It looks at how objects served as expressions of identity for one component of the population, namely, German immigrants and their descendants. I use the term "Pennsylvania German" to describe members of this group, although it is not one with which they or their contemporaries would have been familiar. And I use it to refer to immigrants to the colony or Commonwealth of Pennsylvania from the many German-speaking principalities of central Europe—who, in addition to the more representative Rhinelanders, included among their number Swiss, Bohemians, Alsatians, French Huguenots, and others—and their descendants who remained in the state.[4] Focusing on this diverse group of early Americans, I examine the meaning of material culture both to those who created and used it and to the outsiders who observed them doing so.

In recent years, historians of early America have increasingly recognized the role objects played in self-definition in the years leading up to and immediately following the American Revolution. Before the Revolutionary War, T. H. Breen argues, the consumption of British imported goods—including paper and books, ceramic and pewter table and tea ware, and cloth for adorning beds, tables, and bodies—united American colonists and helped them define themselves in opposition to England. In the 1760s and 1770s, as Americans chose whether or not to boycott British manufactures, their consumer choices expressed their political views.[5] Historian Laurel Thatcher Ulrich, focusing on domestically produced rather than imported goods, finds that objects from spinning wheels to decorative embroideries not only served to convey political meaning but also helped identify their makers and users according to their gender, wealth, education, skill level, cultural heritage, religious affiliation, and virtue.[6] In the formative years of the United States, as these authors make clear, material culture, through its ability to foster personal identity, played a crucial role in bringing people together as well as in tearing them apart. It helped create an American identity, yet it also sustained divisions within the population.

Pennsylvania, with its ethnically and religiously diverse inhabitants, offers an ideal testing ground for determining the role of objects in creating affiliations and disaffiliations in late eighteenth-century America. Prior to 1776, more than eighty thousand men, women, and children from the German-speaking principalities of central Europe arrived in the city of Philadelphia. Many, but certainly not all, had come from the region surrounding the Rhine River and its tributaries. They left Europe as a result of population growth,

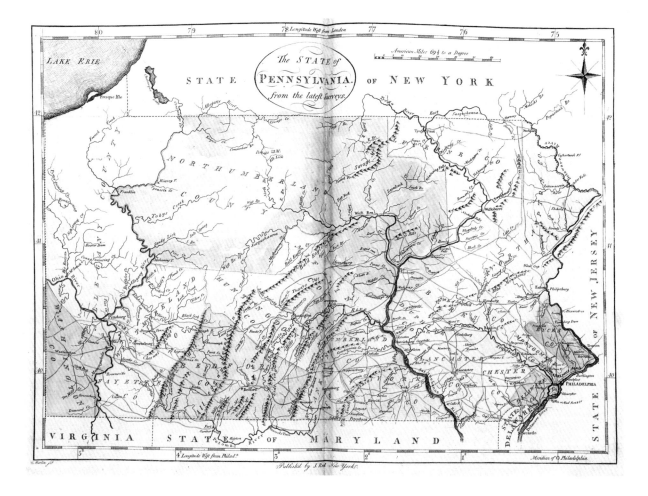

natural disasters, wars, inheritance practices, high taxes, debt, and, occasionally, religious intolerance. During the early colonial period, the majority of the migrants traveled in family groups; single men became a larger percentage of the immigrant group as the century progressed. Although the European occupation of immigrants was seldom recorded, limited data indicate that in the early eighteenth century, fewer than two-thirds of the migrants were farmers, and that tradesmen were becoming increasingly common among immigrants by the end of the century. The proportion of professionals—merchants, clerks, accountants, and doctors—was also on the rise. Although the economic resources of immigrants varied from substantial to extremely meager, in the limited cases where statistical analysis is available, it is clear that the greatest proportion of immigrants had limited financial resources. Literacy rates among male immigrants, however, measured by the ability to sign one's name, were high by eighteenth-century standards, ranging from 60 percent in the 1730s to almost 100 percent by the time of the American Revolution.[7]

Fig. 1 **"The State of Pennsylvania from the Latest Surveys,"** *The American Atlas* (New York: John Reid, 1796), plate 12. This late eighteenth-century map of Pennsylvania illustrates the physical, political, and cultural geography of the commonwealth at the time of the duke's visit with Clements. Montgomery and Bucks counties are located between the Delaware and Schuylkill rivers in the lower-right corner. Other place-names shown on the map will be referenced throughout this work.

German immigrants and their descendants accounted for 50 to 60 percent of Pennsylvania's population in 1760. By the time of the first U.S. census in 1790, roughly a third of the state's population consisted of people of German ancestry. In some counties, such as Lancaster County, they accounted for almost three-quarters of the population. Although some of the immigrants who arrived in Philadelphia opted to settle outside the Commonwealth of Pennsylvania, many stayed. In the early eighteenth century it was common for immigrants to acquire land outside the city, and by 1760 Germans had settled in large numbers in an area extending from present-day Northampton County to York County. Yet, as the century progressed, more immigrants stayed in urban centers, including not only Philadelphia but also Lancaster, York, and Reading. Complicating individual decisions about where to settle was the fact that many German immigrants arrived in Philadelphia as redemptioners who were unable to pay their own passage from Europe. Although the cost of the voyage could be covered by family members or acquaintances after arrival, as many as half of German immigrants were forced into periods of indentured servitude to pay for their travel and had to move to a location determined by their new employer. Regardless of this fact, at the close of the eighteenth century people of German descent tended to live near other Germans, especially in the countryside, and a distinct German region was widely recognized in the counties west of the city of Philadelphia.[8]

Not surprisingly, the areas with the heaviest concentration of German settlement attracted the attention of curious outsiders seeking to discover what made the Germans—the largest group of eighteenth-century non-British European settlers in the colonies that would become the United States—distinct socially, politically, and materially. The region still attracts the attention of outsiders today. Yet as people have begun to study and write about Pennsylvania's ethnic material culture, they have perceived a discrepancy between the documentary evidence provided by period commentators, particularly concerning Pennsylvania German distinctiveness, and the information encoded in actual objects.[9] Reading an eighteenth-century source such as Benjamin Rush's "An Account of the Manners of the German Inhabitants of Pennsylvania," it is difficult not to focus on the reported differences between the British and German residents of the commonwealth.[10] An examination of surviving objects from the period clearly reveals, however, that the goods produced and used by members of the two groups were not always so distinct. In an attempt to explain the divergence, students of material cultures have tended to develop interpretations emphasizing the assimilation of German immigrants and their descendants to English ways.[11]

This work offers a different perspective. Rather than treat ethnic heritage as the primary attribute affecting a person's material possessions, I treat it as one of several factors that influenced the goods a person chose for him- or herself. In addition to ethnicity, characteristics such as social and economic status, religious affiliation, age, gender, familial status, occupation, place of residency, and length of settlement all had the potential to affect an individual's choices about his or her possessions and physical surroundings. In this book, I look specifically at three attributes—ethnicity and European heritage, social and economic status, and religious affiliation and personal piety—to understand the influences on Pennsylvania German material culture. My comparison of the effect of these three personal characteristics suggests that the emphasis on the assimilation of German immigrants and their descendants has been overstated. In the eighteenth century, the material culture of individual Pennsylvania Germans was more overtly influenced by status than by ethnic identity. Grand houses and the activities that went on inside them were understood as tangible manifestations of "improvement," a term that held financial, social, and even moral connotations. In interpreting material cultural as an expression of self, it was this sense of improvement, closely tied to a person's rank rather than ethnic background, that played the prominent role.

Throughout this book, I consider material culture as a physical manifestation of personal identity, that is, as a means of defining self.[12] As a result, I address how people of German descent used objects to express outwardly various aspects of their existence or experience. I do this by using the objects themselves as evidence. Throughout my work, material culture is defined broadly to include anything made, modified, or used by human beings. Much of my focus is on buildings, but I make every effort to analyze structures in their context by including information on both their site and the items found inside them. I treat buildings, particularly houses, as the physical settings where people lived their lives and as tangible evidence of how they wanted to portray themselves. As a result, my emphasis is on how spaces were used for work, sustenance, display, leisure, and other activities. While the artifacts themselves remain mute, the patterns of their use and disuse provide clues to the meaning eighteenth-century people of German descent bestowed on their physical surroundings.

Most of the buildings and eighteenth-century household objects included in this study are well known. Some former houses are now historic sites owned and operated by private nonprofit groups, which make them accessible to the public. Other buildings are held publicly by the National Park Service, the Pennsylvania Historical and Museum Commission, or local municipalities. Many of them are listed on the National Register of Historic Places, either individually or as part of districts, and a few, most notably the religious structures discussed in Chapter 4, have been designated National Historic Landmarks. Interior elements from three buildings, the David and Caterina Hottenstein house, the George and Magdalena Elizabeth Hehn house (better known as the later residence of Captain Conrad Kershner), and the George and Maria Caterina Müller house (the House of the Miller at Millbach), have been relocated to Winterthur Museum and the Philadelphia Museum of Art. In addition to housing the Hottenstein, Hehn, and Müller architectural interiors, those museums are responsible for two of the most extensive Pennsylvania German collections in existence and have produced major publications on the artifacts they hold. Objects examined in this study include those in the collections of Winterthur and the Philadelphia Museum of Art, as well as several other institutions, such as the Hershey Museum, the Moravian Historical Society, and the American Folk Art Museum. Yet despite their inclusion in publicly accessible collections, their meaning to their eighteenth-century makers, owners, and users is not completely understood. This work provides additional insight into how these artifacts of the past should be interpreted.

In studying how German immigrants and their descendants used objects to define themselves in relation to those around them, accounts of the decision-making process regarding the building of a house, the purchase of furnishings, the choice of color schemes, and the preparation of meals would be most helpful. Unfortunately, people rarely take time to record their feelings about their personal property in a medium that will survive for later generations. When studying the material culture of the not-so-distant past, much information can be uncovered through observation and interviews with living subjects. Although we do not have access to this kind of evidence for the material culture of eighteenth-century America, certain documents of the period can begin to provide similarly ethnographic information.

Some of the most enlightening written sources are those directly connected to the people and objects in question. Probate inventories, or lists of movable property and money owed a decedent at the time of death, and wills provide important insight into the monetary value and, occasionally, the cultural significance of some of the items included in this study. Other important sources of information are the date stones that were used to label the buildings themselves. Particularly on grand dwellings erected by Pennsylvania Germans in the late eighteenth century, original owners often included text in addition to the date of construction on the tablet that served to identify a house—and its inhabitants—to the outside world.

Sometimes date stones included scriptural or other spiritual passages written in the German language in Fraktur, or the "broken lettering" of German script, as opposed to English roman characters, thus providing evidence of both ethnic background and religious conviction. The names of the original owners also appeared regularly. The use of German lettering, German spelling, and German grammar was common. It was also customary to include the names of both husband and wife. The date stones indicate that houses were shared architectural spaces during this period, despite a legal structure

that presupposed male ownership during marriage and later cultural conventions that would relegate women to a separate sphere defined largely by
the home.[13] In the late eighteenth century, both Pennsylvania German men
and women worked to fashion their houses, and in many cases both of their
names were prominently displayed on the exterior of the building. This convention does not deny the patriarchal nature of eighteenth-century society or
suggest that men and women had similar roles during the period but rather
demonstrates that most residences were neither exclusively male nor exclusively female places. As a result, when I refer to a house, I have made every
effort to include the name of both the male and female householder. Unfortunately, the latter, if it was not emblazoned on a date stone, has often not been
preserved in other types of sources either.

Apart from probate records and the date stones affixed to houses, the
most accessible written sources about the meaning of the material culture
of eighteenth-century Pennsylvanians were penned by outsiders, especially
European visitors. In a few cases, like that of Clements and the duke, authors
told their readers what an object meant to its male owner. More often, travelers and other observers interpreted goods from their own standpoint. As they
toured an area, they pointed out buildings they felt were of particularly high or
low quality. If they entered a house or tavern, they made notes about furnishings, food, and even articles of clothing that impressed them with their cost,
condition, or another distinguishing attribute. The outsiders who observed
the material landscapes created by Pennsylvanians of German descent drew
conclusions about members of the group based on assessments of their personal belongings. Because the definition of "others" serves as an important
corollary to self-definition, I examine their conclusions here as well.[14]

There are clearly distinctions to be made between accounts produced
by Pennsylvania Germans themselves and those of outsiders. In many cases,
the written word cannot be taken at face value, and its meaning must be
carefully assessed in the light of contemporary polemics. By thoughtfully
studying documentary materials, however, we can achieve a more accurate
interpretation of what these artifacts meant to eighteenth-century Pennsylvania Germans than if we simply postulated what they might have meant
based on modern concepts about how people must have understood the late
eighteenth-century material landscape.[15]

While evidence produced by Pennsylvania Germans and outsiders served
different purposes and often reached radically different conclusions, both
types of sources demonstrate the widespread belief that an individual's ethnic
background, social and economic status, and religious beliefs could all be
encoded in his or her possessions. This work analyzes each of these three
categories to ascertain what kinds of objects were associated with people
of German heritage of various ranks and affiliated with different religious

denominations. It reevaluates the importance of ethnic divisions in late eighteenth-century Pennsylvania and finds that social and economic status, which during the period was often tied to issues of virtue and religiosity, was a paramount concern when it came to choosing a house and household furnishings. While ethnic attributes were often a noticeable part of Pennsylvania German dwellings, they were usually overshadowed in observers' minds by characteristics related to the rank of the buildings' occupants.

The first chapter of this book reviews the scholarship on Pennsylvania German material culture, particularly Pennsylvania German domestic architecture, of the eighteenth century. It examines the general tenor of late eighteenth-century written sources concerning the cultural distinctiveness of the German population in Pennsylvania and demonstrates how scholars working in more recent times adopted similar themes. In assessing the current state of the field of Pennsylvania German material culture studies, this chapter recognizes the pioneering work of twentieth-century fieldworkers who began the process of documenting artifacts of the past as well as the efforts of those who have more recently begun to expand our understanding of the intellectual complexity of the objects associated with Pennsylvanians of German descent.

In the second chapter I begin the process of unraveling the perceived relationship between ethnicity and material culture by examining the eighteenth-century accounts of outsiders. Using documentary sources, I describe just what period authors considered "German" and why they came to the conclusions they did. I argue that most authors' comments had more to do with ongoing debates about the proper ordering of American society than with issues of ethnic distinctiveness. In the postrevolutionary period, as conflicting opinions developed about the relative merits of commerce versus agriculture and aristocracy versus democracy, Pennsylvania Germans as a group became an important illustration. On the basis of their material culture, authors on both sides of the controversy depicted the Pennsylvania Germans as industrious, but often thrifty and uninformed, farmers. Like their contemporaries who made generalized, value-laden statements about Native Americans and people of African descent, the authors who described the Pennsylvania Germans created a stereotype that served their own purposes but was not necessarily accurate.[16] Their comments, which at best held true for a small proportion of Pennsylvania's German population, were intended to be statements about the virtue of farmers generally, regardless of ethnic background. Rather than seeking to reflect accurately the reality of a very diverse national group, these authors were trying to create a serviceable example through their caricatures of Pennsylvania's German population.

The third and fourth chapters of this work move from an analysis of outsiders' constructions of Pennsylvania German identity to an account of how Pennsylvanians of German descent represented themselves. Chapter 3 shifts the terms of the discussion from the issue of ethnic identity to the issue of identity based on social and economic status. It focuses on how individual Pennsylvania Germans used the built environment to define themselves. This chapter supplements information provided by travelers and other late eighteenth-century authors with physical and documentary evidence about actual Pennsylvania German objects. It analyzes Pennsylvania German houses, which European travelers often criticized in an attempt to denigrate American farmers, within the context of late eighteenth-century regional domestic architecture.

While some features of Pennsylvania German dwellings from this period served as manifestations of ethnic background, the buildings were simultaneously part of a much larger process that linked personal and financial improvement with the physical improvement of property. Authors of the period associated certain kinds of "good" and "notable" houses with men and women of elevated social and economic standing. Although scholars have detailed how the construction of such buildings by affluent people of British descent corresponded with the rise of gentility and refinement, little attention has been paid to differences based on rank among Pennsylvania Germans.[17] In this chapter, I demonstrate that genteel forms, such as so-called Georgian houses, crossed ethnic boundaries. They were primarily understood as expressions of status and were used by Pennsylvanians from various national groups. They allowed elite Pennsylvania Germans, for example, to forge unions with non-Germans of similar status and simultaneously distance themselves from subordinates of the same ethnic background.

Chapter 4 continues to explore the topic of Pennsylvania German self-representation by looking at the intersections between religious belief and material culture. It examines how religious ideals concerning the appropriateness of certain belongings and behaviors worked to both unite and divide Pennsylvania Germans. Moving from the realm of the individual to that of the religious community, this chapter analyzes the standards espoused by the members of the numerically dominant Reformed and Lutheran congregations, the Anabaptist "Plain" sects, such as the Mennonites and Dunkards, and atypical communal settlements, such as Conrad Beissel's Ephrata and Moravian communities.[18]

Like most people of British descent who lived in Pennsylvania during the eighteenth century, most Pennsylvania Germans were Protestant in background. As the availability of specialized, often imported, goods associated with polite pastimes increased, a general apprehension about the rise of immoderation and luxury developed among members of most religious groups. Although American and European authors who debated the meaning of the term "luxury" often borrowed ideas from contemporary political rhetoric, including the proper relationship between Britain and her colonies, they also drew on the general religious tenor of the time. This was an era during which concerns about social organization and the economy were regularly tied to concepts of virtue and morality. Particularly among prosperous people of German descent, decisions about material belongings and the behavior associated with them had to strike a balance between high social status and Christian propriety. Most pious Pennsylvania Germans shared a desire to shun what they defined as superfluous and, therefore, ungodly.

Not all people of German descent, however, came to the same conclusion concerning what was and was not appropriate. Differences in religious belief, even among members of Protestant denominations, sometimes resulted in visible differences in the earthly realm. But Anabaptist groups, such as the Mennonites and Amish, whom authors and tourism promoters have often touted for their traditions of simplicity, were not as different from Lutheran and Reformed German speakers in the eighteenth century as is often imagined.[19] By the end of the eighteenth century, members of "Plain" religious communities may have worshipped in spaces that were not as churchlike and stylishly detailed as those of their Lutheran and Reformed counterparts, but outside the meetinghouse, clothing was the primary material indication of religious affiliation. The houses of individual Mennonites could be as large and assigned as high a monetary value as those owned and occupied by members of other religious communities. Pious Pennsylvania Germans from all denominations were known to build grand dwellings for their families. It was only at communal religious settlements, such as Ephrata and Moravian Bethlehem, that the physical environment was truly distinct. At these religious communities, the extremes of the material spectrum, which ranged from asceticism to cosmopolitan sophistication, were in evidence.

The concluding chapter of this work analyzes the influences of ethnic heritage, social and economic status, and religious belief on material culture by examining a number of late eighteenth-century Pennsylvania German objects that I purposely chose because they defy easy cultural categorization. In addition to so-called German-Georgian houses, I look at a communion set from a German Reformed church with components made in London, Cologne, and Philadelphia; a painted chest signed by its maker in both German script and English roman characters; and a ten-plate stove fabricated at Henry William Stiegel's Elizabeth Furnace with a stylish Rococo cartouche containing a scene from Aesop's fables. In summarizing my findings and presenting a model for interpretation, I encourage readers to appreciate surviving eighteenth-century Pennsylvania German material culture for its complexity of meaning. As our twenty-first-century lives attest, our choices about what we create, the items we purchase, and how we use our possessions can rarely be explained in terms of a simple either/or proposition.

While this project defines the term "Pennsylvania German" as encompassing both immigrants from the German-speaking principalities of central Europe and Pennsylvanians descended from them, there is good reason to believe that many of these people would not have defined themselves solely in terms of their national heritage. Although ethnic labels have long been applied to Pennsylvania Germans by outsiders, self-representation was a much more complicated process. Through their material possessions, Pennsylvania Germans created associations and dissociations with others that were grounded in several personal characteristics. Allegiances based on ethnic background were often overshadowed by those based on social and economic status mingled with a sense of appropriateness based on religious conviction. This study cautions against accepting ethnic and racial categories, particularly those applied by nonmembers, as absolute, and it urges a greater recognition of the multifaceted contours of diversity in America. In defining self, as eighteenth-century Pennsylvania German material culture suggests, where one came from may not always have been as important as where one was going in this world and the next.

ir gerß 36=128

269

Dür

Dür

Dien

Dür

Dür

figster   prond Dirt   finster

German or Georgian?

In the second half of the eighteenth century, select members of the Pennsylvania German population chose to build a new type of house. The buildings they constructed were typically two-story masonry structures. What differentiated them from other contemporary dwellings of similar size and building materials was their floor plan, which most notably included a center or side through-passage or occasionally a half-passage—basically a hallway, in modern parlance—that was entered via the front door and provided access to most of the other spaces within the house (figs. 2–3).

For many people charged with their care and interpretation, houses of this type present an analytical dilemma. Often termed German-Georgian, they are viewed as hybrids having a dual and conflicted agenda. On the one hand, many examples of the type preserve certain architectural characteristics that are specifically associated with people who hailed from the German-speaking principalities of central Europe. On the other hand, they incorporate numerous attributes that in a late eighteenth-century American context are generally identified with the Georgian architectural style. This style, although named for three English kings who were imported to the British Isles from the German state of Hanover, is routinely associated with Americans of British descent. From a modern perspective, then, these German-Georgian buildings seem somewhat schizophrenic in their mingling of perceived German and English design traditions.[1]

The German-Georgian house type is representative of a much larger group of objects that present a similar impasse for many students of material

culture. As the eighteenth century progressed, residents of Pennsylvania had access to an increasing number and variety of household goods. Because of colonial trade restrictions, many were produced in England or, if made in another area, were at least imported to America on English ships.[2] Like the Georgian house type, they are often associated with new levels of refinement and gentility but, just as importantly, are typically defined as English. When used by people of German descent, they have raised questions about the ethnic identity of their owners.

Previous students and collectors of the material culture of eighteenth-century Pennsylvania Germans have often chosen to focus on different types of distinctly "German" goods, such as sgraffito-decorated redware plates, Fraktur birth and baptismal certificates, and brightly painted chests.[3] In part, they have classified these objects as German because of the language differences between the region's British and German residents that are reflected in their decoration. The adages adorning many Pennsylvania German objects

Fig. 2 Isaac and Catherine Meier house, Myerstown, Lebanon County, Pennsylvania, c. 1757. Isaac and Catherine Meier embraced a new style of life with the house that they created for their family in the third quarter of the eighteenth century. Possibly a reworking of an earlier house purchased from Catherine's father, within its symmetrical stone façade the Meiers' house had on its first floor a center passage—a hallway, in twenty-first-century language—with two rooms on either side arranged back-to-back or in a double pile. According to Isaac Meier's 1770 probate inventory, filed in Lancaster County, he possessed items such as silver-handled knives, teaspoons, "China & Glass in y. Bufet," a desk, silk clothing, a watch, and £1.4.9 in cash, indicating his wealth, his knowledge, and his concern for display and entertainment. The attached wing served as a kitchen and may have housed some of Meier's six slaves, who facilitated his family's elite lifestyle.

Fig. 3 Center passage, Isaac and Catherine Meier house. The center passage, which ran the complete width of the house, provided access to first-floor rooms as well as to the staircase leading to the second floor. Plaster walls and ceilings, refined woodwork, large sash windows, and domestic objects, in addition to a closed floor plan with entrance to other parts of the house mediated by the passage, would have distinguished this house as above average. The first-floor front parlor, located to one side of the passage, contained a clock, chinaware, a looking glass (mirror), four pictures, a table, a tea table, eight chairs, and firedogs (andirons) when Isaac Meier died in 1770. The Meier house is currently being restored by the Historic Preservation Trust of Lebanon County and is open to the public at several special events.

would have been incomprehensible to anyone who was not familiar with the German language. Even the appearance of individual letters and numbers, which were often printed in German script rather than English roman characters, would have visually distinguished as German an object that was embellished with something as simple as a name or sometimes even a date.[4]

Yet students and collectors have also associated the Pennsylvania Germans with certain kinds of goods based not only on language and handwriting styles but also on aesthetic preference and cultural practice. The objects that have come to be identified with the Pennsylvania Germans are often brightly colored and usually adorned with stylized images of hearts, flowers, and animals. They are fundamentally folk objects, if "folk" is understood to mean something apart from academic or popular culture.[5] They seem to have been produced by a specific group of people who appreciated objects that were vividly decorated and who remained relatively unaware of dominant urban styles. Because of an appreciation for and emphasis on Pennsylvania German folk art, institutions and authors who interpret objects for the public have undertaken numerous projects based on the premise that when German immigrants or their descendants opted for something other than a simply executed, distinctly ethnic form, they must have been abandoning their German identity and assimilating.[6]

The focus on the loss of cultural distinction among the Pennsylvania German population is not completely without precedent. Authors writing during the second half of the eighteenth century often described which purportedly ethnic characteristics residents of the commonwealth maintained and which they abandoned. Referring specifically to people of German descent, they frequently remarked on language. However, their conclusions were seldom clear-cut, and they were often contradictory. As early as the 1750s, German immigrants reported that fellow countrymen who worked as indentured servants for English families often forgot "their native tongues." Yet others, looking at the German population as a whole, portrayed it in a strikingly different way. A European traveler who visited Reading and the surrounding region in the 1790s, for example, noted that "great numbers of the inhabitants of the town and the neighboring country" did "not understand a word of English." He continued, "The greatest part speak no other language than German."[7]

The same types of ambiguity manifested themselves in the realm of manners and material culture. Generally speaking, most authors noted that English tastes and objects were most prominent in British North America. One German immigrant remarked, for example, that "throughout Pennsylvania both men and women dress according to English fashion." Another European traveler more generally noted, "In a country which has belonged to England for a long time, of which the most numerous and nearest connections are yet with England, and which carries on with England almost all its commerce, the manners of the people must necessarily resemble, in a great degree, those of England." He was particularly aware of English trends in clothing, architecture, furnishings, transportation, and foodways. Yet this same author, while visiting Germantown outside of Philadelphia, found that people of German descent in that locale were "particularly averse to leave their old customs." In Maytown, near the Susquehanna River in Lancaster County, he remarked that the residents were all "Germans, who have still remained such."[8]

For various reasons, people who resided in or visited Pennsylvania during the late eighteenth century commented on the relationship among ethnic background and language, behavior, and the material landscape. German immigrants often noted differences between European and Pennsylvania Germans. They were quick to point out when new arrivals began to adopt the English language or wear new English styles of clothing. On the other hand, non-Germans often noted what made Pennsylvanians of German descent different from the rest of the population. They were more apt to notice distinct speech, manners, and objects. The fact that different people during the period could come to such radically different conclusions is even more telling than their actual observations. In assessing the ethnic characteristics of the Pennsylvania Germans, commentary was rarely unequivocal. Conflicting opinions were commonplace, and even supposedly objective statements were often exaggerated.

However, as time passed, the emphasis on the distinctiveness of Pennsylvania's early German inhabitants grew. In the nineteenth century, Pennsylvania Germans themselves began to appreciate and stress the qualities that made them different from their neighbors. A new wave of German immigration, particularly in response to the German Revolution of 1848, forced those of German descent already in Pennsylvania to examine how they defined themselves not only in terms of the English speakers with whom they shared the commonwealth, but also with new German-speaking immigrants from Europe. In 1891, a printed letter addressed "To the descendants of the early German and Swiss Settlers in Pennsylvania" called for the formation of the Pennsylvania German Society in order to preserve ancestral records, bring recognition to forefathers, develop a fraternal spirit, honor little-known history, and preserve "to posterity the old public records, landmarks and memorials, which in another generation will have entirely disappeared." In case there was any confusion about who exactly the Pennsylvania Germans of the Pennsylvania German Society were to be, membership policy made it clear by excluding from full membership anyone who was not "of full age, of good moral character, and a direct descendant of early German or Swiss emigrants to Pennsylvania."[9]

Later organizations, such as the Pennsylvania Dutch Folklore Center, publications, including *The Pennsylvania Dutchman,* and events, such as the Pennsylvania Dutch Folk Festival, continued to publicize the distinctness of the Pennsylvania Germans. When *The Pennsylvania Dutchman* was first published in 1949, its editor, Alfred Shoemaker, explained, "We, the Pennsylvania Dutch, were taught for generations to despise and disrespect our traditional culture. The task that we of THE PENNSYLVANIA DUTCHMAN have set ourselves is to teach NOT hate, NOT disrespect, but UNDERSTANDING, APPRECIATION and, most important of all, A LOVE FOR OUR HERITAGE." Largely as a result of Shoemaker's endeavors, the study of the Pennsylvania Germans and their distinct culture became a model for those interested in documenting ethnic or regional folklife.[10]

While much of the twentieth-century work on the Pennsylvania Germans has been designed to foster an understanding and enjoyment of Pennsylvania German culture, the overarching questions concerning Pennsylvania German objects have come to revolve around issues of ethnic distinctiveness and, when that is not found, assimilation. The simplest interpretations have attempted to pinpoint characteristics that made the creations of the earliest German immigrants particularly "German" and then determine whether these continental European features were abandoned over time. Proponents of this reading of Pennsylvania German material culture view German and English cultural traits as diametrically opposed. They insist that in Pennsylvania, German immigrants and their descendants had to make a choice between either maintaining their German identity or adopting the ways of their English neighbors.[11]

Beginning in the late 1970s, some authors began to reevaluate the degree to which British and German immigrants to Pennsylvania differed in terms of cultural practice. The strongest call for revision came from cultural geographer James Lemon. In his study of eighteenth-century southeastern Pennsylvania, Lemon asserted that previous scholars had often "misstated or exaggerated far out of proportion" the significance of differences in customs, and even language, between members of the ethnic groups that composed the Pennsylvania population. He believed that Pennsylvanians from throughout the British Isles and the German-speaking region of Europe shared such notable qualities as "Protestantism, agricultural techniques, and long-standing dietary preferences." In terms of economic status particularly, Lemon found that the "various national groups did not diverge greatly."[12]

Few authors who followed Lemon went as far as he did in suggesting a comparative lack of distinction between the ethnically diverse European residents of Pennsylvania. They did, however, begin to soften their views on the either/or nature of cultural change. In *America and the Germans,* a 1983 collection of essays that commemorated the three-hundredth anniversary of the first German immigration to Pennsylvania, historian Stephanie Grauman Wolf suggested that in studying the eighteenth-century community of Germantown it was possible to identify simultaneous examples of the preservation and abandonment of ethnic cultural practices. Like the authors of several essays in the compilation, Wolf presented a three-part model for change, which included the option of adaptation or the modification of ethnic patterns to create distinct new forms. Several subsequent scholars, such as Aaron Spencer Fogleman, Philip Pendleton, and Steven Nolt, have all expanded this interpretative framework by emphasizing the Americanization of diverse Pennsylvania communities rather than the Anglicization of German immigrants. In his book *Foreigners in Their Own Land,* Nolt argues that rather than being mutually exclusive processes marked on one end of the spectrum by cultural resistance and on the other by assimilation, creating an ethnic identity and becoming American were in fact integrally related.[13]

Among those devoted more exclusively to the study of material culture, nuanced models suggesting options other than simply the total rejection of or complete assimilation into English culture have emerged as well. In *Arts of the Pennsylvania Germans,* a catalogue of the Pennsylvania German collections at Winterthur Museum, Scott Swank suggests a third alternative, which he terms "controlled acculturation." According to Swank, this middle-of-the-road alternative allowed a significant minority of Germans in Pennsylvania to maintain a sense of traditional culture and to choose what and how change was effected while steadily moving toward acculturation nonetheless.[14] As this model suggests, despite the broadening spectrum of interpretative options, a focus on ethnic background continues to drive studies of eighteenth-century Pennsylvania Germans' material lives.

The field of Pennsylvania German architectural history, for example, has been dominated by the need to identify peculiarly German building methods and materials, floor plans, and decorative details. Lack of, or transformation of, these characteristics is seen as evidence of Pennsylvania German assimilation or acculturation. A significant early study of Pennsylvania German architecture, written by G. Edwin Brumbaugh and published by the Pennsylvania German Society in 1933, was the first to take this approach. Brumbaugh, a trained architect who was responsible for the restoration or reconstruction of numerous important early Pennsylvania buildings, believed that the "simple German peasants [who came to America] had a background of their own, which found expression in plain, almost austere, architecture, of great solidity and primitive detail." More "pretentious structures," which were constructed later, he continued, "began to bear the impress of English ideas" and "show[ed] less pronounced German traits."[15]

Students of Pennsylvania German architecture who followed Brumbaugh continued to search for unique Pennsylvania German features, which

they would often attribute to the folk character and unsophisticated aesthetic preferences of the ethnic group. Robert Bucher and Henry Glassie, for example, relied more extensively on measured drawings, unlike Brumbaugh, who tended to make rather impressionistic observations, to convey the floor plan of a distinct Pennsylvania German house type. Bucher and Glassie referred to the buildings they documented as continental plan houses in order to specify the buildings' links to central Europe rather than the British Isles. According to Bucher, the principal distinguishing characteristic of this traditional German house type was a single large fireplace located near the center of the dwelling and oriented perpendicular to the façade. A narrow *Küche,* or kitchen, was located to the front side of the fireplace. This room provided both a work space and an entrance to the house and now serves as the namesake of the building type—the *Flurküchenhaus,* or entry-kitchen house.[16]

Although an entry-kitchen house could have had as many as four first-floor rooms, in Pennsylvania, most surviving houses of this type had three (figs. 4–5).[17] To the back side of the kitchen fireplace there was a large, usually square room with multiple windows to the front and a smaller, often unheated, rectangular *Kammer,* or bedchamber, to the rear. The larger front room, referred to as a *Stube*—generally translated into English as "stove room"—did not have a fireplace but rather was heated by a closed jamb stove. This stove, which could have been constructed of masonry, tile, or five cast-iron plates, was fed through the back of the kitchen fireplace (figs. 6–7).[18]

Only recently have claims about the origin and pervasiveness of the entry-kitchen house form been challenged. William Woys Weaver questions whether the entry-kitchen house served as a "touchstone with Germany," as Bucher and Glassie had suggested, or whether such buildings' "striking similarities to the Old World [were] in reality counterbalanced by even greater differences." Weaver emphasizes the importance of the stove room in both German and Pennsylvania German houses but asserts that in Pennsylvania, the so-called continental plan house developed a form of its own.[19] Charles Bergengren, in his writings on Schaefferstown, Pennsylvania, suggests that even though the entry-kitchen house form was common, it was not the only model that German immigrants and their descendants used.[20]

Weaver's and Bergengren's work defies previous notions about Pennsylvania German assimilation as expressed through domestic architecture. Weaver asserts that German-American design has always been evolving. Most German immigrants did not arrive in America and indiscriminately reproduce the houses they had occupied in Europe. Bergengren reveals that German-Americans drew on several different, purportedly German, models ranging from the traditional entry-kitchen house to more academic baroque designs. In bringing to light the changes in and multiple influences on German-American

Fig. 4   Bertolet-Herbein house, originally Oley Township, Berks County, since moved to the Daniel Boone Homestead State Historic Site, Exeter Township, Berks County, Pennsylvania, c. 1737–50. This dwelling, probably constructed for widow Elizabeth Bertolet, was built utilizing an entry-kitchen house plan. The door was situated to one side of the façade, providing direct access to the kitchen inside. The chimney, located near the center of the building, served as an outlet for both the kitchen fireplace and the stove that heated one of the two other first-floor rooms. The log walls and limited number of small windows were typical of many domestic buildings in Pennsylvania throughout the eighteenth century.

Fig. 5   First-floor plan, Bertolet-Herbein house. The floor plan of this building typifies the three-room entry-kitchen house plan. Entrance to the building was via the kitchen, which housed a fireplace for cooking and heating and a staircase leading to the loft above. On the other side of the building, there were two rooms that completed the first-floor plan: the *Stube,* or stove room, to the front, and the *Kammer,* or chamber, to the rear. The *Stube* would have been heated by a jamb stove fed from the kitchen fireplace. Floor plan based on plan by J. Michael Everett for the Historic American Buildings Survey, 1958. Library of Congress, Prints and Photographs Division, HABS, HABS-PA, 6-LIMKI.V, 5.

Fig. 6   Jamb or five-plate iron stove, Mary Ann Furnace, Manheim Township, York County, Pennsylvania, c. 1766. A five-plate stove was assembled from five pieces of cast iron that formed its top, bottom, and three sides. The fourth side of the stove was butted against the rear wall of the kitchen fireplace. The stove was "closed" in the sense that there was no access to the fire and embers inside it from the room in which the stove sat. Instead, the stove was fed from an adjacent room, usually the kitchen. Such stoves did not provide the light that an open fire did, but they did eliminate the cold draft common from large fireplace chimneys. Courtesy of Winterthur Museum.

Fig. 7   Kitchen fireplace, originally from the George and Magdalena Elizabeth Hehn house (later the residence of Captain Conrad Kershner), Heidelberg Township, Berks County, Pennsylvania, now installed at Winterthur Museum, 1755. The opening leading to the stove in the adjoining stove room can be seen just under the hanging three-legged pot near the center of the image. The jamb stove was fed and ashes were removed through this opening. Photograph by the author. Courtesy of Winterthur Museum.

buildings, Weaver and Bergengren call for a reevaluation of not just the entry-kitchen house form, but other house types as well, including the grand Georgian houses built by elite Pennsylvania Germans.

Traditionally, sharp contrasts have been drawn between the purportedly "German" characteristics of the entry-kitchen house and the seemingly refined "English" characteristics of Georgian dwellings.[21] The entry-kitchen house, for example, was based on an "open" plan—one entered through the front door directly into a principal workroom, the kitchen. The Georgian house, on the other hand, which had a separate formal entry, was based on a "closed" plan. One had to pass through the entry, an unheated intermediary space, to gain access to the other rooms of the house. In the Georgian house, there were more rooms than in the entry-kitchen house, and these rooms had more specialized uses. On the exterior, while the fenestration on the entry-kitchen house was often asymmetrical, the configuration of openings for windows

and doors on the Georgian house was usually balanced both vertically and horizontally.

I argue that Georgian houses built in America were part of a larger, cosmopolitan trend toward Renaissance design in domestic architecture, which occurred throughout the Western world. I build on the work of historian Cary Carson, who has posited that eighteenth-century Georgian houses were "Georgian" only to the King Georges of England. In a suggestive essay, Carson theorizes that "the dilemma facing Americans of European descent may therefore have been less a choice between ethnic or English than one between folk and formal." He notes that Americans of German descent, like those of Swiss, Dutch, and Scots-Irish descent, were in the late eighteenth century "opening up to the same outside influences that promoted gentility and the use of consumer goods among country people everywhere." Hence, the decision among Pennsylvania Germans to build a Georgian house may have had less to do with their ethnic identity than with their aspirations to refinement.[22]

Surviving buildings and the circumstances that surrounded their construction demonstrate the plausibility of Carson's thesis. The degree to which most German immigrants were able to keep abreast of European news and therefore remain aware of continental architectural style has often been debated. However, among members of Moravian religious settlements, particularly community leaders, there is little doubt that contact was frequent. Moravians in Pennsylvania regularly sought approval from denominational leaders in Herrnhut, Saxony, for any building plans. Nevertheless, when Moravians in Bethlehem constructed their 1744 Single Brothers' house, they based it on a seemingly "Georgian" floor plan. On the exterior, its central door was flanked on each side by two regularly spaced bays of windows. On the interior, the building's first-floor plan consisted of a center passage, which served as the entry, with two rooms arranged back-to-back, or in a double pile, on either side (figs. 8–9). However, unlike the rooms in many English-American buildings of this type, the four rooms surrounding the passage at the Single Brothers' house were all heated by stoves rather than fireplaces.[23]

In size and spatial arrangement, although the 1744 Single Brothers' house included both workrooms and sleeping quarters for over fifty unmarried Moravian men, it was not unlike some single-family dwellings built by well-to-do Pennsylvania Germans. As these individuals constructed substantial residences in the latter half of the eighteenth century, they often found ways, like the Moravians, to combine the refined aspects of Georgian houses and certain more traditional German features. One way that was particularly common was to build a house with a symmetrical façade, an interior space associated with entry, and a more isolated kitchen facility while continuing to rely on a stove, or stoves, for heat. Frequently a closed stove was incorporated in a formal front parlor, a feature that clearly differentiated the eighteenth-century houses of elite Pennsylvania Germans from those of elite Americans of British descent.

Fig. 8 First Single Brothers' house, later converted to the Single Sisters' house, Bethlehem, Northampton County, Pennsylvania, 1744. The Moravian community at Bethlehem designed the first Single Brothers' house to serve as living and work space for roughly fifty Moravian men. The building was fashioned with a five-bay façade, central front door, and gambrel roof. Its masonry construction, multiple stories, symmetrical appearance, and floor plan all became standard in the single-family houses associated with Georgian architecture in America.

Fig. 9 First-floor plan, first Single Brothers' house, from "Entwurf zum Bau des Gemeinhauses in Bethlehem in Pennsylvania mit Angabe der Nutzung der Räume, Grundriss Erdgeschoss," 1751. According to this detailed plan of the first Single Brothers' house, produced just after it had been turned over to the Single Sisters for their use, the building included a center passage and four other first-floor rooms arranged in a center-passage, double-pile plan. Openings in the walls on either side of the passage were used to feed stoves, the locations of which are shown on the plan by rectangular boxes marked with an X pattern. Courtesy of the Moravian Archives, Herrnhut, Germany, TS Mp.216.15.

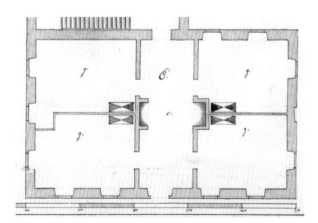

A surviving 1783 building contract between master builder Christian Hagenbuch and joiner Jacob Kratzer demonstrates that even when they did not use stoves, some German-Americans who built houses that departed from the entry-kitchen house model had not stopped thinking about spaces in culturally distinct ways. Illustrations produced in conjunction with the contract show a proposed house with a four-bay façade and a two-bay gable end that included an ocular window at its peak (fig. 10). On the interior, the building's floor plan was to be of what Bergengren has termed the *Kreuzehaus* variety. On its first floor, it would have four rooms: an entry accessible from the front door, a kitchen behind the entry, a large square room to the left side of the entry, and a smaller rectangular room behind that front room (fig. 11). When Hagenbuch and Kratzer referred to these rooms in their written contract they used the German words "*Gang*" (passage or avenue), "*Kich*" (a dialect derivation of *Küche*), "*Stub*[e]," and "*Kammer.*"[24]

What is most significant is the use of the word "*Stub*[e]," to refer to the front room, which was heated by a corner fireplace. Students of Pennsylvania German architecture have often interpreted the replacement of the stove-heated stove room with a fireplace-heated "English" parlor as a sign of the rejection of German identity.[25] However, Hagenbuch and Kratzer did not refrain from using the word "*Stub*[e]," just because the front room of this house had a fireplace. Nor does the lack of a stove seem to have significantly altered the room's function. The contract calls for Kratzer to build two benches, a table, and a small cupboard, the furniture typically found in the stove room of an entry-kitchen house.[26]

Recent scholarship and primary documents such as the Hagenbuch/ Kratzer contract call for a continued reevaluation of the domestic lives of German immigrants and their descendants in late eighteenth-century Pennsylvania. What researchers have often seen as a sharp break in the building practices of Pennsylvania Germans may not have been perceived as such in the eighteenth century. Concerning European and Native American relations, Richard White has argued that "contact opened new possibilities for hybrid cultural identities that probably did not seem hybrid to those who occupied them. There was more continuity across what seemingly were impervious boundaries."[27] Pennsylvania Germans who were building and furnishing new houses in the last decades of the eighteenth century may have experienced that same sense of continuity. Their choices were influenced by more than diametrically opposed concerns involving the rejection or preservation of German cultural practices.

There are several reasons why the issue of national origin has driven so many analyses of Pennsylvania German objects. As illustrated above, one of the contributing factors is the belief that Pennsylvania Germans must have favored a distinct aesthetic, which differed considerably from that preferred

Fig. 10 House designed for Christian Hagenbuch, 1783. This two-story stone house with a four-bay façade was built for Hagenbuch in Allen Township, Northampton County, Pennsylvania. Its façade suggests its interior layout, which consisted of four rooms and did not include a central passage, but rather a front entry room designated as a "*Gang.*" Courtesy of the Winterthur Library, Joseph Downs Collection of Manuscripts and Printed Ephemera.

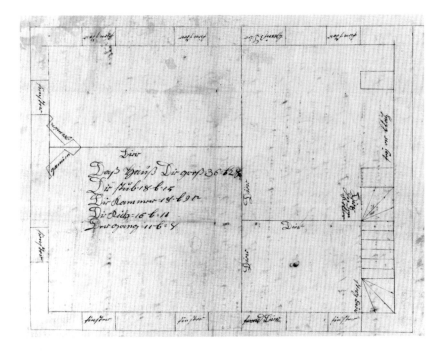

Fig. 11 Floor plan, house designed for Christian Hagenbuch. Hagenbuch's proposed house included four first-floor rooms, which were labeled (starting in the lower left and continuing clockwise) "*Stub*[e]," "*Kammer,*" "*Kich,*" and "*Gang.*" The *Gang* served as an entrance to the building and provided access to the kitchen behind it, the large front room beside it, and the staircase to the second floor. The use of the word *Stub*[e] to refer to the large front room suggests that a preference for using space in traditional German ways persisted despite the fact that this "stove room," as well as the *Kammer,* were heated by corner fireplaces. Courtesy of the Winterthur Library, Joseph Downs Collection of Manuscripts and Printed Ephemera.

by their English neighbors. This interpretation is one that has been put forth in various forms by authors since the late eighteenth century, one that in fact appeals to national stereotypes that had existed in Europe even longer. Today, trends among antiques collectors and tourism promoters continue to encourage it. Since the beginning of the twentieth century, collectors and dealers in the antiques market have placed a premium on unique forms of eighteenth- and early nineteenth-century Pennsylvania German folk art. An active tourist industry in south-central Pennsylvania, better known to some as Pennsylvania Dutch or Amish country, has also fostered the impression that Pennsylvania Germans have always operated apart from the conventions of mainstream America.

Equally significant to the interpretation of ethnic distinctiveness is the mistaken view that the Pennsylvania Germans were a unified, homogenous group in the eighteenth century. Despite their various homelands and dialects, diverse religious beliefs and practices, and distinct stations in life, immigrants from all over central Europe are thought to have come together in Pennsylvania to form a coherent, "non-English" community.[28] While outsiders have long perceived and promoted a collective ethnic experience among Pennsylvanians of German descent, the embrace of a group identity by Pennsylvania Germans themselves has been more limited and more recent. In the nineteenth century, in response to new waves of German immigration as well as pressure from English speakers, descendants of eighteenth-century German immigrants did craft a collective agenda grounded in their shared ethnic background. Pennsylvania German leaders advocated for the use of the German language or in some cases the Pennsylvania German dialect in church services, wrote proud histories of Pennsylvania German communities, and founded the Pennsylvania German Society to recognize the contributions of their progenitors. Townships with significant Pennsylvania German populations resisted the establishment of public schools, which threatened to replace German parochial schools and favored English instruction, in some cases from the inception of the Pennsylvania common school system in 1834 through the early 1870s. During this same time period, distinct forms of material culture, most notably hex signs on barns, began to proliferate as symbols of group ethnic consciousness.[29] This new level of cultural solidarity, while never absolute, was certainly growing in the middle decades of the nineteenth century.

In examining the process of identity formation in the years leading up to and immediately following the American Revolution, I explore the identity thrust on Pennsylvania Germans by outsiders, the identity created by individual Pennsylvania Germans for themselves, and the identity fostered by religious belief among communities of like-minded souls. As Steven Nolt notes, "If ethnicity is partly defined by those outside a particular group, it is cultivated within a group through the formation and perpetuation of *culture*."[30] By focusing on material forms of culture, I conclude that, in the critical years surrounding the formation of the United States, ethnicity, while the focus of outsiders' interpretations of Pennsylvania German domestic landscapes, was not the exclusive, or in many cases even the primary, factor that influenced the way Pennsylvania Germans and Pennsylvania German communities constructed identities for themselves.

Chaff
room.

Stalls for Horses.

Corn Store

Thrash...

Lo...

Mow.

Industry, Economy, and Ignorance

In the eighteenth century, amid a growing wave of nationalism in Europe, Old World residents regularly created stereotypes about one another. According to the author of one period English-language dictionary, for instance, the Swiss and Swedes were robust, the Dutch gentle, and the Spanish haughty.[1] In Pennsylvania, where various European groups came together, commentators continued to note the attributes that they felt distinguished people of diverse national backgrounds. Both American and European authors took particular interest in chronicling what differentiated European-born and America-born Germans from other residents of the New World. This chapter explores the identity that these observers—all outsiders to the Pennsylvania German community—created for members of the ethnic group. Focusing on material culture, it addresses how characterizations of objects—ranging from farms to furnishings and foodstuffs—contributed to common charges about the character of Pennsylvanians of German descent.

Period authors often observed Pennsylvania Germans' buildings and belongings during visits to the countryside in Lancaster, Berks, or more remote Pennsylvania counties. However, the attributes they identified as distinctly German did not typify all of the people of German descent who resided in rural areas, much less all of those who lived in towns or in the city of Philadelphia. In recording the features they believed to be uniquely German, commentators created on paper an imagined landscape that contrasted notably with the real landscape through which they traveled. They ignored the diversity of experience among people of German descent in order to impart a one-dimensional image of members of the group. Their descriptions of Pennsylvania German material culture led period authors to classify German immigrants and their descendants specifically as farmers, who, according to period notions about agricultural workers, were understood to be industrious, economical, and ignorant.

The characterization of Pennsylvania Germans as farmers was pervasive in both Europe and America, particularly among members of the educated classes. This chapter analyzes the written accounts of fifteen Europeans who either visited or became temporary residents of Pennsylvania. It also examines the travel accounts, essays, and memoirs of six Americans who observed, but were not part of, the Pennsylvania German community. Other sources include five geographies or gazetteers that described Pennsylvania's population and material culture.[2] The literary sources in question were directed to both a European and an American readership. They were produced by men of English, French, German, Swedish, and Dutch lineage and as a result were published in a wide variety of European languages. While the tone of the various accounts ranges widely, the similarities in description demonstrate how conventionalized the image of the Pennsylvania German farmer had become by the second half of eighteenth century.

Period authors' descriptions of both material culture and the Pennsylvania German population were influenced by more than mere observation. When describing the characteristics that distinguished Pennsylvania Germans from others, commentators often drew on contemporary rhetoric concerning the process of social and economic development. Theories about the advancement of society from savagery to civilization seemed especially pertinent to those concerned with the creation of the new republic of the United States. European and Euro-American authors readily agreed that hunting and nomadic grazing, forms of subsistence most often associated with Native Americans, typified the more primitive stages of social and economic development and therefore had to be replaced. There was less conformity of opinion about whether agriculture or its presumed "natural successor," commerce, should be the ultimate goal of the American people. Some thinkers who looked to Europe for a model favored mercantilism and the social stratification that normally accompanied it. Others, like Thomas Jefferson, envisioned a more egalitarian society composed of virtuous independent farmers.[3]

Proponents of the two divergent philosophies came to different conclusions about Pennsylvania Germans. Supporters of commerce and social hierarchy generally objected to traits they identified as particularly German. Champions of agriculture and an independent citizenry, on the other hand, often described Pennsylvania Germans in more flattering terms. In both cases, material culture played a vital role in the assessment. Descriptions of the material environments created by German immigrants and their descendants not only allowed opinionated authors to draw conclusions about the ethnic group but also to make larger points about the future of American society.

Late eighteenth-century accounts concerning the objects associated with Pennsylvania Germans fall into two categories. The first focused on characteristics of barns, houses, household furnishings, diet, and attire that emphasized real differences between the material worlds fashioned by some of Pennsylvania's German and British residents. Although period authors often used their observations about distinct house and barn plans, heating schemes, food preferences, and clothing to draw broader conclusions about the Pennsylvania German population, comments that fit into this category at least appear to have recorded—sometimes in exaggerated fashion—visible ethnic differences in the late eighteenth-century landscape. The second group of remarks, rather than describing particular forms or types, often focused on the issue of quality. These portrayals tended to be judgmental and rarely addressed genuine, discernible attributes of Pennsylvania German material culture.

Close Stoves, Feather Beds, and Sauerkraut

Included in the first category of observations are several commentaries that described late eighteenth-century Pennsylvania barns and houses as evidence of ethnic background. Philadelphian Benjamin Rush, for example, elaborated on the distinct form of the German barn in his 1789 essay "An Account of the Manners of the German Inhabitants of Pennsylvania." Rush noted that barns built by Pennsylvania Germans, unlike those built by Pennsylvanians of English descent, often incorporated the functions of grain storage and animal stabling "under one roof." The first American edition of *The Domestic Encyclopædia,* published in 1804, likewise remarked on the "very excellent German [barn] plan," which combined features of a barn for storing grain, a stable, and a coach house, all in one building. The encyclopedia's publishers included floor plans of a German-style barn in Tredyffrin Township, Chester County, to illustrate the form's multiple functions. The two-story structure had stalls for horses and cattle on its first floor and spaces for grain storage and threshing on its second (fig. 12).[4]

Like barns, houses were also seen as visible symbols of national origin. According to Johann David Schöpf, an educated Bavarian doctor who toured Pennsylvania in the years immediately after the American Revolution, it was possible to determine the national origin of a dwelling's residents simply by looking at the building's external features. The distinction was based on the provisions for interior heating, a characteristic that on the exterior was made manifest by the placement of the chimneys. Schöpf explained, "if of one chimney only, placed in the middle, the house should be a German's and furnished with stoves, the smoke from each led into one flue and so taken off; if of two chimneys, one at each gable end there should be fire places, after the English plan."[5]

The typical English house, according to Schöpf, was designed like the surviving Jacob Thomas house in North Coventry Township, Chester County: it had two end chimneys that provided flues for fireplaces in both of its principal first-floor rooms (figs. 13–14). If heated second-floor spaces existed, as at the Thomas house, those rooms would be warmed by fireplaces as well. The typical German house, on the other hand, followed what recent authors have termed the continental, *Flurküchen,* or entry-kitchen house plan. As at the Bertolet-Herbein house, relocated from Oley Township to the Daniel Boone Homestead State Historic Site in Exeter Township, Berks County, a single chimney stack rose through the middle of the house. On the first floor, at least one room was heated by a jamb stove, which abutted the rear wall of the kitchen fireplace (see figs. 4–5). On the second floor or in the attic, another stove or stoves could provide additional heat.[6]

What Schöpf and others most often recognized as German about the latter house type was the heating scheme. Eighteenth-century authors commonly associated wood- and coal-burning fireplaces with the French and English, respectively, and stoves with the Germans. In Pennsylvania, a similar

Fig. 12   Floor plan, John Miller barn, Tredyffrin Township, Chester County, Pennsylvania, as illustrated and labeled in *The Domestic Encyclopædia,* 1804. The Miller barn, like those Benjamin Rush described in "An Account of the Manners of the German Inhabitants of Pennsylvania," incorporated stalls for horses and cattle on its first floor and storage for grain on its second. Floor plan from A. F. M. Willich and James Mease, *The Domestic Encyclopædia; or, A Dictionary of Facts and Useful Knowledge,* vol. 2 (Philadelphia: William Young Birch and Abraham Small, 1804), between pp. 486 and 487.

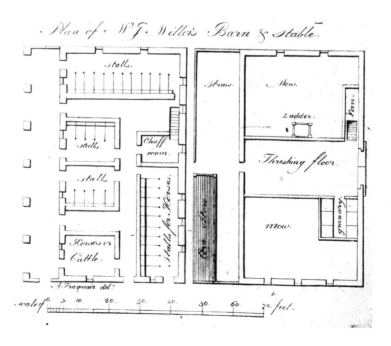

Fig. 13 Jacob Thomas house, North Coventry Township, Chester County, Pennsylvania, c. 1748. The Thomas house was designed as a two-story stone dwelling with two first-floor rooms: a hall, which one entered from the front door, and a parlor. Unlike the owners of some hall-and-parlor houses, the Thomases made some effort to differentiate work spaces from other living spaces by locating their kitchen on the lower cellar level. A modern addition has been appended to the right side of the dwelling.

Fig. 14 Reconstructed first-floor plan, Jacob Thomas house. Fireplaces originally heated both first-floor rooms at the Thomas house, which measured roughly 36 by 24 feet. Floor plan based on fieldwork by Bernard Herman, Gabrielle Lanier, and Cynthia Falk.

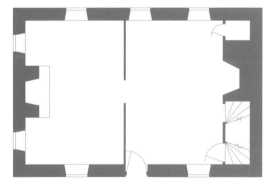

Fig. 15 Ten-plate stove, Oley Furnace, Berks County, Pennsylvania, 1778–1828. When the Historic American Buildings Survey documented the Bertolet-Herbein house (see figs. 4–5) in Oley Township, Berks County, in 1958, this stove, cast at Oley Furnace during Daniel Udree's ownership, remained in the stove room. This freestanding ten-plate stove would have replaced the jamb stove that had heated the room when the house was first built. The new stove type was fed through a door in the front rather than from the kitchen fireplace and was vented via its pipe into a chimney. Ten-plate stoves had a separate interior compartment that allowed for baking, a function not provided for by simpler six-plate stoves. Photograph by Cervin Robinson. Library of Congress, Prints and Photographs Division, HABS, HABS-PA, 6-LIMKI.V, 5–6.

dichotomy developed. Without a coal industry, the English turned to wood-burning fireplaces while the Germans continued to rely on stoves for heat. According to one European traveler, who had observed the interiors of several German-occupied houses in the 1790s, the principal piece of furniture in what he described as "the large fine room" was "an immense stove."[7]

Stoves associated with the Pennsylvania Germans came in several different varieties and were constructed from a number of different materials. Benjamin Franklin, in an essay entitled *Observations on Smoky Chimneys,* described a kind of stove "compos'd of Five Iron Plates scru'd together," which he found used in both Germany and Pennsylvania. The box-like stove's cast-iron plates formed its top, bottom, and three sides. On its fourth side, the stove abutted the rear wall of the adjacent fireplace (see figs. 6–7). In the stove room itself, there were no openings to the stove, and hence this type of stove was sometimes referred to by period authors as a "close" or "closed" stove. As Franklin described it, it was like "a kind of Oven revers'd, its Mouth being without, and Body within the Room that is to be warmed by it." In addition to cast-iron examples, contemporary observers also reported "earthen" and "pantiles or pottery-ware" stoves of this type (see figs. 21, 46).[8]

In the second half of the eighteenth century another kind of stove was also being used by German immigrants and their descendants in Pennsylvania. In February of 1790, David Schultze, a Silesian emigrant who had arrived in America in 1733, recorded in his journal that he "cleaned the stove pipes." In 1777, Lutheran minister Heinrich Melchior Muhlenberg noted that he had "the carpenter cut an opening into the chimney in the front room in order to make it possible to set up a stove with pipes there." Schultze's and Muhlenberg's comments indicate they were using a new type of stove that was not completely "closed" and therefore did not have to abut a fireplace. The fire in this kind of stove was fed through a door in its front and vented through a pipe, which led from the top of the stove to a chimney (fig. 15). According to Schöpf, it was sometimes referred to as a "draught-stove" and could have been made of either cast-iron or "tin-plate." The latter material—sheet iron coated with tin to prevent rust—was so thin that it was more likely used to construct the stove pipe than the stove itself. Although Schöpf reported that this new type of stove was "used more and more by English families" in the last decades of the eighteenth century, he indicated it had been introduced by "the German inhabitants." He attributed its use among the Pennsylvania Germans to "preference and old custom."[9]

Because Pennsylvanians of German descent relied on stoves for warmth, their houses were recognizably different not only in terms of tangible characteristics like floor plan and chimney placement but also in terms of more temporal qualities. Stoves produced a distinct type of heat, and many travelers commented on the difference between houses warmed by fireplaces and those warmed by stoves. Some travelers found the "air of a room heated by a German stove" to be "oppressive," "overheated," or "disagreeable."[10] However, native Germans and even a few Americans praised the stove. Schöpf reported that "winter, with a warm stove and sluggish days" was "indispensable" to a Pennsylvania German's "happiness." Furthermore, both Benjamin Franklin and Benjamin Rush agreed that Pennsylvania German houses were "rendered so comfortable, at all times, by large close stoves" and contrasted these dwellings with those of English families, "where every member of the family crouds near to a common fire-place, or shivers at a distance from it."[11]

The importance of the stove and the heat it provided was particularly noteworthy to early German immigrants. Upon arriving in Pennsylvania in the 1750s, a discontented Gottlieb Mittelberger explained of Pennsylvania dwellings that "one rarely sees stoves in their rooms. Instead, all the houses have French [or wood-burning] fireplaces." David Seibt had written in 1734 to his brother back in Silesia that "if you should come, too, bring with you an iron stove. They are dear here." To European travelers, native-born Americans, and German immigrants, the use of a stove for heat in a principal first-floor room—whether believed to be a positive or negative attribute—was one easily identifiable ethnic feature of Pennsylvania German houses.[12]

Inside the dwellings occupied by people of German descent, there were several other characteristics that period authors identified as specifically German. Not the least of these concerned food and drink. In addition to a warm stove, Schöpf described good beer, "wurst, hog-meat, and sauerkraut" as "national prerogatives" among the Pennsylvania Germans. Soup, a dish Gottlieb Mittelberger believed the English knew "little or nothing about," was also perceived as particularly German, as was dried fruit. Schöpf noted that while people of German descent often gathered to cut and peel surplus fruit for drying, "the English country-people" did not preserve their crops in this way. Another European traveler confirmed this observation when he remarked with some disgust that it was common to find "apples and pears drying on the stove" in a Pennsylvania German's house.[13]

Benjamin Rush also recorded what he discerned as the dietary preferences of Pennsylvania Germans. According to Rush, members of the group ate "large quantities of vegetables," including cabbage, which they made into "sour crout," as well as "a large quantity of milk and cheese." For grains they relied on Indian corn and rye rather than wheat. The Germans' partiality toward rye was additionally noted by miller Thomas May, who wrote a Philadelphia merchant to find out what the "Dutch bakers" who "frequently use it" would pay for flour made from that grain.[14]

Pennsylvania Germans not only partook of specific, reportedly ethnic, foods such as sauerkraut, dried fruit, and rye bread; they also ate and drank from tableware that was perceived to be distinct. Gottlieb Mittelberger was surprised when he came to America and saw people drinking from "china vessels, called bowls." He was not familiar with the form but found that the beverage holders reminded him of "soup plates," a type of tableware which would have been equally foreign to the non-Germans he encountered. One of these outsiders remarked with some surprise that Pennsylvania Germans usually drank their beverages from "tin goblets."[15]

Like their drinking vessels, several kinds of furniture associated with Pennsylvania Germans were specifically singled out for description. Schöpf reported that the dining table where families took their meals was routinely found in one corner of the stove room. Its placement there was deliberate and relatively permanent, since on two sides the benches around it were "fastened to the wall." Pennsylvania German beds, while found in more diverse locations, also warranted comment. Both Benjamin Rush and an unnamed English translator noted that people of German descent generally covered themselves with feather beds rather than blankets when they slept. Perhaps because of the different, particularly thick bedding, bedsteads were also peculiarly constructed. When the estate of German-speaker Michael Roth of Honey Brook, Chester County, was appraised, the inventory takers specifically noted "1 Bedstead made Dutch Fashion."[16] The use of the adjective "Dutch" may refer to something made as if in Holland. However, the term "Dutch" had also been used since the fifteenth century to refer to German-speaking people. The adjectives "high" and "low" were often applied to distinguish the "Low Dutch" of the present-day Netherlands, low on the Rhine, from the "High Dutch" of the German principalities farther south on the Rhine.[17] It is likely, given that Roth was a German speaker, that his bed was of a particularly German rather than Low Dutch form, possibly with side panels to help secure his bulky bedding in place.[18]

In addition to using distinct furniture forms, Pennsylvania Germans also reportedly decorated their household accouterments differently from many of their non-German neighbors. Schöpf noted that inside Pennsylvania German houses "everything [was] daubed with red." He made a similar observation concerning house exteriors. Traveling in south-central Pennsylvania, Schöpf commented that the houses were "painted divers colors." He credited the vivid exteriors to "the taste of the inmates," which he believed was largely reflective of their national origin. He added that the country towns he passed through had "quite the look of our German market-towns . . . for most of the inhabitants are German."[19]

Aside from brightly painted houses, many period commentators also pointed out the colorful nature of Pennsylvania Germans' clothing. That the attire of German immigrants was distinct from that of other Americans was made clear by Heinrich Melchior Muhlenberg, who wrote to his superiors in Europe that "the people here are astonished when they see German dress." In addition to straw hats, "large pulled-down hats," and "boots extending above the knees," color was also a distinguishing feature. As one traveler watched the congregation leaving a rural German Lutheran church in Pennsylvania, he could not help noting that the men wore green or light blue coats "as in Germany." Schöpf likewise recognized the importance of color as an indicator of ethnic costume. He described the attire of a typical "old German countryman" in Pennsylvania as "blue stockings and yellow-leather breeches."[20]

Travelers and the German Farmer

At first it may seem that comments about Pennsylvania German barns, houses, heating devices, foods, furniture, and clothing only represent attempts on the part of their authors to draw distinctions among Pennsylvanians of various ethnic backgrounds. They appear relatively straightforward and free from biases based on national allegiances. However, authors made so many detailed observations about what they believed was distinctly German material culture so that they would be able to draw broad conclusions about the collective character of the group, the place of Pennsylvania Germans in American society, and the social and economic development of the United States. Many of their observations were designed specifically to classify Pennsylvania Germans according to occupation, wealth, and social status—issues of immense importance in the late eighteenth century as Americans experimented with new forms of government and addressed ever-changing social and economic conditions.

Schöpf's remarks about central-chimney Pennsylvania German entry-kitchen houses, for example, while seemingly only intended to identify an ethnic architectural form, would have held deeper meaning for period readers. Other contemporary authors clearly associated the entry-kitchen house type with people of inferior social and economic standing. Benjamin Franklin, for instance, included an illustration of the floor plan of an entry-kitchen house in his publication *Observations on Smoky Chimneys* (fig. 16). In his text, he noted that the form was common among "the lower people among the northern nations of Europe, and among the poorer sort of Germans in Pennsylvania." He was not alone in this impression. A continental European land agent who traveled in America in 1794 associated the entry-kitchen house specifically

Fig. 16 Entry-kitchen floor plan illustrated in Benjamin Franklin's *Observations on Smoky Chimneys, Their Causes and Cure; With Considerations on Fuel and Stoves* (London: I. and J. Taylor, 1793). As Franklin described the image, "*A* is the kitchen with its chimney; *B* an iron stove in the stove-room." Franklin associated the plan particularly with "the lower people among the northern nations of Europe" and "the poorer sort of Germans in Pennsylvania." Courtesy of the Winterthur Library, Printed Book and Periodical Collection.

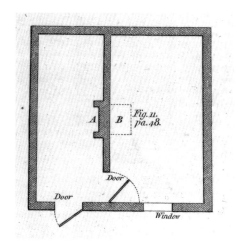

with Pennsylvania German farmers. He observed that the typical German farmhouse was of the entry-kitchen variety with "a kitchen and a large room with . . . the stove" on the first floor.[21]

Remarks about the stoves inside these houses, as well as about Pennsylvania German barns, food, and clothing, were also used by authors to place people of German descent squarely within the category of industrious and economical farmers. Benjamin Rush, for example, explained to his readers that Pennsylvania Germans subsisted "frugally . . . with respect to diet, furniture and apparel." Their stoves and their feather beds kept them warmer than other Pennsylvanians, and their stoves required a smaller quantity of wood than fireplaces did. Furthermore, the rye flour they used was less expensive than wheat flour, and Rush believed more nourishing as well. Pennsylvania German barns, according to Rush, also saved precious commodities, including hay and grain, since animals stabled in the multifunction buildings were kept warmer and therefore required less food. The barns additionally saved labor since they allowed husbandmen to "feed their horses and cattle, and to remove their dung, with as little trouble as possible."[22]

Even seemingly trivial commentary about the use of color contributed to the portrayal of Pennsylvania Germans according to conventional notions about farmers. Schöpf used his description of the "old German country-man" to emphasize the less flattering attributes of those who worked the land. His characterization was part of a story about Pennsylvania German agriculturalists who were elected to the Pennsylvania Assembly but, lacking political astuteness and fluency in English, were nothing but "dumb chair-fillers." The fact that they wore colorful German outfits only distanced them further from English-speaking policymakers and demonstrated what he perceived as their lack of taste and intelligence.[23]

It is not surprising that European and American authors turned to the Pennsylvania Germans to epitomize the farmer in America. During the period the British North American colonies were settled, European Germans were understood to be residents of a vast territory that was not as developed politically, socially, or economically as other parts of Europe. The German-speaking region of the continent had been devastated by the physical destruction and economic and cultural impasses that accompanied the Thirty Years War (1618–48). Military conflicts, both internal and external, continued to plague the area during the next century and a half. Unlike other European nations such as England and France, Germany was not united under a single head of state. The Holy Roman Emperor, the nominal leader of the Empire of German Nations, exercised little control over lands where he was not also territorial lord. As the author of a London dictionary noted, Germany by the mid-eighteenth century was controlled by "upwards of three hundred sovereign princes and states." Territories, which ranged in size from whole regions to individual villages, were part of a complex and often contested network that linked them with other German states, the larger Holy Roman Empire, and more powerful European nations.[24]

While European Germans were commonly believed to be an industrious people, as citizens of what was perceived as a less advanced society politically as well as culturally they were subject to other stereotypes as well. One encyclopedia author reported of the "ancient" Germans that "they do not seem, indeed, to have had a taste for grand and elegant entertainments: they affected in every thing, in their houses, furniture, diet, &c. rather plainness and simplicity, than sumptuousness and luxury." He later reinforced this observation by noting that members of the historic group universally "despised superfluities." In more modern times, although the largely landlocked German provinces were slowly adopting mercantilism and the industry and external trade that accompanied it, many Germans were still characterized as peasants or feudal tenants. Even the Hanoverian Georg Ludwig—descendant of European royalty, elector of the Holy Roman Emperor, and leader of the German Federal troops—was criticized for his unenlightened inclinations when he ascended to the English throne as George I in 1714. According to satirical poems written at the time of his coronation, the new king dressed in dirty shirts made from coarse fabrics, dined on leeks and garlic, and included among the possessions he brought from the continent only a pipe, a closestool, and lice.[25]

In an age when national origin was commonly believed to correspond to certain personal traits and preferences, it was easy for commentators to translate their beliefs about European Germans to people of German descent living in Pennsylvania. In Europe, Germans were perceived as less developed than other Europeans, particularly the French and the English. While "the greatest characteristics" of the "German nation" were thought to be "industry, application, and perseverance," German speakers were also viewed as simpletons, especially by other Europeans who looked to their material culture to prove their contentions. As one Frenchman noted when writing about personal attire, "certainly you would not go [to Germany] in search of models."[26]

As with the material culture associated with European Germans, observers of the Pennsylvania German population often went beyond explanations of real ethnic differences in order to make judgmental statements about the quality of the group's belongings. Despite the great variety of positions occupied by people of German descent in the late eighteenth century, authors routinely chose to focus on the material world created by unpretentious, rural settlers to epitomize the population. In many cases, their observations were made primarily for the purposes of creating a useful stereotype. While traveling in Pennsylvania, commentators were quick to describe bucolic landscape features—rather than elegant urban churches, imposing iron plantations, or even successful merchant grist mills—as German. By emphasizing this selective landscape, they ensured that Pennsylvania Germans would be understood according to predominant notions of the period about farmers and farming.

The most stereotypical characterizations of Pennsylvania German material culture, which fit into a second, less accurate category of commentary, concerned the size and quality of landholdings, barns, and houses. Many observers, for example, commented that Pennsylvania Germans valued large tracts of high quality farmland. According to Schöpf, land was the "chief object" of German immigrants' desires. He remarked that Pennsylvania German landowners saved their money "in old stockings or puncheon chests" until they had the opportunity to buy still more property. Other European visitors also observed a passion for land among Pennsylvania's German inhabitants. In the newly settled territory of central Pennsylvania, an aristocratic French traveler noted in the 1790s that Germans were very "tenacious" of their property. In more mature regions, such as Berks County, a European land agent echoed Schöpf's sentiments when he wrote that Pennsylvania German farmers who accumulated wealth either saved it as cash or used it to purchase more land adjacent to their own. Both of these authors associated the desire to amass land specifically with ethnic background. When comparing the landholding practices of individuals of German and Irish descent, they found that it was the Germans who controlled the sizable tracts.[27]

In addition to accumulating large quantities of land, it was generally believed that Pennsylvania Germans also devoted more attention to their farmland than their non-German neighbors. One European traveler expressed a common opinion when he remarked, "these German farmers take very good care of their farms." The extra effort was believed to be especially apparent in superior fences and gardens. Benjamin Rush explained that the fences on Pennsylvania German farms were "generally high, and well built." They kept horses, cattle, hogs, and sheep from making "inroads" into grain fields and other cultivated areas. Rush likewise praised Pennsylvania German gardens for their size and profitability. He credited the wide variety of vegetables available in Philadelphia to the "settlement of a number of German gardeners in the neighbourhood."[28]

Schöpf, too, reported that Pennsylvania German farms revealed "order and good management in all that concerns the care of the land." Like Rush, he was especially complimentary of the fences and gardens. He also praised the "stabling." Schöpf, along with a number of his contemporaries, found that Pennsylvania German farms often had particularly impressive barns. As European travelers toured the Pennsylvania countryside, they repeatedly described what they perceived to be distinctly German barns as "large" and "good."[29]

Pennsylvania German houses, on the other hand, were routinely described as "small" and "poor." Period authors believed that inside, these farmhouses often lacked important accouterments. One European traveler noted that the typical Pennsylvania German table was generally covered with only "a dirty little napkin instead of a tablecloth." It was a general perception among travelers that Pennsylvania German farmhouses were sparsely furnished and often lacked expendable goods such as nonessential textiles. Other than the stove and table in the stove room, Schöpf reported little else. Another visitor, who was familiar with the French countryside, found that farmers there routinely had "several large wardrobes, filled with clothes and linen, more or less, silver spoons, knives and forks, large silver drinking-cups for each member of the family, father, mother, older children; much linen underwear and table-linen." He did not find the same to be true in Pennsylvania, even among "the rich German farmers." Even in better Pennsylvania German houses, this traveler reported "beds generally without curtains, no mirrors, nor good chairs, nor good tables and wardrobes."[30]

By describing Pennsylvania Germans as the possessors of sizable tracts of land, impressive, large barns, and small, poorly furnished houses, period authors conveyed the perceived priorities of people of German descent. Both supporters and critics of the Pennsylvania Germans felt that members of the group valued agriculture over politics, education, entertainment, or even comfort. According to some commentators, most notably those who understood independent farmers to be ideal citizens, this choice could be endorsed. Others, particularly those like Schöpf who were well-educated noblemen or professionals who embraced the aristocratic social structure of Europe, found the Pennsylvania Germans' priorities displeasing and felt that they resulted in a decidedly inferior population.

Authors from both camps regarded the expansive tracts of land, immense barns, tall fences, and productive gardens that they associated with Pennsylvania Germans as deserving of praise. By contemporary standards, these possessions demonstrated an exceptional proficiency in agriculture. Those who described Pennsylvania German farms often commented on the "industrious" nature of people of German descent. As farmers, Pennsylvania Germans were seldom criticized. However, Pennsylvania Germans were often considered by their detractors to be "economical," "frugal," or even "stingy" in other aspects of their lives.

One of the areas where economy was most often perceived by period commentators was in the Pennsylvania German farmhouse. Benjamin Rush, one of the German's greatest supporters, reported, "they always provide large and suitable accommodations for their horses and cattle, before they lay out much money in building a house for themselves." To Rush, this was an admirable quality. However, many of his contemporaries came to a different conclusion. One Frenchman characterized the Pennsylvania German landscape for his readers by noting, "The houses are small, and kept in very bad order;

the barns are large, and in very good repair." He repeated several pages later, "every where we observe German farms, small houses, large barns."[31]

According to another European traveler, from the yard around a dwelling to the most intimate interior spaces, Pennsylvania German houses were poorly cared for and lacked basic furnishings. This author reported that at the entrance to the typical Pennsylvania German farmhouse there were no trees or flowers but rather stones and mud. The "almost unfurnished" interior was subject to the same perceived level of neglect, where dishes were found on the stove and potatoes and turnips on the floor. The visitor noted that "with the exception of the size of the barn and a larger cultivated area" there was little to "distinguish between the rich Pennsylvania farmer and the poor farmer of other states."[32]

According to this author, Pennsylvania Germans invested their financial resources in land and barns but not domestic accommodations. The decision was believed to be a result of their ethnic background. The traveler recorded in his journal that "probably one of the causes of this slovenliness and lack of comfort is that they do not know any better." He believed that many Pennsylvania German farmers who had been introduced to "English or American clothing" had adopted it and hoped that "from clothes it will pass to house-furnishings, etc."[33]

Schöpf was less optimistic that the Pennsylvania Germans he described would be willing to emulate what he believed to be the superior habits of their non-German neighbors. Although the Bavarian's belittling descriptions of Pennsylvania German houses were perhaps influenced by regional German prejudices, his comments indicate that such buildings were not simply poorly judged because they were misunderstood by those unfamiliar with their heating scheme and form. While Schöpf praised Pennsylvania German dwellings as "better-built" and "warmer" because of their stoves, he found that inside their occupants lived "thriftily, often badly." Schöpf, influenced by his professional position and negative opinion of those who worked the land, told his readers that "the economy of the German farmer in Pennsylvania is precisely the same as that customary in Germany—even when his next neighbor every day sets him a better example." According to Schöpf, in their dwellings Pennsylvania Germans lacked "the simple unaffected neatness of the English settlers, who make it a point, as far as they are able, to live seemly, in a well-furnished house, in every way as comports with the *gentleman*."[34]

Especially troubling to Schöpf was the lack of reading material he perceived in Pennsylvania German houses. In this regard, German farmers reportedly demonstrated not only their thriftiness but also, allegedly, their ignorance. Schöpf believed that in Pennsylvania "the universal German farmer's library" included a Bible, two prayer books, a songbook, and an almanac. In even the poorest English houses, on the other hand, Schöpf assumed that larger libraries—which would include journals, magazines, and dictionaries—were common. The perceived lack of reading materials in German farmhouses was, in Schöpf's mind, indicative of a larger difference between people of German and English descent. He wrote, "In the same circumstances and with the same facilities the Englishman invariably shows more information." Schöpf reported the German, on the other hand, was more inclined toward "superstitions and prejudices" and was "less intelligent in political matters."[35]

As Schöpf toured the Pennsylvania countryside, he recorded examples to support his claim that Pennsylvania Germans trusted superstition rather than learned knowledge. In the mountainous region of northeastern Pennsylvania, he noted that German immigrants put their faith in stories of elves and secret treasures. Schöpf argued that such fairy tales, which they "brought with them" from Europe, led German settlers to "[dream] of mines and sudden wealth" rather than learn the practical requirements of developing "fine plantations." Schöpf was joined in his assessment of the Pennsylvania Germans as believers in fables and the magical beings described in them by the author of *The American Geography,* published in 1789. This reference book reported that is was not uncommon to see Pennsylvania Germans "going to market with a little bag of salt tied to their horses['] manes, for the purpose, they say, of keeping off the witches."[36]

The observations of period writers concerning the belongings of Pennsylvania Germans—from barns to books and bags of salt—contributed to an assessment of members of the group that matched popular conceptions about those who worked the land. People of German descent living in late eighteenth-century Pennsylvania were perceived as industrious in their work, economical in their accommodations, and ignorant in their beliefs. Those who championed the Pennsylvania Germans praised the first two traits and found ways to excuse the third. Benjamin Rush, for example, wrote, "It has been said, that the Germans are deficient in learning; and that in consequence of their want of more general and extensive education, they are much addicted to superstition, and are frequently imposed upon in the management of their affairs." However, Rush believed that this fault would soon be eradicated and told his readers of a new college that had recently been established "for the purpose of diffusing learning" among the next generation of Pennsylvania Germans. Another period author agreed with Rush about the fleeting nature of Pennsylvania German ignorance. Writing in 1795, he observed that although "the body" of the group still lacked education, a "literary spirit" had "of late been increasing among them."[37]

To period commentators who found Pennsylvania German material culture and therefore Pennsylvania Germans distasteful, only their industrious nature was viewed in a positive light. Economy, often presented as frugality or stinginess, was interpreted as a common shortcoming and ignorance as a consistent failing. After observing the landscape created by German immigrants and their descendants, one traveler concluded of the Pennsylvania Germans that "they are all very laborious, and extremely industrious, having improved this part of the country beyond conception; but they have no idea of social life, and are more like brutes than men." Another added, "they are thrifty to the point of avarice. . . . They deny themselves everything costly. . . . They are remarkably obstinate and ignorant." Even the native German Schöpf found his Pennsylvania brethren unappealing. He summed up his impression of the Pennsylvania Germans by writing that "on the whole they show little or no zeal to bring themselves up in any way except by small trade or handicrafts or farming. To use their gains for allowable pleasures, augmenting the agreeableness of life, this very few of them have learned to do, and others with bad grace."[38]

Schöpf and others indicated that German immigrants brought traditions of frugality in domestic accommodations and personal betterment from central Europe and therefore believed that the English in Pennsylvania must have lived in superior houses that were "neater" and better furnished than those of their German neighbors. Rarely did they point to specific individuals to prove their points, however. Despite numerous period accounts concerning Pennsylvania Germans' experiences, in only one case was a "typical" Pennsylvania German farmer mentioned by name. In November of 1794, a European traveler visited a Pennsylvania German by the name of Leonard Elmaker in Salisbury Township, Lancaster County. According to the amateur ethnographer, Elmaker was a "very rich farmer" who owned 320 acres of land as well as a flour mill and a saw mill. However, when he entered the Elmaker house, he reported that "the whole family (7 children) were having a very bad dinner around a very dirty little table, and the furniture in the main room was not worth 200 dollars." Based on other passages in his text, it is clear that this author associated the Elmaker family's perceived shortcomings with their German background. The Elmakers reinforced the stereotype that Pennsylvania Germans, while industrious in their work, were overly thrifty, particularly in their domestic accommodations.[39]

Through the Tax Assessors' Eyes

Other, less impressionistic documentary records produced in the late eighteenth century suggest why Leonard Elmaker was the only Pennsylvania German singled out by name to illustrate the conventional image of the Pennsylvania German farmer. To possess significant resources and still live in a poor-quality house, as Elmaker reportedly did, was very unusual for anyone in late eighteenth-century Pennsylvania, regardless of ethnic background. By turning to 1798 Federal Direct Tax records, we can directly compare the dwellings occupied by members of different ethnic groups.[40]

While tax records do not provide information about the floor plan or color of a house, how it was heated or furnished, or what its habitants ate or wore, the assessments from 1798 do include detailed data about the dimensions and assessed value of buildings. Although there is much that tax records cannot confirm about Pennsylvania German material culture, they can be used to challenge travelers' observations about the size and quality of the buildings occupied by members of the group.[41] What the records demonstrate is that people with British surnames did not always live in larger houses or in houses that were more highly assessed than those occupied by people with German surnames. In late eighteenth-century Coventry Township[42] in northern Chester County, for example, the average size of houses owned by people with British surnames was approximately 700 square feet, while the average for householders with German surnames was over 830 square feet. The average value for houses, including house lots and domestic outbuildings, was $284 for the British; for the Germans it was $347. In this locale, it was actually the Germans, not the British, who tended to have superior domestic accommodations.[43]

The Coventry Township pattern of house ownership, however, was no more universal than the travelers' stereotypical claims. In her work on Lancaster County, Gabrielle Lanier found that an overriding proclivity toward larger houses was hard to substantiate for either Germans or non-Germans. Based on the 1798 records, in Conestoga Township, Lancaster County, as in Coventry Township, the average German-occupied dwelling was larger than the average dwelling occupied by a non-German. Yet in nearby Hempfield Township, the trend was reversed, with non-Germans residing in houses that averaged more square footage.[44]

Based on the information recorded in tax returns, the imagined landscape travelers created on paper—dotted with small, "bad" German houses—seems far removed from the physical landscape they must have observed as they toured Pennsylvania. In reality, people of both German and British descent occupied small houses in poor condition. Members of both ethnic groups also resided in larger houses that were highly appraised by tax assessors.[45] The tax records indicate that, depending on the locale, the houses of one group may have been on average slightly bigger and more valuable than those of the other. However, the differences in size and assessed value were not substantial enough to be easily recognizable, nor were they absolute.

A similar discrepancy existed between the imagined world of the travelers and the tangible world through which they passed in regard to landholdings and agricultural buildings. Period commentators repeatedly identified large tracts of land and large barns with people of German descent. In some places, such as Hempfield and Conestoga townships in Lancaster County, late eighteenth-century tax records indicate that people with German surnames did average more acreage than their non-German neighbors. However, in other locales the opposite was true. In Coventry Township, Chester County, for example, the average British settler possessed more than 104 acres of land while the average German possessed fewer than 90.[46]

Just as tax records challenge period authors' beliefs about landholding patterns, they also dispute popular perceptions about barns. Sizable barns were not common on the majority of Pennsylvania German farms nor were they unknown on the farms of non-Germans. The assessments produced in conjunction with the 1798 Federal Direct Tax do not provide as much information about barns as they do about other types of buildings such as houses; what they frequently do include, however, are measurements of overall length and width. From these dimensions, it is possible to get some idea of a barn's size, although total square footage is impossible to determine since the number of stories is rarely included.

Even with the limited available data on barn size, it is clear that large barns were rare in southeastern Pennsylvania. In predominantly rural Coventry Township, Chester County, one-third of all households had no building identified by the 1798 tax assessor as a barn. Another group of property holders possessed barns that measured 20 by 36 feet or less; in all but one case these buildings were specifically described for assessment purposes as "small." Only 16 of 179 householders could boast of a barn at least 30 by 60 feet in size. Many of these large structures were described as "good," and several were additionally distinguished because they were "new."[47]

The wide variety of barn sizes in Coventry Township is difficult to explain in terms of the barn owners' ethnic background. People with German surnames possessed both the largest barn in the township and the smallest. Barns owned by individuals with British surnames also appeared at both ends of the spectrum. Overall, Germans in the township possessed barns that averaged a little over 100 square feet larger in footprint than the barns of their British neighbors. Gabrielle Lanier found that the same pattern was even more pronounced in Hempfield Township, Lancaster County, where barns held by Germans averaged over 400 square feet larger in footprint than those held by non-Germans. However, in Conestoga Township, Lancaster County, the opposite was true. There the average barn possessed by a non-German was close to 100 square feet larger than that possessed by a German.[48]

What tax records demonstrate is that large barns, which travelers and other eighteenth-century authors specifically associated with Pennsylvania Germans, were neither unique to members of the group nor common among them. A small minority of Pennsylvanians from various ethnic backgrounds possessed a sizable barn in the late eighteenth century. Many more individuals had no barn or a small- to mid-sized barn on the property they owned or rented. While in Hempfield Township the barns possessed by people with German surnames were on average significantly larger than those possessed by their non-German neighbors, in other locales ethnic patterns were not as pronounced. In Coventry and Conestoga townships, differences in average barn size based on ethnic background were slight and would not have been easily noticed by even the most careful observer.

Not only did Pennsylvania Germans reside in both large and small houses and possess both large and small barns, but the juxtaposition of a small house and large barn, so often commented upon in eighteenth-century accounts of the Pennsylvania German landscape, was also exceedingly rare. In Coventry Township, of the sixteen householders who had barns measuring at least 30 by 60 feet, only three lived in one-story houses, and only one of those dwellings had less than 450 square feet of interior space. The remaining thirteen large barn holders all resided in one-and-a-half- or two-story dwellings, which, with combined first- and second-floor spaces, each amounted to over 1100 square feet of interior area. Furthermore, of the sixty-seven householders who lived in small houses with less than 450 square feet of space, only one-fifth possessed barns that were larger than 20 by 36 feet and therefore exceeded the assessor's definition of a "small" barn. Only two had barns that measured at least 30 by 60 feet. Not surprisingly, farmsteads composed of humble houses and at least mid-sized barns were occupied by people with both British and German surnames.[49]

Many of the descriptions of Pennsylvania German material culture that saturated late eighteenth-century literature were not supported by the physical landscape that people of German descent actually created.[50] Commentators chose to depict Pennsylvania's German inhabitants as hard-working farmers who devoted few resources to their physical comfort or personal advancement. The adage about small houses and large barns, which supported stereotypes of industry, economy, and ignorance, applied to less than 10 percent of the 111 householders with German surnames in Coventry Township in 1798.[51] More common scenes included properties with small houses and no barns or small houses and small barns. Generally when a farm had a large barn, it also had a sizable dwelling.

The Pennsylvania German and Republican Ideals

The prolific authors who so often identified attributes of the so-called German landscape did so with specific goals in mind, goals that did not necessarily include the desire to accurately reflect the reality of Pennsylvania Germans' material existence. As late eighteenth-century thinkers debated the relative merits of a commercial versus an agricultural society and the extent to which democracy should replace aristocracy in both politics and society generally, they created in the Pennsylvania Germans a useful example. Rather than reflect on the diversity of the Pennsylvania German experience, made tangible by the great variety of structures and other objects that people of German descent possessed, they chose to portray members of the group according to a rigid formula.

Beginning in the 1750s, French and Scottish political economists, writing about the progression from savagery to civilization, posited that societies advanced through four stages of development. In their theory, which served as a springboard for European thought through the end of the century, the stages they defined were marked by four kinds of subsistence: hunting, pasturage, agriculture, and commerce.[52] People of German descent living in late eighteenth-century Pennsylvania came to represent a specific component of the American population that was not defined by its ethnic background but rather by its place in the four-stage progression—Pennsylvania Germans became the farmers. When period authors wrote about members of the group, they were more generally referring to those who worked the land and largely avoided nonessential commercial relations. In describing Pennsylvania German material culture and in using it to characterize the Pennsylvania Germans as industrious, economical, and ignorant, they were most notably making judgments about agriculture and commerce rather than about ethnic traits. Depending on the author, people of German descent came to be presented as either virtuous husbandmen or brutish toilers of the soil.

In equating the Pennsylvania Germans with agriculture, late eighteenth-century authors frequently compared them with members of another ethnic group that had settled in Pennsylvania, the Scots-Irish. In German immigrants and their descendants, writers found a group they considered more dedicated to the land, to honest labor, and to the unpretentious lifestyle of the farmer. When one author compared the two groups, he observed, "The Irish are, with a few exceptions, the worst of them all. Being less industrious than the rest, they are consequently poorer; and the property of an Irishman is constantly at the service of such as wish to have it. The Germans are more tenacious of theirs; and, for this reason . . . where they reside in considerable numbers, estates are dearer." Another noted, "it is only fair to say that German farmers give farms to their sons as soon as they are of age, for their marriage, and even if they have 10 sons, they all become farmers,—while Irish farmers, if they make a fortune, bring up their children for the cities." While depictions of the Scots-Irish, usually referred to by European authors as simply the Irish, were likely as exaggerated as those of the Germans in Pennsylvania, they painted a picture of a group that was ready to forsake the hard work of the countryside in favor of the commercial city. In the Germans, on the other hand, authors envisioned a group devoted to agriculture in this generation and the next.[53]

In the new United States, those who supported the extension of agriculture rather than the expansion of cities and industry often identified themselves with Thomas Jefferson's Republican party. They championed the independent farmer and denounced the extremes of social hierarchy that were marked by great luxury and abject poverty. They also tended to praise Pennsylvania Germans and Pennsylvania German material culture. Even the Virginian Jefferson had positive things to say about members of the group. When contemplating the peopling of Western lands, he wrote to colleagues that he preferred German immigrants to other European settlers since they did "the best for themselves," and their offspring readily became "good citizens."[54]

In Pennsylvania, Benjamin Rush perhaps best articulated the Jeffersonian Republican platform by repeatedly highlighting the virtues of agriculture. In an address concerning the proposed establishment of a college to serve Pennsylvanians of German descent, Rush pointed out that vices "always prevail[ed] in large towns." In rural areas, however, they were much less common. Rush in fact argued that political leaders should be chosen from among "the cultivators of the earth" since "their manner of life" best shielded them from corruption.[55]

Unlike some of his contemporaries, Rush found no incongruity between agriculture and education. He believed that it was only by "diffusing learning" that "aristocratic juntos" could be destroyed and "a true commonwealth" established. Furthermore, among farmers he concluded that knowledge from "books containing an account of the improvements and discoveries in agriculture and rural economy" would advance cultivation "to a degree of perfection hitherto unknown." According to Rush, farmers were not to be categorized among the lowly but rather among the most virtuous. They were free from the corruption and vices common in the city and were soon to be inundated with knowledge that they would use to advance the "utility and beauty" of their "fields, gardens, fruit trees, and meadow grounds." To Rush, who identified himself as "A Friend of Equal Liberty and Learning," this knowledge would additionally be used to put an end to government based on aristocracy.[56]

It is not surprising that Benjamin Rush found the Pennsylvania Germans to be among "the best members of republican governments." Rush was fond of the Germans' "republican manners" and their "republican virtues of industry and economy." Perhaps more than many other authors, Rush, who included among his friends Pennsylvania German clockmaker and scientist David Rittenhouse, understood that the German population of the commonwealth included artisans, merchants, and learned professionals in addition to farmers. Furthermore, he observed that German agriculturalists regularly participated in market relations when they sold their grain and other produce in Philadelphia, even if at the same time he saw in them a group primarily composed of "skillful cultivators of the earth" who strove to avoid the excess made possible by unrestrained commerce.[57]

As Rush described Pennsylvania German material culture, he emphasized that German economy prevented luxurious living and encouraged economic independence. According to Rush, Pennsylvania German furniture was "plain and useful," much of what members of the group ate could be produced on their farms, and their clothing and bedding was also homemade. Overall, the Pennsylvania Germans, as Rush characterized them, were largely self-suffi-cient, avoiding both waste and superfluous expenditures. They were the inde-pendent farmers that Republicans felt should form the backbone of American society.[58]

Rush's opinion of the Pennsylvania Germans was shared by those who agreed with his political philosophy, including the French revolutionary Jacques-Pierre Brissot de Warville. Brissot saw the new United States as a model for his European homeland. He detested luxury in the form of gilded ceilings, rich carpets, and expensive wines and advocated rural life to resurrect "private and public morals." He believed that the reason Americans had "such pure morals" was because "nine-tenths of them live[d] dispersed in the country." Not sur-prisingly, as Brissot described the Pennsylvania Germans he encountered on a tour of the United States in 1788, he praised their multifunction barns, their warm stoves, and their homemade clothing. Both he and Rush additionally remarked on the Pennsylvania Germans' sobriety.[59]

The desire among critics of commerce to present the Pennsylvania Germans as ideal citizens was so strong in the late eighteenth century that it even affected Benjamin Franklin's assessment of the group. Just a few decades earlier, at midcentury, Franklin had repeatedly berated people of German descent. He characterized the Pennsylvania Germans as being "of the most ignorant Stupid Sort." He found their "dis[s]onant Manners" intoler-able, their women "disagreeable," and their "Ideas of Beauty" bankrupt. While he believed some of the earliest German immigrants had been "good sober industrious honest People," he described more recent immigrants as poor "Refuse Wretches" or deceitful "Knaves and Rascals." In fact, Franklin charged that many of the new arrivals had come directly from German prisons. In a 1751 essay on population growth, Franklin made perhaps his most derogatory, and best remembered, remarks about the Pennsylvania Germans. Calling for an increase in the "Purely white" population in America, Franklin identified Germans (excluding Saxons) with Africans, Asians, and Native Americans because of their "swarthy" skin tone. He asked his readers, "why should the *Palatine Boors* be suffered to swarm into our Settlements and, by herding together, establish their Language and Manners, to the Exclusion of ours? Why should *Pennsylvania,* founded by the *English,* become a Colony of *Aliens,* who will shortly be so numerous as to Germanize us instead of our Anglifying them, and will never adopt our Language or Customs any more than they can acquire our Complexion?"[60]

During the first half of the eighteenth century, Franklin had made his own unsuccessful efforts to anglicize the Germans of Pennsylvania by publishing a German-language newspaper that failed after only two issues and establishing a system of "charity schools" that met with equally poor results. Much of his concern with the Pennsylvania Germans revolved around the internal political contest to control the Pennsylvania Assembly and the impending international contest to control western settlement. By the late 1760s, however, several factors had caused Franklin to change his mind about the swarthy-skinned Pennsylvania Germans. The French and Indian War, which had served as an impetus for many of his anti-German remarks, had ended. It had become clear to Franklin that people of German descent were not all pacifists who were unwilling to defend their new homeland, nor were they going to align themselves slyly with the French to defeat their British neighbors, as he had once suspected. Furthermore, as a politician Franklin had learned that he needed the support of his German constituency. His unflattering remarks about the "Palatine Boors" had been resurrected by his opponents during the 1764 provincial election and had cost him his seat in the Assembly. According to Franklin, "about 1000 Dutch" had voted against him that year because they believed that he had called them hogs.[61]

While this remark demonstrates that Franklin still believed the Pennsylvania Germans uneducated, his increasing dissatisfaction with English authority caused him to rethink his other views about them. Many of Franklin's midcentury remarks denigrated German immigrants because they were either poor British subjects (who did not speak or read English, for example) or because they took precious resources away from British settlers. Yet as England turned increasingly to an economy based on mercantilism, Franklin's pro-British sentiments wavered. He believed that wealth achieved through the export of manufactured goods was by nature acquired dishonestly. Not only were foreign consumers cheated, but domestic workers were exploited as well. "Manufacturing Life," according to Franklin, was "Unwholesome," and England's reliance on commerce had created a society marred by great disparities in wealth. With the negative English model in mind, Franklin, like Rush and Brissot, came to believe that "Farmers who manufacture in their own Families what they have occasion for and no more, are perhaps the happiest People and the healthiest."[62]

It is not surprising then that Franklin's later comments about the Pennsylvania Germans took a more positive tone. In his midcentury writings

Franklin had recognized people of German descent as "excellent husband-men." However, he neutralized his compliment by insisting that Pennsylvania Germans seemed to "under-live" and were "thereby enabled to under-work and under-sell" their English neighbors. By the end of the century, what Franklin perceived as the Germans' inclination toward frugality had taken on a more positive cast for him, as it became associated with self-sufficiency and the shunning of luxury. Rather than focusing on German/English divisions as he had earlier, Franklin began to focus on the contrasts between an economy based on agriculture and an economy based on commerce, particularly on the export of manufactured goods.[63]

Nowhere is Franklin's shifting attitude toward Pennsylvania Germans more noticeable than in his assessment of their material culture, particularly their stoves. Franklin, who wrote extensively on the scientific principles of fire and heat, had long been interested in the types of heating devices used in continental Europe. In 1744, when he began advertising his newly invented Franklin stove, known at the time as a "Pennsylvania Fire-Place" because it replicated the form of an open hearth in iron, Franklin described the kinds of stoves used in both Holland and Germany. Not surprisingly, the author-inventor found numerous problems with the German example. The people who employed it could not see or use the fire inside and were "moreover oblig'd to breathe the same unchang'd Air continually, mix'd with the Breath and Perspiration from one another[']s Bodies." By the 1780s, however, Franklin no longer emphasized the lack of firelight, poor air circulation, or odors that accompanied the use of a closed German stove. Instead, he announced to the members of the American Philosophical Society that "in Germany, you are happy in the use of stoves, which save fuel wonderfully." On Pennsylvania German farms, he reported, "the whole house is warmed at little expense of wood, and the stove room kept constantly warm; so that in the coolest winter nights they can work late, and find the room still comfortable when they rise to work early." The closed stove had become for Franklin a symbol of economy, which allowed for increased industry and personal independence among even the poorest farmers.[64]

For the group of late eighteenth-century writers that included Rush, Brissot, and Franklin, material culture identified as "German" was virtuous in its practicality. They emphasized both the possessions that saved labor and resources and those that could be produced at home. Both types of goods contributed to the economic independence of farmers by limiting their dependence on imported goods as well as on hired help. Although such belongings were often described as manifestations of ethnic background—and some, like the stove and the featherbed, were used primarily by people of German descent in late eighteenth-century America—what was more important was that they also represented industry and economy. The Pennsylvania Germans, according to this group of commentators, were an example to all Americans, regardless of national origin.

Just as champions of the independent farmer turned to people of German descent for a model, those who believed that the United States must continue to develop socially and economically according to the European example also relied on the ethnic group for an illustration. To them, the Pennsylvania Germans came to represent all that was wrong with a society that promoted equality rather than appropriate forms of hierarchy and fostered agriculture at the expense of industry. It must be noted, however, that the most outspoken members of this group of detractors were complete foreigners to the Pennsylvania German community. Unlike the Germans' supporters, a group that consisted of both long-term Pennsylvania residents and tourists who visited the commonwealth only briefly, critics of the ethnic group were invariably from more remote regions of the United States or from Europe. The Federalist Party, which often supported manufacturing interests and aristocratic government, depended in Pennsylvania on the leadership of individuals of German descent and on the support of a constituency that was at least one-third German. As a result, it was only a New England Federalist such as Uriah Tracy who could boldly proclaim that he considered Pennsylvania Germans "both stupid, ignorant, and ugly."[65]

Europeans who were further removed from the Pennsylvania German population were even more likely to provide details of what they found displeasing about the people of German descent they encountered while visiting America. Often their criticisms centered on the very material symbols of economy others had praised. One traveler, for example, noted that on their farms, people of German descent "cultivate[d] enough flax and hemp and also raise[d] what sheep they need[ed] for making their linen and cloth." Yet unlike Rush and Brissot, who found the resulting "homespun" clothing a sign of virtue, this traveler remarked on its "coarse" quality. He found it a sign of Pennsylvania German obstinacy and ignorance. He noted with distaste that even farmers worth £20,000 went to market in Lancaster wearing their unfashionable "long linen-trousers."[66]

For European authors, economy in the material world frequently took on negative connotations. Those who belittled the Pennsylvania Germans in the late eighteenth century were often European professionals or noblemen who were accustomed to social hierarchy. They equated large landholdings with a certain lifestyle, which included a grand house, expensive furniture, fine clothing, and refined dining. Furthermore, they associated affluence with education. Their descriptions of the Pennsylvania Germans presented an enigma. Here was a group that seemed to prefer agricultural to personal improvement. Among people of German descent, the accumulation of land and wealth was not believed to correspond with better quality food, shelter, or clothing, or with the advancement of knowledge. As one commentator put it, "The highest delight of the German countryman in Pennsylvania is—drink . . . having made a good sale, he is certain to turn in at some grogshop on his way home—drinks in good spirits a glass of wine, drinks perhaps a second, and a third, recks no more and often leaves his entire wallet at the bung."[67]

These remarks about the Pennsylvania Germans, which contrasted notably with the positive appraisals of the industrious, frugal, and sober Germans in the accounts of people like Rush and Brissot, expressed deep concerns among certain Europeans about the future of American society. In Europe, increased social and economic hierarchy had accompanied the rise of industry and mercantilism. In America, such stratification seemed almost nonexistent. Schöpf explained, "People think, act, and speak here precisely as it prompts them; the poorest day-laborer on the bank of the Delaware holds it his right to advance his opinion, in religious as well as political matters, with as much freedom as the gentleman or scholar." He went on to explain that neither wealth nor posts of honor nor family affiliation corresponded with rank in America.[68]

Travelers' remarks about Pennsylvania Germans specifically critiqued the place of farmers in this more democratic American society. Farmers, regardless of ethnic background, lacked "taste and sensibility." Furthermore, they demonstrated a "total lack of education." Their failings were evidenced by their material surroundings, particularly the "lack of neatness and of furniture in their farmhouses." In fact, one traveler believed it an "impossibility" for a farmer to have "a neat or comfortable home." In America, farmers may have been able to acquire wealth in the form of cash and land, but their new-found riches did not translate to the lifestyle of the upper class. While some commentators like Rush found the perceived material simplicity of farmers' houses refreshing, these European tourists were confounded and dismayed by what they presented as an ignorant rejection of comfort and refinement. Farmers in their estimation were certainly not America's most virtuous citizens; rather, with laborers, they were among its lowliest.[69]

Thus while contemporary thinkers did not agree on whether Pennsylvania Germans should serve as a positive or negative example for other Americans, they did agree on how the group should be depicted. Both champions of the independent American farmer and defenders of European aristocracy and mercantilism painted a picture of an ethnic group typified by industry, economy, and ignorance. Commentators on both sides of the equation relied heavily on material culture to prove their points. They provided genuine—if sometimes exaggerated—descriptions of distinctions in house and barn form, diet, and wardrobe as well as less accurate generalizations about the quality of Pennsylvania Germans' property.

It must be remembered, however, that these authors were using their characterizations of Pennsylvania German material culture to make larger points about American society. Rather than being precise in their observations, they developed a conventional image that helped them defend their positions on the future of both agriculture and equality in the new United States. Although they spoke in ethnic terms about a national group, these commentators were in reality expressing their opinions about a people defined not by place of origin but rather by means of subsistence and style of living. In order to make Pennsylvania Germans fit their formula, they had to overlook the vast majority of people of German descent. They were undoubtedly influenced by previous stereotypes of European Germans, but, even more importantly, they built on one another's increasingly similar descriptions of what they believed to be the norm among Germans in Pennsylvania.

Some of these authors' portrayals certainly pointed to real differences between the material culture of some of the region's German and English residents. Comments about multifunction barns, stoves and the house forms associated with them, feather beds and unique bedsteads, certain types of food such as sauerkraut, and particular kinds of apparel such as straw hats suggest recognizable ethnic practices and traditions that worked to distinguish at least a portion of the Pennsylvania German population. However, in the writings of late eighteenth-century travelers and other observers, not all remarks about ethnic difference can be taken at face value. Published and unpublished sources were filled with commentary about politics, economics, and social organization that was expressed in ethnic terms although it had little to do with ethnicity. In an age when national prejudices and stereotypes were accepted with little question, Pennsylvania Germans as a group became farmers in the minds of many. Their houses, at least in terms of quality, came to represent the typical farmer's house, and their personal possessions were thought to exemplify the farmer's lifestyle.

For outsiders, both those who encountered the Pennsylvania Germans only briefly as tourists and those whose knowledge of the group was developed over a longer period as residents in Pennsylvania, it was not uncommon to put all individuals of German descent in the same category. Identity based on ethnicity became intrinsically tied to occupation and its associated qualities—in this case industry, economy, and ignorance. The congruence was so strong that when Schöpf encountered Pennsylvanians of German descent whose conversation was interesting and pleasing—unlike the conversation he expected from uneducated farmers—he insisted they were "no longer Germans" and had "become English quite."[70]

In the ethnically diverse Commonwealth of Pennsylvania, conclusions about an individual's identity went beyond a simple determination of where that person was born or from where his or her ancestors had come. Although authors frequently used ethnic categories as if they applied universally, their descriptions and criteria for inclusion were in fact much more limiting. In the case of the Pennsylvania Germans, articulate thinkers familiar with contemporary debates about political economy created for the group an identity that made them a useful example. Rather than reflect on the diversity among people of German descent, they developed a stereotype that applied to only a small percentage of the population. In all their travels, these commentators pointed out only one individual who could serve as a concrete example. That industrious, economical, and perhaps ignorant farmer was Leonard Elmaker. Yet, as the next chapter will demonstrate, that Lancaster County resident did not feel confined to the conventionalized role that had been created for him. Rather, he was part of a dynamic multiethnic community that was continuously working toward material improvement at the close of the eighteenth century.

From Awkwardness to Civility

In characterizing Pennsylvania Germans as farmers who lived in small, poorly furnished houses, late eighteenth-century authors overlooked the great diversity among members of the group in terms of both occupation and material culture. Like other Pennsylvanians, men and women of German descent occupied various social and economic strata. Their positions in American society were generally reflected in their houses and the objects that filled them. While a cursory reading of many published travel accounts would imply that differences in house quality were based on the ethnic background of a building's residents, surviving structures as well as various documentary sources suggest differently. As new types of houses were adopted by elite Pennsylvanians in the second half of the eighteenth century, buildings reflected national origin less and increasingly became symbols of social and economic status.

Houses in late eighteenth-century Pennsylvania directly mirrored their owners' or occupants' wealth. Significant financial resources were required to build, or even rent, a large, two-story masonry dwelling of the best sort. Such buildings were seen as expressions of social rank. Owning a highly valued house was a sign not only that the occupants had discretionary income, but also that they possessed education, social grace, and leadership potential. The specialized, often imported, objects used inside such buildings for refined rituals like tea drinking were likewise viewed as symbols of affluence. They were often expensive, but just as important, they served as manifestations of the taste and knowledge of the men and women who bought and used them.[1]

Among Pennsylvania Germans who built notable houses and purchased consumer goods such as imported ceramic tea services, such procurements reflected at least two aspects of personal identity. Although evidence provided by many period commentators and modern authors would suggest otherwise, they did not necessarily signal a rejection of German culture. Many affluent Pennsylvania Germans erected buildings that incorporated continental European construction techniques as well as prominently located stoves and quite noticeable German-language date stones.[2] Yet while these structures exhibited certain German features, they also bore features that connected their owners to a broader multiethnic community of people of similar social and economic status. The buildings were part of a cosmopolitan trend that linked improvement in the realms of finance, deportment, and knowledge with the improvement of the material landscape.

The European land agent who pointed to Leonard Elmaker as a typical Pennsylvania German farmer after a visit to his property in November of 1794 was appalled by the Elmaker family's material circumstances. He observed that their dinner was "bad," the table around which they ate "dirty," and collectively the furniture in the main room of their house not worth even $200. From his comment that "the whole farm is like those already mentioned," it is safe to assume that this traveler considered the Elmakers' property to be generally lacking in neatness and comfort and to reflect the frugality and simple-mindedness he associated with Leonard as well as with his wife, Elizabeth.[3]

Other historical records provide little additional information about the physical appearance of the Elmakers' house, the kind or condition of the furnishings they owned, or their behavior during domestic rituals such as dining. Tax records do indicate that Leonard and his family had arrived in Salisbury Township, Lancaster County, some twenty-four years earlier and had brought with them from neighboring Earl Township a fifteen-year-old slave. By 1782, the Elmakers had acquired close to 300 acres in the township, constructed two water-powered mills on the Pequea Creek, and in addition to their "Negro" had added to their household a mulatto who was probably not free, even though the state had recently enacted a gradual emancipation law. Despite their ownership of land, mills, and labor, however, the Elmakers may have still proved the exception to the rule by residing in a modest house. While their visitor indicated that their dwelling possessed both a "main room" and presumably one or more other rooms, it was very likely a one-story log structure, the most common kind of house in late eighteenth-century Pennsylvania. It is additionally plausible that to a European professional, the interior of the abode would have appeared poorly furnished and its inhabitants' dietary preferences poor.[4]

If their guest had arrived only four years later, however, his assessment of the Elmakers and their material culture would probably have been quite different. The 1790s were years of great change for the Elmaker family. By 1792, Leonard, like many other Pennsylvanians, was no longer a slave owner.[5] At the end of the decade, the structure of his household was different not only because it included both black and white free workers but also because the role of head was increasingly being assumed by his son Peter. Peter was thirty-one years old in 1797 when he replaced his father on township tax lists. He was a justice of the peace and an extensive lender of funds in the form of bonds and notes. Additionally, both Peter and his father had taken on leadership roles in their nearby church.[6]

Along with the Elmakers' changing household composition and increasing leadership roles in the community came a marked change in the material circumstances of the family. From an inventory produced as a result of "esquire" Peter's untimely death in August 1798, it is clear that when the Elmakers dined they had the option of using costly accouterments such as china dishes and silver table- and teaspoons. Furthermore, they did not have to crowd around what their guest had described as one "dirty little table," since they possessed a dining and breakfast table, a tea table, and a card table. The value of the belongings in their main room had increased as well. The "House Clock & Case" was by itself worth £20 (approximately $53), roughly equal in value to their road wagon or their yoke oxen. The increase in the number and cost of household goods was not just a result of son Peter taking over household expenditures. When Leonard died "an old man" at eighty-eight years of age in 1829, his estate also included a wide range of expensive and specialized forms, such as silver teaspoons, sugar tongs, and a waiter, or tray, for serving tea; kitchen, dining, and breakfast tables; and an eight-day clock.[7]

It is difficult to gauge just how quickly the Elmakers' material world was changing during this period. In 1794, did their European visitor fail to see—because of either preconceived ideas or limited access—certain kinds of goods used in the Elmakers' home? Or was much of what was recorded in son Peter's inventory purchased only after his visit? One fact suggests the latter might have been the case. During the summer of 1798, just months before the inventory was taken, the family commenced an extensive building campaign to construct both a "complete stone barn" and a new, two-story stone house. Presumably silver and china, multiple tables, and a tall case clock could have been purchased specifically to furnish the new building.[8]

To the European traveler who stopped at the Elmakers' in 1794, the family's older Salisbury Township residence served as a symbol of their German heritage. It may have used an entry-kitchen plan, but of more importance to their visitor was the fact that it was small and under-furnished. It fit prevailing period stereotypes concerning Pennsylvania German dwellings and confirmed the popular belief that Pennsylvania Germans such as the Elmakers lived frugally in regard to their domestic accommodations. Their new dwelling, however, would have had quite a different meaning. The house was constructed of masonry, contained a full two stories, and measured a sizable 30 by 40 feet.[9]

The house built by the Elmaker family in 1798, while certainly above average for the area, was not unique in terms of either its square footage or its durable stone construction. While most Pennsylvanians resided in much smaller, humbler one-story dwellings built of log, a select group of residents in the region were constructing larger, more elaborate houses during the last half of the eighteenth century. Furthermore, like the Elmakers, they were furnishing their new houses with increasingly specialized and expensive household accouterments. During the eighteenth century a profusion of goods, many of which were associated with genteel forms of entertainment, were introduced, particularly among members of the upper classes. Elaborate meals were eaten around an increasing variety of function-specific tables by people seated in matched sets of chairs, ideally constructed of imported mahogany. Food was consumed by each diner using her or his own spoon as well as a newly introduced utensil, the fork, and its companion, the table knife. Fine wines were served in matching imported wine glasses, and tea was consumed from sets of Asian or English ceramics. Rooms where rituals such as dining took place could be embellished with floor coverings, wallpaper, and a variety of imported textiles.[10]

The people who built highly valued houses and purchased new kinds of domestic furnishings often shared a number of attributes. Those who lived in rural areas generally held extensive tracts of land, had ready access to labor, and owned mills or other buildings that suggest they received income from activities other than farming. As a group they were wealthy—they frequently lent money out at interest, for example—and took on leadership roles in government, the military, or religious or educational institutions. In the late eighteenth century, when commentators were trying to define just what characteristics typified Pennsylvania's better sort, these individuals could have been singled out for a number of reasons. Because of their financial resources, property holdings, occupations, public services, and intellects, they exemplified what many period authors referred to as the "first class."[11]

While the owners of these houses and belongings had much in common, they did not share similar ethnic backgrounds. Some were European-born immigrants while others were American-born. Moreover, they could trace their roots to various parts of Europe, including England, Ireland, Scotland, France, and even the German principalities. Although many period authors told their readers that people of German descent invariably lived in small, poorly furnished dwellings, this was not always the case. Some Pennsylvania Germans, just like some of their non-German neighbors, opted in the last decades of the eighteenth century to construct notable houses, which often incorporated new floor plans and were furnished with costly objects that served specialized functions.[12]

Houses of the Best Sort

The buildings that were singled out for their exceptional qualities in the late eighteenth century, whether they were occupied by Germans or non-Germans, usually shared several traits. Edward and Catherine Hand's house, built just outside of Lancaster in 1794, serves as an example of what period commentators expected in a grand house (figs. 17–18). The same traveler who visited Leonard Elmaker and his family also had occasion to stop at the Hands' during the fall of 1794. In contrast to the way he described the Elmakers' dwelling, this commentator specifically referred to the Hand house as "good."[13]

Edward Hand, the owner of the house, was a physician who was born and trained in Ireland. He served in the Continental Army during the American Revolution and by 1781 had achieved the rank of adjutant general. Following the war, he occupied a number of positions in state and local government. The house he built on the bank of the Conestoga River in Lancaster County was constructed of brick with five symmetrically arranged bays of windows across its front. It rose a full two stories over a cellar where the kitchen facilities were located. Its floor plan was of the center-passage, double-pile variety. On the first floor, an unheated passage ran the full width of the building and housed an open, dogleg staircase. It was flanked on each side by two rooms arranged back-to-back, or in a double pile. Furnishing these spaces were items such as a mahogany card table, ten mahogany chairs, several gilt frame looking glasses, and sets of both queensware and china.[14]

Houses such as Edward and Catherine Hand's are generally termed by architectural historians "Georgian" and are associated with people of English, or in Edward Hand's case British, descent.[15] However, Britons did not have a monopoly on the form in late eighteenth-century Pennsylvania. Such buildings did not serve primarily as a reflection of ethnic background but provided a new way to symbolize divisions based on social and economic status. Most Pennsylvanians of British descent in earlier decades, regardless of wealth or power, had resided in more traditional buildings that utilized an open plan, such as the hall-and-parlor plan (see figs. 13–14).[16] By stepping through the front door of a house of this type, a guest entered directly into the hall, a multifunctional room that often incorporated a hearth for cooking. The new "Georgian" houses that were adopted by increasing numbers of affluent Pennsylvanians in the eighteenth century were based on closed plans. A

Fig. 17　Edward and Catherine Hand house (Rock Ford), Lancaster, Pennsylvania, c. 1794. When a European land agent visited the Hands in 1794, he described their new house as "good." Constructed of brick, it rose a full two stories. On the exterior, jack-arch lintels over the windows with stone keystones and a brick belt course between the first and second floors contributed to the building's refined appearance.

Fig. 18　First-floor plan, Edward and Catherine Hand house (Rock Ford). The Hand house was based on a center-passage, double-pile plan. The four rooms to the sides of the passage were all formal, fireplace-heated spaces. The kitchen facilities were located on a lower level. Floor plan based on plan by Harold P. Warfel for the Historic American Buildings Survey, 1961. Library of Congress, Prints and Photographs Division, HABS, HABS-PA, 36-LANC.V, 1.

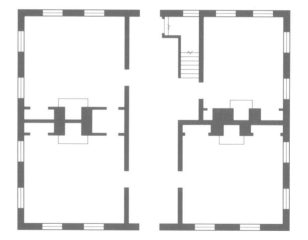

passage, which functioned specially as an entrance, ran back from the front door and provided access to all the rooms on the first floor as well as to the staircase leading to the second.[17]

Just as people of British descent were making the transition from hall-and-parlor or other open-plan houses to Georgian houses based on center-passage, double-pile or similar floor plans, people of German descent were also adopting new architectural forms. In the first half of the eighteenth century, Pennsylvania Germans who chose to distinguish themselves by building a grand masonry house often simply constructed larger-than-average dwellings based on the entry-kitchen plan.[18] In 1719, for example, Christian and Anna Herr erected a sizable entry-kitchen house in what would later become West Lampeter Township, Lancaster County (figs. 19–21). Built of stone, it measured approximately 30 by 38 feet and had a partial cellar, four first-floor rooms, a lower attic level with additional sleeping spaces, and an upper attic level for storage. In the second decade of the eighteenth century, far west of any extensive European settlement, the Herrs' house must have

Fig. 19   **Christian and Anna Herr house, West Lampeter Township, Lancaster County, Pennsylvania, 1719. The Herr house, although only one full story in height, was a large example of the entry-kitchen type when it was built, containing four rooms on its first floor and two attic levels. It is now operated as a museum by the Lancaster Conference Mennonite Historical Society.**

Fig. 20 First-floor plan, Christian and Anna Herr house. Beginning in the lower right and continuing clockwise, first-floor rooms in the Herr house included an entry-kitchen, stove room, chamber, and workroom (or pantry). Floor plan based on plan by Jeffrey C. Bouke of the office of John D. Milner, National Heritage Corporation, published in Margaret Berwind Schiffer, *Survey of Chester County, Pennsylvania, Architecture: 17th, 18th, and 19th Centuries* (Exton, Pa.: Schiffer Publishing, 1984), 376.

Fig. 21 Stove, Christian and Anna Herr house. The stove room of the Herr house was heated by a stove fed from the kitchen fireplace. This reproduction stove approximates the original, which was probably constructed of brick and covered with earthen plaster. It may have been referred to during the eighteenth century as an "earthen" stove.

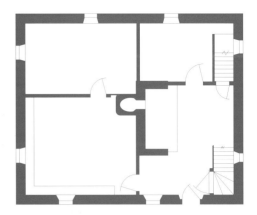

contrasted noticeably with the predominantly small log houses erected by most of their neighbors. According to R. Martin Keen, who has analyzed economic stratification in the early settlements of Lancaster County's Conestoga Valley, "Christian Herr represented the elite" in terms of both taxable property and land ownership. His family's house reflected his position as a wealthy community leader as well.[19]

Other prominent Pennsylvania Germans who built during the first half of the eighteenth century used certain decorative embellishments, as well as size and building materials, to distinguish their dwellings—and therefore themselves—from others. In 1745, for example, Heinrich and Anna Maria Zeller constructed an entry-kitchen house, now popularly known as Fort Zeller, west of present-day Newmanstown in Lebanon County (figs. 22–25). The stone dwelling included a partial cellar that housed a spring, a three-room first-floor plan, and two attic levels. Measuring roughly 34 by 30 feet, the masonry building was not as large as the Herr house but was still quite substantial for the period. The fact that the house was built over a spring distinguished it as the home of people of continental European lineage. The crest over the front door, however, communicated a different meaning. Zeller included over his elaborately carved entrance a coat of arms that demonstrated his family's claims to greatness even on the Pennsylvania frontier.[20]

Large entry-kitchen houses with ambitious decorative details were still being built during the second half of the eighteenth century by some affluent Pennsylvania Germans. Miller George Müller and his wife Maria Caterina, for instance, constructed an entry-kitchen house of stone in 1752 near Millbach, in what is now Lebanon County (figs. 26–28). Measuring 40 by 30 feet, the building incorporated a cellar; a kitchen, stove room, and chamber on its first floor; several additional chambers on its second floor; and two attic levels. In addition to its large size and multiple stories, the building was further distinguished by its gambrel roof, a feature that was generally reserved among eighteenth-century Pennsylvania Germans for religious buildings.[21]

Changes made at the Müller house in 1784 by George and Maria Caterina's son Michael demonstrate the new ideas about domestic architecture that were increasingly being incorporated by elite Pennsylvania Germans even as the original dwelling was built. Michael extended the east wall of his parents' house to create a wider kitchen and then added a partition lengthwise across the room to form a separate space that would serve as a distinct entry (fig. 29).[22] The resulting structure was similar in plan to the house Christian Hagenbuch and Jacob Kratzer discussed in their 1783 building contract, except in this case the principal first-floor room continued to be heated by a stove. The change in configuration demonstrated the desire on the part of many Pennsylvania Germans, as well as other Americans, of the "better sort" to live in dwellings where work spaces were less visible and access

Fig. 22   Heinrich and Anna Maria Zeller house (Fort Zeller), Newmanstown, Lebanon County, Pennsylvania, c. 1745. The center chimney at the Zeller house provided an outlet for both the kitchen fireplace and the stove in the stove room. The Zeller house would have appeared somewhat different in the eighteenth century since it had a half-hipped rather than a gable roof.

to principal rooms was achieved only through some kind of intermediary space. Although houses with combined entry-kitchens continued to be built by people of German descent throughout the eighteenth and even into the nineteenth century, new types of floor plans began to be adopted by many of the most esteemed members of the group during the second half of the eighteenth century.

The creation of a distinct entry room like that at the Müllers' house was only one option available to people of German descent who had been familiar with the entry-kitchen house form. Another alternative was explored by Peter and Rosina Margaretha Wentz, who in 1758 built a large stone dwelling house in Worcester Township in what is now Montgomery County (figs. 30–33). The Wentz house, like Edward and Catherine Hand's, was based on a center-passage, double-pile plan. The centrally located front door led to a long, unheated passage that ran the full width of the building. On either side of the passage, two rooms were arranged back-to-back.[23]

The Wentz house incorporated some features from the entry-kitchen house form while abandoning others. On the exterior, the two types of buildings looked quite different. At entry-kitchen houses, the front door was located to one side of the façade, and openings for windows could be irregularly arranged. At the Wentz house, the front door occupied a central position and was flanked on either side by two evenly spaced bays of windows. Inside the Wentz house, the insertion of a passage and the relocation of kitchen facilities clearly differentiated it from entry-kitchen houses. However, the Wentz family and those who built houses like theirs still maintained the integral

relationship between the kitchen and the stove room that existed in the more traditional house form. The kitchen was discreetly moved to the rear of the building on the north side of the central passage, with the kitchen fireplace placed so that its rear wall abutted the more formal front room. A five-plate stove in that room fit snugly against the rear wall of the fireplace and thus could be fed from and vented into the kitchen fireplace, as it would have been in an entry-kitchen house.[24]

When the Wentz house was restored to its mid-eighteenth-century appearance in the 1970s, later modifications to the floor plan, such as the removal of the kitchen fireplace and five-plate stove, were addressed. In addition, the wall surfaces were analyzed and the painted decoration that had adorned them was reproduced, which was crucial to recreating the appearance of the house. When Johann David Schöpf characterized the stove room of the thrifty Pennsylvania German farmer's house by describing "everything daubed with red," he was remarking on a preference that some more elite Pennsylvania Germans, such as the Wentzes, displayed in their dwellings as well. Paint analysis revealed that in the center passage of the Wentz house the dado, or lower part of the wall, was painted red with white spots. To the south of the passage, the front room also had a red dado with white spots, and the back room had a white dado with black spots. The kitchen, to the north side of the passage, had white walls with black spots from floor to ceiling. Upstairs, the bedrooms and the hall had painted decoration on the lower portion of the walls, which in various rooms included spots, lines, and comma-shaped forms in white, red, and black. The out-kitchen behind the main house had black spots over the entirety of its wall surfaces, similar to the kitchen within the house.[25] Like the use of a five-plate stove, the use of painted decoration on interior walls differentiated this house from other buildings with a similar floor plan that were built by people of British descent.

Unfortunately, the Wentzes sold their house prior to Peter's death, so the contents of the building were not inventoried as part of the probate process. However, many of the items listed in Peter Wentz's 1793 probate inventory were likely in his possession from 1758 to 1784 while he resided in the building.[26] Some express the Wentz family's ethnic heritage. The presence of a "large German bible," valued at £1.10.0, suggests that the family was able to read the German language. A cabbage knife and cabbage cutter, as well as rye in the sheaf and in the ground, indicate German foodways; a feather bed and clothes press reflect distinct ways of using and storing textiles. The clothes press, or wardrobe, was a form in early America specifically associated with continental Europeans and their descents. The form was most typically found in colonial New York, where the Dutch called it a *kas;* in eighteenth-century Pennsylvania, where the Germans called it a *Schrank;* and in the Mississippi River Valley, where the French called it an *armoire.* People

Fig. 26 George and Maria Caterina Müller house, Millbach, Lebanon County, Pennsylvania, 1752. The Müller dwelling is actually part of a house-mill. The mill portion of the structure projects forward to the right of the front door. The current mill building may have been the second building constructed on the site, since it bears a date stone that reads 1784. The Müller house is distinguished on the exterior by the use of stone quoins at the corners and by the gambrel roof, a feature more commonly found in Pennsylvania on public buildings, such as religious structures, during this time period.

Fig. 27 Original first-floor plan, George and Maria Caterina Müller house. As constructed in 1752, the Müller house included an entry-kitchen, stove room, and chamber on its first floor. The original location of the stairs to the second floor is not known. Floor plan based on plan by Donald Miller in Joseph Downs, *The House of the Miller at Millbach: The Architecture, Arts, and Crafts of the Pennsylvania Germans* (Philadelphia: Pennsylvania Museum of Art, 1929), plate 1.

Fig. 28   Interior of entry-kitchen, George and Maria Caterina Müller house. The interior woodwork from the entry-kitchen, as well as a second-floor chamber, was removed from the Müller house, also known as the House of the Miller at Millbach, and relocated to the Philadelphia Museum of Art in the 1920s. Architectural features from the entry-kitchen, including the fireplace, raised panel doors, and elaborate staircase, provide a period-room setting. The heavy baroque balusters at the stairs, like the quoins on the exterior of the house, indicate a knowledge of and desire for sophisticated design elements. Paint remnants indicate that the woodwork may once have been painted a vibrant blue. Philadelphia Museum of Art, Gift of Mr. and Mrs. Pierre S. du Pont and Mr. and Mrs. Lammot du Pont, 1926.

Fig. 29   Amended first-floor plan, George and Maria Caterina Müller house. In 1784, the second generation of Müllers to own the Müller house made substantial changes. The gable-end wall in the entry-kitchen was relocated in order to create a larger room, and then that space was divided so that the entry and kitchen would be distinct. The front door served the entry; a secondary door in the kitchen led to the attached mill. Floor plan based on plan by Donald Miller in Joseph Downs, *The House of the Miller at Millbach: The Architecture, Arts, and Crafts of the Pennsylvania Germans* (Philadelphia: Pennsylvania Museum of Art, 1929), plate 1.

who came to America from the British Isles in the seventeenth and eighteenth centuries tended to store their textiles not in wardrobes but in chests or chests of drawers. Peter Wentz's ownership of a clothes press, valued quite highly at £2.10.0, and no chests of drawers, suggests that a preference for the continental form persisted through the eighteenth century.[27]

The ownership of other items, however, seems less related to Peter Wentz's German heritage and more to his family's social and economic status. With a maple tea table, tea kettle, six silver teaspoons, and coffee mill, he clearly was familiar with the fashion for serving hot imported beverages. In a corner cupboard, probably located in a formal room rather than a work space like the kitchen, he displayed "China, queens ware and Glasses" for consuming food and drink. The location of his china, perhaps Chinese export porcelain, and queensware, or creamware—an earthenware manufactured in

ARCHITECTURE AND ARTIFACTS OF THE PENNSYLVANIA GERMANS

England with a light-colored body and creamy glaze—suggest a degree of refinement as well as conspicuous consumption. The Wentzes also owned tableware of pewter, including eight plates, thirteen spoons, a tankard, two basins, and two dishes, but while they may have used it regularly they did not display it as prominently. The objects exhibited inside the house made statements about the family's social and economic position, just as the building itself did. Imported tablewares and corner cupboards for showing them off, textiles such as Peter Wentz's two tablecloths and almost £7 worth of wearing apparel, and new genteel forms, evidenced by a "Knife box and knives and forks" in the Wentz inventory, made important statements. At the time of Peter's death, other household furnishings that communicated his elite status were his twenty-four-hour clock, which allowed him to know the time of day, his looking glass, which provided a means of checking his appearance, and his "Desk and Cover" and £2 worth of books in addition to his German Bible, which indicated his ability to both read and write.[28]

In time, variations on the center-passage, double-pile plan increasingly came into use among prosperous Pennsylvania Germans, including ironmasters, millers, and civic and religious leaders.[29] The invention of six-plate and ten-plate stoves, which allowed greater flexibility in placement, permitted

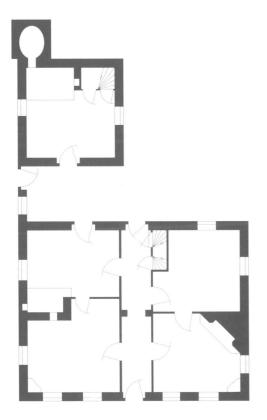

Fig. 32 Center passage as viewed from the front door, Peter and Rosina Margaretha Wentz house. Paint analysis has indicated that the walls of the Wentz house were elaborately decorated. In the center passage, a classically inspired entablature painted yellow separated the front and rear of the space. The wall surface below the yellow chair rail in both parts of the passage was painted red with white spots. The staircase to the second floor was not a prominent feature in the passage, as at some other center-passage houses, but rather was located to the side of the passage and accessed through a doorway. Photograph © Geoffrey Gross for the *Stone Houses: Traditional Homes of Pennsylvania's Bucks County and Brandywine Valley* (New York: Rizzoli, 2005) project.

more variation in floor plan. These new kinds of stoves were freestanding, vented into a chimney with a pipe, and fed through a small door in the front (see fig. 15). Since they did not have to adjoin a kitchen fireplace, kitchen facilities could be further removed from the core of a house. Without giving up stove heat, the kitchen could be located in the cellar or in an attached kitchen building to the side or to the rear of a central-passage, double-pile house.

Fig. 33 Kitchen, Peter and Rosina Margaretha Wentz house. Like most rooms within the Wentz house, the kitchen also included painted decoration. In the kitchen, as well as the out-kitchen behind the main house, that decoration was not limited to the lower portion of the walls; rather, the walls were decorated with black dots from floor to ceiling. The fireplace in the kitchen provided a cooking hearth as well as access to the jamb stove in the front room. The opening for feeding the stove, trimmed with brick, can been seen to the left of the tea kettle. The smaller hole above that opening provided a vent for the smoke from the stove. Photograph © Geoffrey Gross for the *Stone Houses: Traditional Homes of Pennsylvania's Bucks County and Brandywine Valley* (New York: Rizzoli, 2005) project.

With the adoption of six-plate and ten-plate stoves, houses with stove rooms could also be constructed according to a side-passage, double-pile plan (figs. 34–35).[30] At buildings of this type, a passage ran from the front door, located in one of the outermost of three bays on the façade, along the length of the gable-end wall. To one side of this passage, there were two rooms, arranged back-to-back. One of these rooms—usually the front room—was heated by a six- or ten-plate stove. The kitchen facilities would be

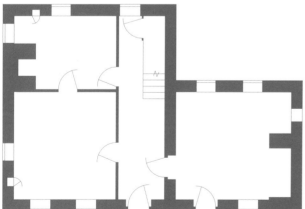

Fig. 34   Ulrich Switzer house, North Coventry Township, Chester County, Pennsylvania, before 1798. The Switzer house originally was a side-passage, double-pile dwelling (on the left), which measured approximately 26 by 30 feet, with a one-story attached kitchen (on the right) of roughly 19 by 19 feet. The kitchen building has since been expanded to include a second story. While the façade was constructed of uncoursed rubble stone, the corners of the building were highlighted through the use of large stone quoins.

Fig. 35   Reconstructed first-floor plan, Ulrich Switzer house. The front room to the left of the side passage was originally heated by a pipe stove, which was vented into the chimney of the rear room's fireplace. Floor plan based on fieldwork by Bernard Herman, Gabrielle Lanier, and Cynthia Falk.

Fig. 36   David and Caterina Hottenstein house, Maxatawny Township, Berks County, Pennsylvania, 1783. The façade of the Hottensteins' house included a central front door, four large sash windows on the first-floor level, five sash windows supported by decoratively carved wooden brackets on the second-floor level, jack-arch lintels with keystones over all the windows, and two date stones. The Hottenstein house is owned by the Historic Preservation Trust of Berks County.

located in a separate purpose-built structure that was often attached either to the side or to the rear of the building.

The introduction of six- and ten-plate stoves also allowed houses that had been built with fireplaces to be adapted for stove heat. David and Caterina Hottenstein, for example, erected a center-passage house in Maxatawny Township, Berks County, in 1783 (figs. 36–41). Each of the principal rooms on both the first and second floors was equipped with a fireplace. The fireplaces were designed with paneled surrounds, which in some cases featured pilasters and dentil molding. The quality and academic inspiration for the woodwork around the fireplaces was echoed in other places inside the house, including the stair banister, corner cupboards, door surrounds, and the entablature in the passage just in front of the stairs, as well as on the exterior in the cornice and the brackets under the windows. What is unknown is whether the majority of the woodwork was painted in contrasting shades of blue and white with the panels fancifully grained, as they were upstairs on at least two fireplace surrounds and two corner cupboards.[31]

By the time of David's death in 1802, his probate inventory indicates that the Hottensteins had chosen to heat two spaces within the house not with the fireplaces that were integral to the structure but with ten-plate stoves that were vented with pipes inserted through the paneled fireplace surrounds into the flues.[32] This, coupled with the painted decoration on at least some of the woodwork, indicates that the Hottensteins were combining features

Fig. 37 David Hottenstein date stone, David and Caterina Hottenstein house. The date stone, to the left of the second-story center window, is labeled "ANNO / DOMNY / 1783 / TAVIDHOTT / ENSTEIN." The number "1" in 1783 is crossed in typical German fashion, and David's name is spelled with a "T," indicating the German accent of its delineator.

Fig. 38 Caterina Hottenstein date stone, David and Caterina Hottenstein house. The date stone, to the right of the second-story center window, is labeled "ANNO / 1783 / CATARINA / HOTTEN / STIN." Both Caterina's and David's stones are also embellished with two hearts and architectonic designs.

Fig. 39   Center passage, David and Caterina Hottenstein house. An entablature supported by pilasters created a division in the Hottenstein house's center passage just in front of the prominently located staircase to the second floor. Doorways throughout the passage were capped with classical pediments, the lower portion of the wall was paneled, and the staircase railing included turned balusters and carved details.

Fig. 40   Second-floor fireplace surround, David and Caterina Hottenstein house. On the second floor, evidence remains of blue painted decoration on the fireplace surrounds and corner cupboards in two rooms. The woodwork from one of the rooms was removed from the Hottenstein house in the 1950s and reinstalled at Winterthur Museum as the "Fraktur Room." Woodwork in the other room, including this fireplace surround, remains in the house. The circular disturbance above the fireplace mantel marks the spot where a stove pipe for a freestanding stove was fed through the surround to the chimney.

related to both their ethnic identity and their social and economic status within their house. They, like several of their contemporaries, were experimenting with a new architectural form that communicated their status, but they also found ways to utilize certain features that were associated with their ethnic heritage.

A wardrobe made for David Hottenstein in 1781, two years before the house was constructed, represents a similar mixing of Pennsylvania German and more widely accepted fashionable elite styles (fig. 42). Listed as a "Cloath Dresser" in Hottenstein's 1802 probate inventory, this typically continental European form was crafted to incorporate more cosmopolitan design elements. Its top simulated the type of broken-arch pediment found on many other pieces of eighteenth-century furniture, and its corners were fluted to resemble classical columns. Furthermore, in four separate locations its design included inlaid or carved seashells, another stylish decorative motif of the period.[33]

At first glance the wardrobe, built from walnut, appears somewhat awkward in design. Yet its squat proportions are the result of the decision to include a fashionable broken pediment on the wide wardrobe form, which normally would have had a flat top. The decision to execute the majority of

Fig. 41   Corner cupboard, David and Caterina Hottenstein house. The Hottensteins incorporated several built-in corner cupboards in their new house for the storage and display of their belongings. Those on the first floor, such as this one in the dining room, had solid doors allowing the contents of the cupboard to be seen only when the doors were opened. Upstairs, two corner cupboards had doors with glass panes.

Fig. 42   *Schrank,* 1781. Made for David Hottenstein, this "Cloath Dresser," or wardrobe, included fluted corner columns, a broken-arch pediment, and inlaid and carved shells. It represents a traditional continental European form updated with more cosmopolitan design elements. Courtesy of Winterthur Museum.

Fig. 43   Ceiling construction, George and Magdalena Elizabeth Hehn house (later the residence of Captain Conrad Kershner), Heidelberg Township, Berks County, Pennsylvania, 1755. In the process of moving portions of the Hehn-Kershner house to Winterthur Museum, the construction of the building was carefully documented. This photograph shows the use of mud and straw insulation wrapped around wooden staves, or pales, which were inserted in grooves carved into the larger joists. In this dwelling, this technique was used not only between the cellar and the first floor but on upper floors as well. Courtesy of the Winterthur Library, Winterthur Archives.

Fig. 44   Johannes Lesher house (Oley Forge Mansion), Oley Township, Berks County, Pennsylvania, c. 1750–55. Ironmaster Johannes Lesher experimented with the center-passage, double-pile plan, creating a house that included to the right of its center passage a stove room and kitchen, and to the left, two rooms heated by corner fireplaces. The four-bay asymmetrical façade may reflect the need for more natural light in a room heated by a closed stove than in one heated by a fireplace with an open flame.

the decorative embellishment in inlay may reflect the lack of skilled carvers in rural Berks County, or a tradition of using inlay on *Schrank,* or the fact that in 1781 the three-dimensional surfaces of the rococo style were being abandoned in favor of smoother neoclassical façades. While the wardrobe appears somewhat unsophisticated compared to Philadelphia furniture of the same period, its owner and crafter clearly made a concerted effort in a rural location to adapt a German form built with German construction techniques by refashioning its top and adding decorative elements based on academic styles of the day. The wardrobe probably held the wearing apparel, fifteen tablecloths, seventeen linen sheets, twelve towels, three sheets, eight pillow and bolster cases, twenty-nine yards of linen cloth, two coverlets, two bed curtains, and possibly the seven window curtains that were listed before it in David Hottenstein's probate inventory. The wardrobe itself was valued at £5.5.0, while the textiles were worth more than £48.[34]

The center- and side-passage houses that were built and occupied by Pennsylvania Germans in the second half of the eighteenth century could incorporate certain features found in entry-kitchen houses, such as stoves for heating. They could include fancifully painted interior elements, and they likely housed objects that spoke of the ethnic background, as well as the social and economic status, of their occupants. They might also utilize par-ticularly German construction techniques. In the cellar, for instance, it was not uncommon for the ceiling to be heavily insulated with mud and straw, which was held in place by pales, or wooden slats, placed in grooves in the joists (fig. 43). It was also possible to build a cellar with a vaulted stone ceiling (figs. 44–47). Both the use of insulation between the cellar and first floor and the use of vaulted cellar ceilings seem to be related to the propensity among Pennsylvania Germans to create cool spaces for food storage. The creation of a cellar space with a barrel-vaulted ceiling may relate to the use of vaulted ceilings in separate structures known as root, ground, or cave cellars (figs. 48–49). The use of insulation between the cellar and first floor was also a way to keep the coolness and dampness of the cellar from penetrating the upper floors of the house. Some entry-kitchen houses, such as the Heinrich and Anna Maria Zeller house, and numerous outbuildings were designed with springs on their lowest levels to provide a water source as well as a place to cool dairy products (see fig. 23). Given this tradition of cellar springs, the cre-ation of a barrier between the cellar and first floor was a frequent practice.[35]

Characteristics such as vaulted cellar ceilings, cellar springs, and cellar ceiling insulation distinguished the houses of German settlers from those of members of other ethnic groups. In the attic, ethnic building practices might be used as well. Roofs were sometimes carried by a heavy framing system, known in German as a *liegender Dachstuhl* (see fig. 47). Unlike the roof frames favored by Pennsylvania carpenters of English descent, which

Fig. 45 Barrel-vaulted cellar, Johannes Lesher house (Oley Forge Mansion). Some of the center-passage houses erected by Pennsylvania Germans were built over cellars with vaulted ceilings. A barrel-vaulted cellar was normally under only part of the house, in this case the center section.

Fig. 46 Stove, Johannes Lesher house (Oley Forge Mansion). Twentieth-century owners Kenneth and Hope LeVan used photographs of surviving German and Pennsylvania German stoves and archaeological fragments from Ephrata Cloister as models to construct a closed stove faced with tile, which was made from local clay. The resulting stove approximates the type of tile stoves available in eighteenth-century Pennsylvania and referred to in period documents as "pantiles" or "pottery-ware" stoves.

Fig. 47   Roof framing, Johannes Lesher house (Oley Forge Mansion). The two-tiered system of heavy roof framing at the Lesher house is known in the German language as a *liegender Dachstuhl*. The heavier lower section consists of large principal rafters, principal purlins, collar beams, and braces. The smaller common rafters and collar beams form the upper level of framing, which rests on top of the lower support system.

were usually composed of a series of common rafters all of similar size that were joined in pairs with collar beams, in this German framing system the common rafters were supported by a lower level of roof framing. The overall effect was a much heavier roofing system that was essentially composed of two layers of timber framing, one on top of the other.[36]

While elements such as insulation in the cellar and roof framing in the attic would not have been noticeable to people who did not have access to those spaces, other ethnic features would have been. A German-language date stone on the façade, for example, would have been visible to even the casual passerby. Although such stones were not used universally on center- or side-passage houses, they were not uncommon either. A house built by Johann Peter and Maria Magdalena Troxell in Egypt in what is now Lehigh County, for instance, originally included a plaque next to the second-floor middle window of its five-bay façade. The German inscription on the tablet included a house blessing that read, "Gott behüt dis haus fur aller gefahr, führ unser Seel ins himmels Saal" (God protect this house from all danger, lead

Fig. 48 Philip Erpff house, Schaefferstown, Lebanon County, Pennsylvania, c. 1758. Not truly symmetrical in plan or elevation, the Erpff house was designed with five bays at the first-floor level of the façade and only four at the second. The center passage of the house was not quite in the center of the building, and the rooms to the right were larger than those to the left. When Philip Erpff signed a rental agreement with Jacob Grubb in 1800, the "large Front Room," presumably that on the right, was heated by a ten-plate stove. Photograph by Diane Wenger.

Fig. 49 Root cellar, Philip Erpff house. Root, ground, or cave cellars provided a cool place to store perishables and often had barrel-vaulted ceilings. Photograph by Karen Green.

our soul to heaven's fold) as well as the names of the building's first owners, Johann Peter and Maria Magdalena, and the date of construction, 1756 (fig. 50).[37] At David and Caterina Hottenstein's center-passage house, two date stones were incorporated into the second-floor level of the symmetrically arranged façade. As at the Troxell house, the stones included the distinctly German names of the Hottensteins. The date 1783, preceded by the Latin phrase "ANNO DOMNY" on one stone and "ANNO" on the other, was written in German form with a crossed "1." The stones were further embellished with hearts and architectonic designs (see figs. 37–38).[38]

While many of the center- and side-passage, closed-plan houses Pennsylvania Germans built shared particularly German characteristics with more traditional types of Pennsylvania German dwellings, they were quite distinct in form and finish from these other structures. On several levels, they expressed a marked departure from the open-plan houses that had been erected earlier in the eighteenth century and were still being built right into the nineteenth. With their orderly façades, passages, and sequestered kitchen facilities, side- and center-passage dwellings did as much to distinguish their occupants

Fig. 50   Johann Peter and Maria Magdalena Troxell house, Egypt, Lehigh County, Pennsylvania, 1756. The inscription on the original date stone on the Troxell house included a house blessing that read, "1756 Gott behüt dis haus fur aller gefahr, führ unser Seel ins himmels Saal, Johan Peter Trachsel und Maria Magdala" (1756 God protect this house from all danger, lead our soul to heaven's fold, Johann Peter Troxell and Maria Magdalena). The original date stone deteriorated, so it was replaced with a recreated date stone that is located on the front of the building, which is administered as a historic site by the Lehigh County Historical Society.

Fig. 51   David and Mary Deshler house (Deshler-Morris house), Germantown, Pennsylvania, 1772. Built as a country seat for German immigrant David Deshler, the Deshler-Morris house was used as a temporary residence by British general William Howe and American president George Washington. The house is now part of Independence National Historical Park.

Fig. 52   First-floor front room, David and Mary Deshler house (Deshler-Morris house). Fireplaces within the Deshlers' house were designed with marble surrounds and crosseted, or "eared," overmantels. In the dining room, interpreted by the National Park Service to the period of George Washington's residency, a built-in cupboard provided storage space for household wares.

from the people who lived in entry-kitchen houses, or even smaller one-room houses, as to unite members of these groups.[39]

Perhaps for this reason, some Pennsylvania Germans chose to build closed-plan houses with either center or side passages that did not have stove-heated front rooms, German-language date stones, or ethnic construction techniques. Some people of German descent, or even German immigrants like David Deshler, built houses that in form and finish were analogous to those of their elite British neighbors (figs. 51–52). Deshler's country house in Germantown, enlarged in 1772 to include a prominent two-story, five-bay, center-passage core fronting the Great Road to Philadelphia, may have been consciously fashioned as a means to renounce his immigrant identity. However, its location in a community that was transitioning from an ethnic village where craftspeople plied their trades to a fashionable neighborhood where Philadelphians from a variety of European backgrounds built grand summer residences suggests other factors were at work as well. Unfortunately, neither David nor his wife, Mary, recorded whether they conceived of the fireplace-heated front room in their country house as a parlor or a *Stube*. However, what is clear is that in opting for such a dwelling in the early 1770s, Deshler was communicating his elite status. His family claimed standing among the German nobility, his father had served as an aide-de-camp to Prince Louis of Baden, and in Philadelphia David himself became a successful merchant and community leader. The elite nature of Deshler's house was not lost on those who had the opportunity to use the structure in ensuing years. The building served as residence and headquarters for British general

William Howe during the Battle of Germantown in 1777 and American president George Washington during the yellow fever epidemic of the summer of 1793. Both presumably considered it an appropriate setting for their activities in Germantown, even though it had been erected for a German.[40]

Wealth, Knowledge, Manners, and Material Culture

Houses based on the new forms, whether occupied by people of German or non-German descent or heated with fireplaces or stoves, differed considerably from many other dwellings in Pennsylvania that, according to period authors, were of extremely poor quality. Upon visiting Berwick on the Susquehanna River in northeastern Pennsylvania, a French duke commented on the "twenty miserable houses," or "huts," that made up the village. In Shippensburg in the south-central part of the state, another European traveler noted that of "about 140 buildings or houses," only thirty were "two-stories high and built of stone." The others, he added, "are all wretched huts of wood and log and clay."[41]

Generally, the poorest houses that travelers observed in Pennsylvania and elsewhere in America were referred to as "cottages" or "huts." That these buildings were associated with those of the lower class is evidenced by Benjamin Franklin. In an article in *Poor Richard's Almanac,* Franklin asked his readers to consider, "*What denominates Men* GREAT *and* GLORIOUS?" Franklin explained that in late eighteenth-century Pennsylvania, people valued titles, education, and military victories. However, he speculated, "WERE Angels, if they look[ed] into the Ways of Men, to give in their Catalogue of Worthies, how different would it be from that which any of our own Species would draw up!" Only celestial beings, he said, could recognize "the Philosopher in the Cottage, who possesses his Soul in Patience and Thankfulness, under the Pressures of what little Minds call Poverty and Distress." From a human perspective, the resident of a cottage could not be great and glorious. Living in a cottage was at odds with holding a title, receiving a good education, or serving in a position of leadership in the military. To anyone but an angel, living in a cottage meant living in poverty and distress.[42]

Other period writers provide further evidence of the perceived lack of refinement among the residents of small, poor-quality houses. The buildings themselves were felt to be lacking in neatness, cleanliness, and comfort. Those living inside were generally characterized as dirty and ignorant. One traveler referred to a one-room inn in Pennsylvania between Harrisburg and Sunbury, both on the Susquehanna River, as a "dirty hole." Of its proprietors, he commented, "The uncleanliness, stupidity, and rudeness of the whole family can hardly be conceived." Near the border of Pennsylvania and New Jersey, another tourist noted the "astounding indifference" of the residents who were rarely exposed to "anything neat and comfortable."[43]

Both of these travelers recognized the role women played in the residences they were describing. The eighteenth-century women who resided in small, poor-quality houses were generally uneducated and overworked. The guest at the one-room inn reported seeing "four or five girls who were either the daughters or servants" of his host. These young women "perform[ed] the business of the inn," but, according to their visitor, there was not one of them who could "distinguish one letter from another" to write a bill or receipt. At the dwellings near the Pennsylvania–New Jersey border, it was also the women who did the domestic work. The traveler who observed them wrote, "The wives have the care of the house, and besides they have a number of children, 5, 6, 7, 8. So they have more work than they can do, with no help, except one or two old and dispirited colored women. That is why the wives are indifferent, tired." He noted that if it were not for "the wise institution of the day of rest, and church service, may be the farmers' wives would never wash." Burdened by other work, these women did not have the time or the inclination to clean themselves or their dwellings.[44]

At the other end of the housing spectrum, women found themselves in quite different positions. It is not surprising that dwellings like the Troxells' and the Hottensteins' were embellished with date stones that included the names of both husband and wife, since women played a key role in creating and maintaining a high-quality domestic environment. Houses of those of the upper class were usually larger, better furnished, and also notably cleaner. The women of the house were aided in their domestic duties by servants, hired help, and, before gradual emancipation was enacted, slaves. They were therefore able to spend more time perfecting their own appearance and manners. In Middletown, twenty-two miles from Philadelphia on the Neshaminy Creek in Bucks County, Jacques-Pierre Brissot de Warville visited the house of William and Elizabeth Richardson in 1788. In addition to housing William and Elizabeth, the building served as residence for the couple's nine unmarried children, one additional white male and one additional white female (possibly their married daughter and her husband, but more likely non-family members), and a free person of color.[45]

Brissot wrote of his visit to the Richardsons that "never was I so much edified as in this house; it is the asylum of union, friendship, and hospitality. The beds were neat, the linen white, the covering elegant; the cabinets, desks, chairs, and tables, were of black walnut, well polished, and shining." The residents of the house, particularly the women, were equally pleasing to Brissot. He remarked, "I was really charmed with the order and neatness of this house, and of its inhabitants. They have three sons and seven daughters. One of the latter is married; three others are marriageable. They are beautiful, easy in their manners, and decent in their deportment." The Richardsons and their house were everything Brissot expected from the Pennsylvania upper class. The Richardsons, with the help of the nonwhite resident of their house and possibly others, kept the furniture polished, the linen white, and the beds neatly arranged. Adding to this refined interior finish were the family members themselves. In Brissot's assessment, the three oldest unmarried daughters were particularly well mannered and well groomed.[46]

The indicators of elevated status, including, for women, the time and skill to awe a visitor such as Brissot with one's deportment and appearance, went hand in hand in late eighteenth-century Pennsylvania with the ownership of a distinguished house. The European traveler who described Edward and Catherine Hand's house as "good" was quick to recognize a correspondence between the admirable physical characteristics of the building and the refined attributes of its inhabitants. Immediately after characterizing the house, he noted that the Hand family was "very polite."[47]

It is not clear what travelers would have thought of women from families of German descent—such as Caterina Hottenstein—who helped fashion grand houses, albeit with certain distinctly German elements. In the 1750s,

Benjamin Franklin had shared his overwhelmingly negative opinion of Pennsylvania German women as a group, writing of them, "The German Women are generally so disagreeable to an English Eye, that it wou'd require great Portions to induce Englishmen to marry them." However, by the end of the century, perhaps his assessment would have softened. Théophile Cazenove, usually critical of Pennsylvania's German population, recognized at least some redeeming features among a select group of women in Lancaster. While he found the grace and manners of the female youth generally lacking, he reported, "The young ladies I saw here are very well dressed, very much like Philadelphia ladies. Generally the young women and girls of this district seem to me to have a rather pretty figure, good carriage, [and] beautiful teeth and hair." He further recognized that the "most notable" among them were "beginning to learn a little music" and that "tea parties" were becoming common. Women of German descent, just like other Pennsylvania women including the Richardson daughters and the Hands, could participate in activities such as the ritualized consumption of tea and performances on the harpsichord and could pay more attention to clothing, hygiene, and posture, which communicated their elite status. The Hottensteins' two tea kettles, two coffee pots, and six silver teaspoons suggest that Caterina had begun to embrace this new standard in her fashionable house, which included formal rooms for dining and entertaining.[48]

As articulate travelers scrutinized the late eighteenth-century Pennsylvania landscape, they repeatedly observed congruence between house quality, household behavior, and the social status of house occupants, both female and male. In Spring Mill, on the Schuylkill River in what is now Montgomery County, Brissot noted that the "best house" was occupied by "Mr. L," a Frenchman. He described the house as "very well built in stone, two stories high, with five or six chambers in each story." In addition to this "great house," Mr. L also owned "several small houses for his servants, his barns and his cattle." Brissot informed his readers of Mr. L's elevated status by noting, "He is attentive to the subject of meteorology; it is he that furnishes the meteorologic tables published every month in the Columbian Magazine: they are certainly the most exact that have appeared on this continent."[49]

There were, of course, some exceptions to the correlation between the quality of a dwelling and the rank of the family that occupied it. Because these deviations challenged common assumptions about the relationship between architecture, wealth, and social standing, they were considered anomalies and were frequently the subject of commentary. In the mid-1760s, for example, blacksmith John Miller began work on a three-story brick house on Queen Street in Lancaster (fig. 53). Edward Shippen reported in 1766 that the house, which was located "very near the Court-House," was "as good . . . if not better than his own." Three years later, he noted that it was "the best in

Fig. 53 John Miller house, Lancaster, Pennsylvania, c. 1766. The house John Miller built was a three-story brick building with large sash windows. Those on the façade facing Queen Street were capped with decorative stone jack-arch lintels with keystones. While the exterior of the Miller house has been restored to its appearance when it was constructed in the 1760s, the interior has little historical integrity, and it is therefore difficult to determine its original floor plan.

the Town." He believed, however, that "John Miller the Smith" had "built two [*sic*] large an house for his circumstances." Shippen, a former mayor of Philadelphia who had recently relocated to Lancaster and become an esteemed member of that community, did not feel that Miller was worthy of such a grand house. Despite the fact that Miller had accumulated significant wealth, as a tradesman (or mechanic) he was not supposed to occupy a three-story brick dwelling near the center of town.[50]

On the other hand, sometimes extremely poor houses were inhabited by individuals who had once been members of the upper class but later found themselves in difficult economic circumstances. Such was the case for the members of the Dash family, who lived in the vicinity of Northumberland in central Pennsylvania in the 1790s. Mrs. Dash was an English "lady" who had left Europe with her three daughters after her husband went bankrupt. When a French duke discovered the Dashes in Pennsylvania, they were living in a small "wooden house, built against the side of a high mountain." The disparity between the status of the Dashes, as evidenced by their manners, knowledge, and character, and the state of their dwelling was readily apparent to the duke. He commented on the "strange contrast" of the circumstances of one of the Dash daughters, who had played the pianoforte for him. He noted, "She performs very well, is young, pretty, unfortunate, modest, possesses no property on earth, and, in a wooden hut, plays upon one of the finest instruments, that ever came from Longman's shop [in London]."[51]

Generally, people like the Dashes, who had been educated in the manners of upper-class eighteenth-century society, did not live in small wooden huts. Rather, they occupied larger houses that were usually constructed of masonry and based on a closed floor plan. When the duke encountered the Dashes, they were in the process of securing such a house. The duke believed that when completed, their new stone dwelling, while still "humble," would represent a "decent habitation."[52]

The reason the Dashes had not built a better house sooner was that they lacked the financial wherewithal to undertake the construction. Wealth, more than any other attribute, was necessary to erect a large masonry house. Soon after arriving in Pennsylvania in the 1740s, the Lutheran clergyman Heinrich Melchior Muhlenberg noted in his journal, "It is not a good thing to build of wood here because it decays quickly, and it is expensive to build of stone." Because of the cost of building a durable house of either stone or brick, such dwellings were equated with wealth throughout the eighteenth century. When a European visitor traveled to Chambersburg, Pennsylvania, he noted in his journal, "The place is very pleasant, and from the quantity of new brick houses, neatly built, it appears that the place is prosperous." In Middletown, Bucks County, after Brissot visited with William and Elizabeth Richardson, Jacob Shoemaker, the Richardsons' son-in-law, took their guest to see the site where William Richardson was going to build a house for his oldest son. According to Shoemaker, the construction of this house was an indicator of William and his son's wealth. Brissot recorded the conversation: "You see, said he to me, the wealth of this good farmer. His father was a poor Scotchman; he came to America, and applied himself to agriculture, and by his industry and economy amassed a large fortune. This son of his is likewise rich."[53]

The correlation between the quality of a house and the wealth of its owner was so certain that when the U.S. government decided to tax individuals according to their means, it looked to houses as one of the most accurate measures. Faced with an impending war in the 1790s, Federalists, guided by Alexander Hamilton, advocated for a shift from indirect taxes on goods purchased to a direct tax on property to raise revenue. During a debate in the House of Representatives on the feasibility of a land tax, John Williams, a representative from New York, observed that such a tax would have "no way of reaching the moneyed men, who lived in great cities; and, though large holders of land, their land was in the hands of their tenants, who must pay the tax." In a report to the House, Oliver Wolcott Jr., who continued Hamilton's policies as secretary of the treasury after Hamilton resigned from the post, made another suggestion. Wolcott began describing a proposed tax on houses by stating, "In a scientific view, a tax on houses can only be considered a tax on expense, and in no sense as a tax on capital or revenue." He considered "the houses and other buildings of the great body of farmers and laborers of a country" as "objects of *necessary expense,*" which were not "the most eligible objects of public revenue." However, he continued, "Such houses . . . as exceed in value the average of those occupied by farmers and laborers, may be regarded as among the most suitable objects of taxation. Perhaps there is no single criterion by which the comparative expenses of individuals can be so fairly estimated as by their dwellings." A basic dwelling could satisfy the physical need for shelter; houses that possessed greater monetary value because of their size, plan, or finish served as status symbols for those aspiring individuals who could afford to build them.[54]

In the House of Representatives, the proposal to tax houses met with some resistance. William Craik, of Maryland, believed that houses "were an equivocal representation of property, and a tax on them would fall on some parts of the country much heavier than on others." John Swanwick, a Republican from Pennsylvania, remarked that the "injustice of such taxes was not greater than their hateful nature, since a rich man by no means paid his portion of them." Despite these objections, in 1798, the federal government initiated a direct tax to raise $2 million—$1,315,000 of which was to be obtained through a tax on dwelling houses, associated outbuildings, and house lots. To lighten the burden on farmers and laborers whose houses were merely "necessary expenses," dwellings of minimal value were considered "indicators of poverty," and their owners were exempt from liability. More valuable houses were divided into nine classes and subject to a graduated tax.[55]

In Pennsylvania, the 1798 Federal Direct Tax and other Federalist programs, such as the Alien and Sedition Act, sparked a wave of resistance, which reached its pinnacle in the Lehigh Valley with Fries's Rebellion. Yet many Americans, particularly those aligned with the Federalist Party, believed that taxing wealthy members of the upper class by applying a tax to houses was reasonable. One Pennsylvanian remarked in his nineteenth-century memoirs that the house tax established a "policy of favoring the industrious and frugal at the expense of the luxurious." He added, "the farmer paid very little for his property in proportion to the idle gentleman or inhabitant of the city, who gratified himself in the enjoyment of a sumptuous house." In December 1798, *The Oracle of Dauphin and Harrisburg Advertiser,* a Federalist newspaper, published the federal tax rates as well as a description of how the new impost would work essentially to tax the rich and spare the poor. The author, who identified himself simply as "A Farmer," wrote:

> Thus—Suppose there is in Boston, or Philadelphia, a Mechanic, whose house and shop are worth 500 dollars—he will pay a tax of one dollar.— Suppose their [*sic*] are five hundred such mechanics—they will, of course, pay a tax of five hundred dollars.
>
> Suppose further—That one man owns a house and out-buildings worth 50,000 dollars—he then will have to pay a tax of five hundred dollars— That is, he will pay as great a tax for property worth only 50,000 dollars, as the FIVE HUNDRED Mechanics will pay for property worth 250,000 dollars!
>
> Or thus—My neighbor's farm house and barn are worth 500 dollars— My house and buildings (I am a farmer too) are worth 5000 dollars— Now my neighbor will pay a tax of one dollar; and I a tax of twenty five dollars—That is, I shall pay as great a tax for property worth 5,000 dollars, as TWENTY-FIVE such brother farmers will pay for property worth 12,500 dollars.
>
> And if the palace of the great and illustrious FARMER OF MOUNT VERNON is worth 50,000 dollars, he will pay as great a tax for it, as five hundred other farmers, of the above description, will pay for property worth 250,000 dollars[.]
>
> The foregoing statements shew clearly—That the Federal Government have consulted the interest of the poorest classes of citizens—and have aimed in this, as indeed they have in all their fiscal laws, to draw the public revenue from the purses of the wealthy.[56]

In an effort to place the tax burden on wealthy members of the upper class, national, state, and local tax policy in the late eighteenth century focused on material goods, such as highly valued houses, that were associated with genteel activities. However, graduated direct taxes that penalized those who owned the best houses were just one element of the equation. On the federal level, congressmen—both Federalists and Republicans—called for indirect taxation, akin to a sales tax, on bottles and the fine beverages they held as well as on imported fabrics, particularly silk, which were used to embellish dwellings and bodies. In Pennsylvania, in addition to imposts on land, buildings, and cattle, the state also taxed slaves and servants, wrought silver plate, billiard tables, and "travelling or pleasure carriages." According to one commentator, the last impost "upon carriages kept for comfort and pleasure" revealed "beyond all others" the government's "discrimination in behalf of *the mouth of labor.*" During the late eighteenth century, officials often chose to raise revenue not by taxing items that were required by everyone, regardless of rank, but rather by taxing nonessential goods that were specifically associated with the upper class. Temple Franklin, Benjamin Franklin's grandson, expressed a common sentiment of the period when he stated, "if any thing ought to be taxed, it is pleasure." For this reason, imposts were placed primarily on articles used by individuals of elevated rank who had discretionary income to spend as well as time and knowledge to participate in leisure activities.[57]

The Stages of Improvement

In the late eighteenth century, Americans and Europeans traveling in America had clear ideas about the types of goods members of the various classes used and the types of entertainment they sought out. In large measure, members of the lower sort were believed to restrict their consumption to items of necessity. They were not supposed to own imported fabrics or tableware because the purchase of such items required significant financial resources. Furthermore, the objects themselves were associated with a lifestyle in which those who occupied lower social stations were not expected to participate. In the congressional debates about taxation, Joseph B. Varnum, a Republican from Massachusetts, stated, "the poor and the industrious people, whose income and labor barely [supply] them with the common necessaries of life, do not pay any part of the tax or duty on wines, teas, silks, carriages, and a great variety of other matters." According to Varnum, a poor man was too occupied with "supply[ing] his children with bread, to assuage their hunger, and buy[ing] clothing to guard them against the inclemency of the weather" to purchase a carriage, silk cloth, or certain taxable wines and teas. These commodities were simply not supposed to be possessed by people of limited means. These were items reserved for people of the better sort and were specifically associated with wealth and status.[58]

Travelers in late eighteenth-century Pennsylvania recognized that when it came to personal possessions, the type and appearance of goods was often related to the rank of their owners. After visiting several stores in inland Pennsylvania towns, one European traveler remarked, "You find everything necessary in utensils, clothing, and furniture, for the lower class, but nothing dainty or choice." His statement indicates that there was a real disparity between the "necessary" goods used by the lower class and the "dainty or choice" items preferred by those of more elevated status. Traveling in Philadelphia, a Frenchman observed the type of possessions that might fit into the latter category. He noted, "The rich man loves to shew the stranger his splendid furniture, his fine English glass, and his exquisite china." According to this tourist, people with money did not have just furniture; they had "splendid" furniture. They did not eat and drink from homemade or locally made tableware but rather from "fine" imported English glasses and "exquisite" imported porcelain dishes.[59]

Another recently arrived European noted that even in death, material distinctions were evident among people of different stations. Gottlieb Mittelberger observed that in Pennsylvania coffins were generally made of "beautiful walnut wood, stained quite brown, and shiny with varnish." However, he added, "Wealthy people attach four beautifully worked brass handles to the coffin." Presumably, these handles, which Mittelberger noted made the coffins easier to carry to the cemetery, also bestowed distinction on the families of the individual who had died.[60]

In the late eighteenth century, houses with center or side passages, which were furnished with fine furniture, imported glassware, and china, became increasingly common in Pennsylvania. Yet such buildings and the objects in them were associated specifically with certain kinds of individuals. Their occupants were expected to be wealthy. However, as the case of Lancaster's John Miller suggests, money did not automatically convey the social status that was expected of the residents of elaborately furnished, closed-plan houses. During the period in question, these kinds of material objects were commonly understood to transmit information about other attributes, including occupation, education, social graces, and leadership ability. Even something as simple as a brass coffin handle held deep meaning for those who observed it. Buildings and other belongings regularly served as symbols of "improvement." In the late eighteenth century, ideas about the enhancement of property in the form of land, houses, and furnishings were often conflated with ideas about progress, power, and virtue.

In this period, many Americans and European visitors to America understood the process of settling and improving the American countryside as a visible, multistaged endeavor. Personal possessions provided one of the most discernible measures of progress. Perhaps no personal possession was more often remarked on as an example of improvement than the house. During the first stage of settlement, domestic accommodations were understood simply to fulfill the basic need for shelter. Gradually comfort became a more important attribute. By the final stage of settlement, comfort had the potential to give way to elegance and spaciousness, and perhaps even ostentation and luxury.

According to the entry for "Pennsylvania" in the *United States Gazetteer* of 1795, the first houses in the state's new settlements were generally built of log. Another author, writing in the same year, indicated that these earliest log houses customarily took six men three or four days to build and cost their owners roughly ten guineas, or £10.10.0. He wrote that the "first care" of a settler "removing into the back country" was "to cut down a few trees to build his log-house." A French traveler described the next step in the process by noting that after these felled trees were used to build the walls of a dwelling, then often "the interstices between the trunks [were] filled up with earth." In other cases, he observed that stone, plaster, or clay could be used to chink the spaces between the logs. Not surprisingly, regardless of chinking material, this author concluded that most of the houses of this type had "a mean appearance."[61]

With time, improvements were made to existing houses, or new dwellings were built to replace them. After traveling in the 1790s between Carlisle and Shippensburg in south-central Pennsylvania, a European land agent concluded, "The new farmers all live in wretched log houses without windows, and with chimneys of sticks and clay, but as the land they acquired yields good wheat, the price of which is so high, they are beginning to have comfort." Another tourist, in this case a French duke, noted an even more drastic change. Writing later in the decade, he remarked of the country along the Schuylkill River between Pottstown and Reading that "those marks of the increasing improvement of the country, which are observable as far as Bethlehem and the Delaware, are also perceivable here. Log-houses, constructed of trunks of trees, laid one upon another, the interstices of which are filled up with clay, are seen no longer, having been replaced by framed houses, consisting however of balks, properly hewn and shaped, and covered with boards." The newly constructed buildings that the duke observed were signs of an advancement to a second stage of "civilization," which, according to this foreign visitor, had occurred throughout much of the countryside in eastern Pennsylvania by the end of the eighteenth century. The new buildings were not built of round logs hastily produced from tree trunks but rather of "balks," or carefully shaped, squared logs. Furthermore, their log construction was concealed by boards, which created a more refined exterior finish.[62]

In Philadelphia, as well as several inland Pennsylvania towns, the process of improvement, as expressed by dwelling houses, had progressed still further. Founded by William Penn in 1682, Philadelphia in the first decades of the eighteenth century contained many buildings described as "poor," "ordinary," or "tolerable"; some early eighteenth-century Philadelphia dwellings had even been characterized as "hutts." However, by the late eighteenth century, numerous authors remarked favorably on the new dwellings being built. In the 1790s, the author of "Observations on the City of Philadelphia" commented that "modern" houses in the metropolis were constructed of brick, not wood or log. The same was true in older inland Pennsylvania towns such as Reading and York, both founded in the 1740s. In the former, the European traveler who visited the Elmakers and Hands observed in 1794 roughly fifty houses "newly built, of bricks, and neatly decorated like the Philadelphia houses." Of the approximately four hundred houses in York, he noted about sixty that were "brick and newly built."[63]

In the late eighteenth century, differences in material culture clearly existed between older towns, which had been "improving" for several decades, and new towns, which were often surrounded by wilderness. In 1788, as Jacques-Pierre Brissot de Warville approached the city of Philadelphia from Bucks County, he could not help marveling at the prospect before him. He observed in his published journal that "passing the river Shammony [Neshaminy], on a new bridge, and then the village of Frankford, we arrived at Philadelphia, by a fine road bordered with the best cultivated fields, and elegant houses, which announce the neighbourhood of a great town." Several years later, as a French duke journeyed from the new state capital of Harrisburg to the central Pennsylvania town of Sunbury, which had been founded in 1772, he found himself recording very different impressions. He wrote of Sunbury, "This town, which is not so large as Harrisburg, and in its buildings less elegant and compact, is seated on the left bank of the Susquehanna. . . . The prospect of the town, on descending from the mountain, is neither grand nor pleasing; in point of size the houses, viewed from the heights, resemble a camp, rather than a town."[64]

To contemporary observers, the built environments of Philadelphia and Sunbury conveyed radically different messages. To Brissot, Philadelphia appeared a "great town"; to his contemporary sojourner, Sunbury appeared "a camp." Both authors based their conclusions concerning their destinations in large measure on the houses they observed. In the vicinity of Philadelphia, Brissot encountered "elegant houses." Although he did not explicitly describe the residences, it is safe to assume that many of the buildings he passed were constructed of brick or stone and contained multiple rooms and even multiple stories. Approaching Sunbury, the duke observed very different structures. He told his readers that the buildings generally were not elegant and that the houses were small. If the houses in Sunbury were anything like those in the neighboring town of Northumberland, the majority were probably built of inferior materials as well. Describing the buildings in Northumberland, the duke noted, "All of the houses are of wood, chiefly log-houses; only two are built with stone."[65]

To argue that period observers perceived a correlation between house quality and length of settlement may seem to contradict the assertion that Americans and European visitors to America understood houses, and other forms of material culture, as representations of their owners' ranks. However, in the late eighteenth century, the two assertions were not believed to be in tension. The most detailed late eighteenth-century treatise on the improvement of Pennsylvania, "An Account of the Progress of Population, Agriculture, Manners, and Government in Pennsylvania," helps explain how this could be so. Published by several authors in several different formats, the essay has been credited to Benjamin Rush, who published it in the *Columbian Magazine* in 1786. Its title begins to suggest the conflation of the diverse topics of leadership, deportment, and improvement.[66]

According to Rush and those who borrowed from him, settlement in Pennsylvania progressed through three distinct stages, which were characterized by three distinct types, or "species," of settlers. The first kind of settler was poor: he had "outlived his credit or fortune" and routinely suffered from a "want of money." Furthermore, the first settler lacked good character and proper conduct. Rush stated that this type of settler participated in a "licentious manner of living" and that he was "nearly related to an Indian in his manners." By all accounts, because of his poverty and behavior, an individual who fit Rush's description of the "first settler" conformed to the characteristics that eighteenth-century Pennsylvanians and others used to distinguish the lower sort. Not surprisingly, it was this type of settler who lived in the most basic, unembellished type of house. As Rush described it, the typical dwelling of the first species of settler was "a small cabbin of rough logs" with a dirt floor, split logs for a roof, and perhaps a small window "made of greased paper" rather than a wooden sash with glass panes. The clothing and standard of cleanliness of the typical first settler were equally poor. According to Rush, "he eats, drinks and sleeps in dirt and rags in his little cabbin."[67]

In terms of wealth, manners, and material culture, the second species of settler was in a more esteemed position than the first. Whereas the first settler had often been a tenant, the second was able to pay "part in cash" for his land and "the rest in gales or installments." Moreover, "the Indian manners" of the first settler had become "more diluted" in the second. Yet, the second species of settler had still not achieved financial security or social polish. According to Rush, although members of this group were usually landowners, they frequently contracted debts. Furthermore, Rush stated that they were seldom "good member[s] of civil or religious society."[68]

The dwellings occupied by members of the second "species" of settler suggested to readers their position somewhere between the more lowly first settlers and the more lofty third and final group of settlers. According to Rush, many members of the second species took the path spelled out in period travel accounts: they replaced the first settlers' cabins with more substantial dwellings constructed from hewn, or squared, logs. Rush noted that these new residences usually had board floors, clapboard roofs, cellars, and stone foundations and were often two stories tall. Yet, despite all the improvements, Rush also commented on deficiencies that were inherent in this kind of settler's house. He remarked, "His windows are unglazed, or, if they had glass in them, the ruins of it are supplied with old hats or pillows." Overall, Rush concluded, "His house, as well as his farm, bear many marks of a weak tone of mind."[69]

It was only with the third species of settler that, Rush claimed, "we behold civilization completed." According to Rush, the typical settler of this type was "a man of property and good character." His house and other belongings reflected the elevated status he had gained by means of his wealth and deportment. Rush associated a "large, convenient" stone house with the third species of settler. Other structures on his property might include a large stone barn, a milk or spring house, and possibly a smokehouse. Rush described the inside of the typical third settler's house as being "filled with useful and substantial furniture." He noted that "his table abounds with a variety of the best provisions." If, to Rush, the material environment of the second species of settler had indicated a "weak tone of mind," the holdings of the third species of settler suggested that he did not suffer from the same deficiency.[70]

Rush argued in "An Account of the Progress of Population, Agriculture, Manners, and Government in Pennsylvania" that the stages constituted a linear progression. Although he recognized exceptions, the general pattern he established was of the first settler and his buildings being replaced by the second and his buildings being in turn replaced by the third and his buildings. Many period authors agreed with this assessment of the development of Pennsylvania, particularly as it related to the succession of buildings. They observed in newly populated areas basic log structures, which did little more than provide shelter from the harshest weather conditions. In regions where there had been a somewhat longer history of settlement, dwellings built of logs made quickly from tree trunks were replaced or amended to provide their occupants with more comfort. In Pennsylvania towns and some rural areas that had still longer histories of settlement, commentators believed a third transition from small or medium-sized wood houses to larger masonry houses had taken place. As the author of the *United States Gazetteer* noted of Pennsylvanians, "Their houses in the old settlements are chiefly built of limestone, or brick, two stories high."[71]

It is relatively clear that few areas made the transition through the three types of houses as neatly as period authors claimed. Historian Billy G. Smith has found that even in Philadelphia, many people were still living in houses constructed of wood at the end of the eighteenth century. Although some inhabitants of the city owned three-story brick town houses as well as lavish country seats, other urban residents resided in one-story structures with no more than 154 feet of interior space. Yet most observers who described the metropolis pointed out the best buildings rather than the worst. As early as 1740, one author reported that of the fourteen hundred to fifteen hundred houses in the city, most of them were "well built with Brick." At the end of the century, another commentator related that many Philadelphia houses were five or even six stories high. Remarks about small, poor-quality, log houses were reserved for those in locations on the more distant Pennsylvania frontier.[72]

The concept of describing the settlement of Pennsylvania as a three-tiered progression, when it was in fact much more observably complex, was, at least in part, related to the belief that the quality of a house denoted its occupants' rank. As the clergyman Jacob Duché wrote to the Right Honourable Lord Viscount P—— in Westminister, "The progress of the human mind may here likewise be observed to keep equal pace with the external improvements." Duché believed that as the "gradual polish of manners" in America progressed "from aukwardness itself even to courtly civility," the physical environment would also improve.[73]

Duché, Rush, and numerous others expected individuals who headed into the wilderness, squatted on or rented land they did not own, and seemed to behave more like "uncivilized" Indians than Europeans to occupy small, poor-quality houses. Failing to possess an education, polite manners, professional skills, wealth, or any of the other characteristics associated with the upper class, period commentators readily identified these people with buildings that provided little comfort or convenience, and certainly no luxury. However, they also expected these first settlers and their buildings to give way to a new class of residents and new types of dwellings as time progressed. Rush and his contemporaries felt that as the population increased, laws were established, wild beasts were replaced by domesticated animals, and fences were made necessary by the cultivation of grain, the early settlers would make way for the next stage of improvement. Initiated by people of more elevated status, people who had greater financial assets and who behaved more "civilly," this next stage would logically bring with it better-quality houses.[74]

The progression would continue until finally individuals of "property and good character," who erected "commodious" masonry dwellings, inaugurated what in the late eighteenth century was perceived as the third and final stage of improvement. Unlike the pioneers who typified the first or even the second "species" of settlers, members of this group possessed many of the characteristics period authors associated with the elite. As Rush and his imitators noted, they enjoyed "affluence and independence." They supported schools, churches, and government, and presumably were educated, at least in agriculture. In their manners they were not "nearly related to an Indian," but instead represented "civilization completed." It was this third species that possessed the degree of refinement that period authors associated with the ownership of a multistory, masonry dwelling house, particularly of the closed-plan variety.[75]

Pennsylvania German Refinement

When discussing houses and furnishings of the best sort, commentators rarely made mention of ethnic background. Occasionally, they might note that the occupants of a building were of a particular nationality—the Richardsons of Middletown in Bucks County, for example, were said to be of Scottish descent, and "Mr. L" of Spring Mill, in what is now Montgomery County, was reportedly French. However, such remarks were only incidental. In describing the owners of so-called "Georgian" buildings, period authors were really not concerned with issues of ethnicity. Instead they saw the buildings as manifestations of social and economic status. Two-story, masonry houses with symmetrical façades, center or side passages, and increasingly segregated kitchen facilities were viewed as signs of the improvement of physical property, which was believed to correspond with the improvement of mind and manners.

Although many period authors repeatedly and specifically indicated that Pennsylvania Germans lived in poor-quality, sparsely furnished dwellings, some documentary evidence and numerous surviving buildings suggest otherwise. For example, the German blacksmith John Miller, who was criticized for building the best house in Lancaster, was censured not because he was German but because he was a mechanic by trade. In other locales, people of German descent were clearly recognized as the owners of notable dwellings. Daniel Hiester's two-story brick center-passage house in Upper Salford Township, in what is now Montgomery County, was described in the *Pennsylvania Gazette* as "one of the best houses in that part of the country" (fig. 54). And in Middletown, Dauphin County, "the only stone building in the town" in the late 1790s was a two-story, 30-by-40-foot house with an adjoining 17-by-29-foot stone kitchen building, which was owned by the German miller George Frey (fig. 55).[76]

Daniel Hiester house, Upper Salford Township, Montgomery County, Pennsylvania, c. 1757. Daniel Hiester's two-story brick house, located near Sumneytown, was described as "one of the best houses in that part of the country" when it was advertised for sale in 1783.

Fig. 55 George Frey house, Middletown, Dauphin County, Pennsylvania, before 1795. George Frey's house, with its façade of coursed stone, was reportedly the only stone building in Middletown when a French duke toured the area in the last decade of the eighteenth century. A successful owner of a merchant mill for grinding grain into flour, Frey was "rich, and grows daily richer" (François Alexandre-Frédéric, duc de La Rochefoucauld Liancourt, *Travels Through the United States of North America, the Country of the Iroquois, and Upper Canada, in the Years 1795, 1796, and 1797; With an Authentic Account of Lower Canada* [London: R. Phillips, 1799], 1:50).

Houses like those owned by Miller, Hiester, and Frey were distinguished from the exterior because of their size, materials, and symmetrical façades and from the interior because of their floor plan, architectural finish, and level of cleanliness, the latter facilitated by the women of the house and, significantly, their hired or enslaved "help." Such houses were additionally singled out because they were furnished with the kinds of objects that period authors associated specifically with the upper class. Closed-plan dwellings that were occupied by Pennsylvania Germans were often equipped with the same assemblages of specialized, "nonessential" goods that non-Germans used in their houses. An 1803 probate inventory for Philip Erpff, who lived in a center-passage, double-pile house in Schaefferstown (see figs. 48–49), in what is now Lebanon County, illustrates the kind of items that often filled the interior spaces of buildings of this type. Erpff's walls were adorned with "Pictures" and "3 Looking Glasses," and his furniture included a "House Clock & Case" and six tables. He could store tea in four tea canisters and use his queensware dishes, six silver teaspoons, and silver sugar tongs to serve it. Wine could be kept in white, green, and clear glass bottles and poured into nine wineglasses. Erpff's estate appraisers additionally recorded "a Lott Books" and several items of noteworthy apparel, including two black silk handkerchiefs, one pair of silver knee buckles, three pairs of sleeve buttons, and two pairs of shoe buckles.[77]

Yet suggesting that Erpff's house was outfitted exactly like the houses of his affluent non-German neighbors would be an overstatement. From Erpff's inventory and a contract between him and Jacob Grubb, which was signed in 1800, it is clear that in addition to the items just described, Erpff's household accouterments also included a ten-plate stove, which was found in his "large Front Room."[78] As Pennsylvania Germans such as Erpff began to build and occupy new kinds of houses in the late eighteenth century, they often embraced objects that demonstrated a continued preference for certain ethnic customs. Heating devices such as five-plate, six-plate, and ten-plate stoves, for example, were often incorporated in prominently located first-floor stove rooms.

The inclusion of a stove in a closed-plan house such as Erpff's begins to demonstrate the multiple identities people of German descent could convey by constructing a center- or side-passage, double-pile house. A stove-heated room differentiated many German-occupied houses of the type from similar houses owned by non-Germans such as Edward and Catherine Hand. Construction techniques also served as expressions of ethnic identity, as did prominently placed German-language date stones. However, physical manifestations of ethnic background did not prevent this type of house from accumulating other kinds of meaning. By building large masonry closed-plan residences, Pennsylvania Germans, like members of other ethnic groups living in late eighteenth-century Pennsylvania, defined themselves largely according to prevalent ideas about improvement. They did not necessarily forsake traditional ethnic building techniques, heating schemes, or decorative preferences, but they did opt for a new house type that spoke to a different type of identity.

The construction of a two-story, masonry, center- or side-passage structure required significant financial assets. More importantly, however, the finished product symbolized the power and prestige that were felt to accompany education, good manners, and the shunning of manual labor. By furnishing such houses with expensive, often highly taxed, items that were associated with refined rituals of entertainment such as tea drinking, esteemed Pennsylvania German men and women made statements about more than just from where they or their ancestors had come. Being able to construct a new house, such as the Elmakers did in 1798, was a sign of personal advancement. It allowed a certain group of Pennsylvania Germans to distinguish themselves from the stereotypical image of the ignorant and frugal farmer.

Luxury

The decision some Pennsylvania Germans made to set themselves apart by building a grand house—characterized by a closed floor plan, spaces for entertaining and display, segregated work areas where nonfamily members provided much of the labor, and furnishings including objects associated with tea drinking and dining, reading and writing, and timekeeping—must be analyzed in light of period religious beliefs. Religious communities in eighteenth-century Pennsylvania created standards, some codified in written records, many communicated orally or simply understood, that regulated the way people expressed themselves materially. While there were always instances of divergence and disagreement, the general rules provided a sense of unity and conformity among members of religious groups. On one level, they separated Mennonites from Moravians and Lutherans. On another, they served to unite multiple Protestant religious denominations in a common visual language of piety. Particularly in the late eighteenth century, in light of the events leading up to the American Revolution, moderation in the material realm became tied to issues of morality and virtue. Material excess, on the other hand, was a sign of vice in the form of luxury.[1]

In this chapter, I explore the relationship between religious belief and material culture in the eighteenth century. Among Protestant Pennsylvania Germans, different religious groups advocated different material expressions. Those best known today, such as the buildings that Conrad Beissel constructed at Ephrata in Lancaster County and those built by Moravians in towns such as Bethlehem, represented the extremes on a spectrum that ranged from strict asceticism to cosmopolitan sophistication. I also demonstrate that the process of identity making was shaped by communities. In previous chapters, I have shown that outsiders referenced the material landscape to create identities for those they defined as Pennsylvania Germans and that individual Pennsylvania Germans used material culture to fashion identities for themselves. Communities, or groups of like-minded individuals often united by geography as well as common beliefs and practices, also played a part in identity formation.

The German-speakers who immigrated to Pennsylvania in the eighteenth century represented a wide variety of religious groups. Some were Catholics or Jews, but the vast majority adhered to Protestant beliefs. Yet even among Protestants—ranging from Lutherans to Amish—differences abounded.[2] Two broad categories, designated by the adjectives "Plain" and "Church," have been used to describe and group many Pennsylvania Germans based on their religious affiliation. Members of Lutheran and Reformed congregations are known as "Church" people, due to their membership in churches that were recognized state institutions in continental Europe. Historian Steven Nolt argues that "though representing historically distinct Reformation traditions, Lutheran and Reformed churches in Greater Pennsylvania developed close relations, often shared church buildings, and lived within a common cultural context that often meant more than their dogmatic differences." By 1740, the two denominations had more than sixteen thousand communing members. Eighty thousand German Reformed and Lutheran immigrants had arrived in the British North American colonies by 1776.[3]

Since the nineteenth century, commentators have often grouped the Mennonites, Amish, and Brethren—the last better known in early Pennsylvania as Dunkards—together as "Plain" people. Those affiliated with these religious groups had much in common in the eighteenth century. As Anabaptists, they baptized adults, in some cases by immersion, following a profession of faith. Furthermore, they took a radical approach to Christ's directive of nonresistance, advocating nonviolence and nonparticipation in war.[4] Yet the adjective "Plain," by which they are often identified, is misleading. Certainly Mennonites, Amish, and Dunkards were all concerned about the relationship between worldly goods and Christian devotion. However, so were Lutheran and Reformed believers. The plainness of the "Plain" sects tended to be most apparent in the liturgy of worship. Outside worship spaces, apparel may have been the only material element that began to distinguish the so-called "Plain" folk from "Church" folk in the eighteenth century.[5]

Previous studies of Pennsylvania German material culture have often emphasized traditions of simplicity among Anabaptist groups, including the Mennonites and the Amish. They have additionally focused significant attention on the unusual eighteenth-century communal assemblies at Ephrata and the Moravian settlement at Bethlehem in what is now Northampton County.[6] Often overlooked are the affluent Pennsylvania Germans of various faiths who chose to build grand houses. Pennsylvanians of diverse religious and ethnic backgrounds who strove to improve their property and refine their manners during the second half of the eighteenth century were aware of the opinions of their neighbors, both those who had similar religious beliefs and those who did not.

Community standards were often established by clergy and church leaders, but the laity played an important role in interpreting and negotiating what was acceptable and what was not. Concerns about religious devotion and virtue, and how one would be perceived by others, helped define the upward limits of material display. Clergy and their congregants contemplated the destructive power of worldly goods and condemned excess in household furnishings, personal attire, and diet. Furthermore, they admonished coreligionists to avoid certain activities, most notably dancing and inebriation, which they considered evidence of luxury and the worship of earthly pleasures. As people of elevated status embraced the belongings and behaviors associated with gentility, they were ever aware of the boundaries imposed on them by contemporary standards of godliness and propriety.[7]

Ephrata and the Moravian Settlements

Because of divergent denominational tenets concerning material display and the acceptability of certain pastimes, a person's religious identity could be expressed visually. The Moravians, who were led by Count Nicholas Ludwig von Zinzendorf and whose American membership included other members of the lesser German nobility, were the most likely to embrace new aesthetics associated with the elite, particularly in the closed communities they created before Zinzendorf's death in 1760.[8] At the other end of the continuum were the followers of Conrad Beissel at Ephrata, who lived secluded, disciplined, and austere lives. Both Beissel's followers at Ephrata and Zinzendorf's Moravians complicate the seemingly simple divide between "Church" and "Plain" folk. The Ephrata settlement traced its religious roots to the Dunkard faith. In fact, during the second half of the eighteenth century, many travelers referred to Ephrata as Dunkard Town.[9] However, several aspects of Beissel's theology, including recognition of Saturday as the Sabbath, avowal of celibacy, and insistence on asceticism, distinguished Ephrata residents from other Dunkards and superficially connected them with Jewish or monastic Catholic practices.[10]

The Moravian leader Zinzendorf, on the other hand, insisted that the Moravians were part of the Lutheran church. Yet eighteenth-century Moravians defy easy categorization, perhaps in part because Zinzendorf aimed to create an ecumenical religious movement among Germans in Pennsylvania. Moravians rejected violence, like many Anabaptists; formed communities where property was owned collectively, yet supported worldwide missionary activity and commerce; and supported a high percentage of well-educated male and female religious leaders. Compounding their unique religious position, Moravians hailed not only from the Rhine River valley, like many of their Pennsylvania neighbors, but also from throughout central Europe, with the greatest number of German speakers tracing their roots to Moravia and Silesia. Moravian immigrants also included non-Germans from Europe, including most notably immigrants from England and Denmark, and to a lesser extent from the Caribbean, Ceylon, and Guinea. At least eighteen Moravian families in the North American colonies were members of the European nobility, an aristocratic influence unknown among other Pennsylvania Germans. While the Moravian North American headquarters and industrial center was at Bethlehem, founded as an exclusively Moravian community in 1741, even in the mid-eighteenth century Moravian immigrants, their offspring, and converts lived and worshipped in both exclusively Moravian settlements and in areas where multiple religions were practiced, such as Philadelphia, Lancaster, and the Oley Valley.[11]

The contrasts between the closed religious communities at Ephrata and Moravian towns such as Bethlehem, Nazareth, and Lititz and the religious communities formed by other Protestant groups in Pennsylvania are instructive. While most Pennsylvania Germans lived in single-family houses and joined together for worship, the communal environments created by the Moravians and by Beissel's followers at Ephrata in the 1730s and 1740s resulted in a different type of living arrangement. At Moravian settlements and at Ephrata, typical familial relationships and households were suspended. At Ephrata, men and women led celibate lives cloistered according to their sex. At Moravian communities, where marriage and sexual intercourse were encouraged, members were divided into "choirs" based on their age, sex, and marital status and worked, ate, slept, and worshipped in choir groups until at least 1760 and, in the case of the Single Sisters' choir in Bethlehem, as late as 1841.[12]

Almost as unusual as their living arrangements were the groups' interactions with material goods. Moravians and Ephrata residents represented two extremes. Those who lived at Ephrata lived "extremely austere" lives, according to one period author. In closed Moravian communities, on the other hand, the landscape reminded contemporary observers of the estates created by European nobility. When Israel Acrelius, the provost of the Swedish Church in America, arrived in Bethlehem in 1754, for example, he stated that the town "shows itself in a glory which is not much inferior to that of Konungahof," the summer residence of the Swedish king. The visual contrasts between the environments that the two groups created demonstrate their members' differing religious attitudes toward the material world. Ephrata residents embraced ascetic design, while those at Moravian communities favored more sophisticated, modish styling.[13]

According to religious historian Jeffrey Bach, the buildings at Ephrata can be divided into three distinct architectural phases: the first involved a hermetic lifestyle, the second communal living, and the third the transition to a new form of congregation under new leadership. During the first phase, which began in 1725 when members of the group were living in the Conestoga Valley, solitary congregants lived in small isolated houses. As the group's numbers continued to grow, individual solitary dwellings became impractical and perhaps undesirable. During the second architectural phase, between 1734 and 1746, four large convents and four adjoining worship spaces were built at Ephrata to accommodate celibate Brothers, celibate Sisters, and householders who had formerly been married but had chosen to dissolve their unions.[14]

During the construction process, Beissel and his followers found themselves balancing the need for sizable and therefore potentially ostentatious buildings with beliefs about asceticism. The challenge of negotiating spiritual and material wealth caused one member, Israel Eckerlin, the prior of the celibate Brethren, to be expelled from the community in 1745. Much disagreement at Ephrata stemmed from the appropriateness of the large dormitories and worship spaces. In 1743, for example, Conrad Weiser, a prominent Ephrata resident, reported at the time of his decision to leave the community that he and others had been "compelled to protest for a considerable time . . . against the prevailing pomp and luxury, both in dress and magnificent buildings." In 1751, outsider Christopher Sauer referred to the "great buildings" at Ephrata that had been erected under Eckerlin's leadership.[15]

Yet the only surviving convent at Ephrata indicates attempts on the part of its designers, including Eckerlin, to choose more humble building materials, limit decorative detailing, and use an open rather than a closed floor plan (figs. 56–58). The 71-by-29-foot building, originally known as Hebron, was constructed not of stone but of hewn logs, which were covered with clapboard. Other dormitories at Ephrata that both predated and postdated Hebron were also built of wood. Kedar, constructed in 1735, was probably an earth-fast wood frame building that, unlike Hebron, did not even have a stone foundation. Bethania, built in 1746, measured 72 by 36 feet and was of half-timber construction. The fact that these buildings were constructed of wood rather than masonry, as might be expected for such large and important community structures, was not lost on outside observers. One remarked of Ephrata's architecture, "The buildings for the Brethren and Sisters are of timber, but spacious"; another, "everything is wooden and yet durable."[16]

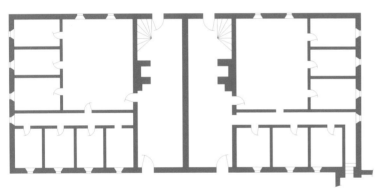

Fig. 56 Hebron/Saron and *Saal,* Ephrata, Lancaster County, Pennsylvania, 1743–45. Hebron, on the left, was originally designed in 1743 to house married couples who wished to dissolve their marriages and live at Ephrata. Hebron's *Saal,* on the right, provided a worship space for the building's residents. In 1745, Hebron was remodeled in order to accommodate Ephrata's celibate Sisters and renamed Saron.

Fig. 57 Reconstructed first-floor plan, Hebron, c. 1743. Hebron's original plan included two entry-kitchens, two large stove-heated common rooms, and individual sleeping cells. The plan was, in essence, two entry-kitchen houses arranged end-to-end and adapted through the incorporation of multiple cells for the use of a group of individuals rather than a single family. Based on plan in Patrick O'Bannon et al., *Ephrata Cloister: An Historic Structures Report,* 3 vols. (Philadelphia: John Milner Associates, 1988).

Hebron, which was meticulously documented and restored in the twentieth century, lacked decorative moldings or flamboyant ironwork, and individual 6-by-10-foot sleeping cells were furnished with only two wooden benches and a small closet. The building was basically two large entry-kitchen houses joined together and surrounded by cells for individual use. Originally intended for formerly married householders, one of the house-like sides was inhabited by men and the other by women. When the building was converted for use by the celibate Sisters in 1745 and renamed Saron, the interior wall separating the two "houses" was removed.[17]

The restraint that Ephrata residents exercised in fashioning their living spaces in terms of construction materials, decoration, and plan was further evidenced in other aspects of their material world. Beissel recommended bread and other grains for food and water for drink. In a desire to decrease sexuality and purify the body, he cautioned against the consumption of meat,

Fig. 58 Third floor, Hebron/Saron. The surviving buildings at Ephrata are now part of Ephrata Cloister, a historic site operated by the Pennsylvania Historical and Museum Commission. The third floor of Hebron/Saron has been stabilized and preserved rather than restored to an earlier appearance. The doors from the common room lead to individual sleeping cells.

leafy vegetables, and legumes. Although a community leader reported to a visitor in 1753 that "we forbid none among us who desire it to eat meat," he also explained that "the brethren do not incline to the eating of flesh. Our food is usually of vegetables, such as cabbages, roots, greens, also milk, butter, cheese, and good bread always." For clothes, a 1764 world history explained, "Their garb is the most simple that can be imagined, being a long white woolen gown in winter, and linen in summer, with a cape, which serves them for a hat, like that of a capuchin, behind, and fastened round with a belt." When one of Beissel's followers appeared at market in 1734, the *Pennsylvania Gazette* described him as wearing "the Habit of a Pilgrim," with a "Hat of Linen, his Beard at full Length, and a long Staff in his Hand." Not surprisingly, the distinct clothing, diet, and sparsely furnished cells of Ephrata residents were often a subject of comment among people who visited the community.[18]

Not long after the Ephrata settlement's founding in 1732, a German immigrant noted that the community's residents "practice[d] voluntary poverty." This prospective member was told that in order to join the Ephrata group, he would first have to sell all he owned "and give it to the poor." According to Bach, "As Beissel aged and the number of celibates dwindled, mystical interpretations faded from the rituals and ascetic rigor abated considerably." Yet decades later, commentators were still remarking on the unique, unpretentious lifestyle of Ephrata's few remaining residents. The people who lived there continued to "use great plainness of dress and language." A leader of the community reported to a French traveler that adherents to the faith took a "vow of poverty and chastity," "live[d] with the utmost frugality," and shared property communally. As a result, the visitor noted, they were not supposed to drink coffee or tea or sleep on feather beds. Although digressions were reportedly commonplace, ideally Beissel's instructions to regulate "eating and drink, sleep and waking" were to prevail. At eighteenth-century Ephrata, self-denial was the norm, and the built environment, despite its scale, was designed to reflect discipline and humility, as were Ephrata residents' meals, clothing, and lack of personal property.[19]

Contrasting with the restrained architectural expressions at Ephrata were the buildings erected by the Moravians at their religious settlements of Bethlehem and Nazareth, in what is now Northampton County, and Lititz, in Lancaster County. A 1755 map of Bethlehem and the surrounding area shows numerous multistory residential, commercial, and religious buildings with symmetrical façades carefully laid out along the banks of the Lehigh River and its tributary, the Monocacy Creek (fig. 59). As at Ephrata, at closed Moravian communities, buildings had to not only serve as worship spaces but also house and provide work spaces for members of the community. However, the overall impression produced at the Moravian town of Bethlehem, which was

Fig. 59 "Bethlehem Tract with All the Adjacent Land," attributed to Andreas Hoeger, 1755. By 1755, when this map was created, the Moravian community at Bethlehem included numerous commercial, residential, and religious structures. Most were multiple-story buildings constructed of stone. Many had symmetrical façades and closed floor plans. Photograph, Metropolitan Museum of Art. Courtesy of the Moravian Historical Society, Nazareth, Pennsylvania.

founded less than a decade after Ephrata, was different from that at Beissel's settlement. One European traveler who visited the community in the 1780s went to the top of the Single Brothers' house to survey the area from a lookout on its roof. In describing the landscape before him, he noted that the buildings in the area were "all handsome and built of stone" and that each had "a garden cultivated with care." Perhaps at least in part because of the buildings and grounds they fashioned, the Lutheran clergyman Heinrich Melchior Muhlenberg repeatedly insisted that the Moravians, whom he referred to as "Herrnhuters" or "Zinzendorfers," always attracted the "wealthiest and most important people" to their faith.[20]

While residents of Ephrata were supposed to shun worldly dress, rich foods, and elaborate buildings in an attempt to distance themselves from the world and be more Christ-like, Moravians often embraced the contemporary culture of refinement. Schools run by the Moravians in Bethlehem and Nazareth, for example, were of "great repute" and took in "genteel" students, including non-Moravians, from throughout North America and the Caribbean. At the girls' school, which often had a waiting list for admission, young women were taught the polite skills of needlework, painting, and music as well as reading and writing, arithmetic, history, geography, and literature. Boys were taught four languages—English, German, French, and Latin—in addition to drawing, music, mathematics, history, and geography. Architectural designs produced by young men at the Moravian school in Nazareth demonstrate a commitment on the part of their teachers to train students in fashionable design traditions rather than shield them from the ways of the world (fig. 60).[21]

Fig. 60   "Plan and Elevation of a Country House," Jacob Weiss, 1794. While a student at the Moravian school Nazareth Hall in Nazareth, Weiss created this plan for an expansive country house of 76 by more than 32 feet. Rooms in the central main block were to include the entrance with a library and "eating parlour" to either side and a "best stair case," a "with drawing room," and china closet to the rear. The wing to the left in the drawing was to house the kitchen and pantry. That to the right would provide a "servants hall" and washhouse. This watercolor image, and others like it, demonstrates a desire on the part of Moravian teachers to instruct their pupils in cosmopolitan academic design. Courtesy of the Winterthur Library, Joseph Downs Collection of Manuscripts and Printed Ephemera.

Fig. 61   Sun Inn, Bethlehem, Northampton County, Pennsylvania, 1758–60. The Sun Inn was designed in 1758 with a seven-bay symmetrical façade. The door in the middle bay led to a center passage. The inn was highly regarded by visitors to the Moravian community at Bethlehem.

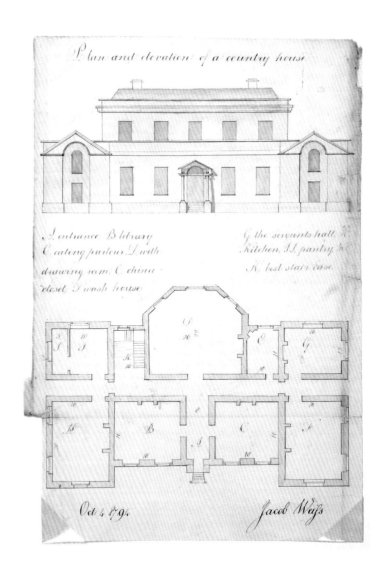

Not only were the Moravians instrumental in teaching a generation of young men about trends in polite architecture, but they also made it a point to construct stylish buildings in their own settlements. As tourists visited Moravian communities throughout the second half of the eighteenth century, they routinely recorded their positive appraisals of the built environment they observed. In 1754, Acrelius portrayed the second Single Brothers' house in Bethlehem as "not unlike a castle, built of sandstone, five stories high, containing about seventy rooms, large and small." Travelers who visited Bethlehem later in the century often specifically described the Sun Inn, which the Moravians began erecting in 1758 to provide lodging for their guests (fig. 61). According to one observer, the inn, which had a center passage leading to "convenient apartments," was based "upon an exceeding good plan." Another

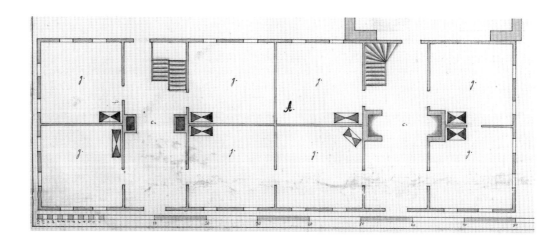

Fig. 62   First-floor plan, *Gemeinhaus,* from "Entwurf zum Bau des Gemeinhauses in Bethlehem in Pennsylvania mit Angabe der Nutzung der Räume, Grundriss Erdgeschoss," 1751. Built from 1741 to 1743, the Moravians' log *Gemeinhaus* was designed as two center-passage, double-pile buildings joined end-to-end. Courtesy of the Moravian Archives, Herrnhut, Germany, TS Mp.216.15.

Fig. 63   Candlesticks (two of set of four or six), Johann Christoph Heyne, Lancaster, Pennsylvania, 1757–81. Heyne was born in Saxony and trained as a pewterer in continental Europe. He spent his first years in America living and working at the Moravian settlement of Bethlehem. He left Bethlehem in 1750 and started his own pewtering shop in Lancaster in 1757. Heyne may have made these ornate baroque candlesticks for the Most Blessed Sacrament Roman Catholic Church in Bally, Berks County. Courtesy of Winterthur Museum.

guest reported that the "commodious" structure was "the neatest and best" tavern "in any part of America." Generally, while Moravians may have built variations on the entry-kitchen house form for some individuals, the choir and other community buildings they erected in Pennsylvania were of a closed plan. The first Single Brothers' house, dating to 1744, and the Sun Inn are but two examples of the prevailing type. Even the *Gemeinhaus* at Bethlehem, the first community building erected at that settlement, utilized a closed plan. Built from 1742 to 1743, the building was constructed of log. Unlike Hebron at Ephrata, whose core was two adjoining entry-kitchen houses, the first-floor plan of the contemporary *Gemeinhaus* was basically two center-passage, double-pile buildings arranged end-to-end (fig. 62). The second floor included a large worship space. Dormitories were located in the lower attic level, and kitchen facilities were housed in the basement.[22]

Among the German speakers who came to Pennsylvania, the Moravians were probably the first to use a closed plan, as all the houses with a central or side passage discussed in Chapter 3 were constructed after 1750. The Moravians' familiarity with this new type of spatial ordering may have been the result of the presence of German-born nobility in their communities. Other types of Moravian material culture further suggest an inclination toward high-style objects. Maps and architectural drawings produced at midcentury by Andreas Hoeger had cartouches in the fashionable rococo style (see fig. 59). Furthermore, a set of four surviving candlesticks crafted by pewterer Johann Christoph Heyne exemplify the full curves of the baroque style (fig. 63). While the candlesticks were somewhat outdated when they were made, sometime between 1757 and 1781, the baroque shaping of the objects indicates a knowledge of modish form and ornament. For the Moravians, surviving material culture demonstrates that the creation of stylish and sophisticated buildings and objects was not at odds with religious dictates.[23]

Worldliness and Denominational Difference

Pennsylvania Germans of other faiths developed their own ways of reconciling religious belief and material displays. They usually fell somewhere between the two extremes represented by Beissel's followers and the Moravians. As students of Pennsylvania's historic Quaker material culture have noted, it is often hard to understand how members of the Society of Friends visually interpreted religious dictates advocating plainness. Although the group, whose adherents were largely of British descent, periodically recorded *Rules of Discipline* that insisted on plainness, minutes of meetings for business and discipline shed little light on how these were understood, since members were rarely cited for failing to adhere to the doctrine. When deviations did

occur, they frequently concerned speech and dress rather than other material forms.[24]

Like Quaker documents, the writings produced by Lutheran and Reformed clergy and church members are difficult for the modern reader to interpret, although they often include directives against worldliness. Lutheran clergyman Heinrich Melchior Muhlenberg repeatedly warned his parishioners about focusing too much attention on earthly goods. He counseled a "poor old miner," for example, "to cease looking for the treasures of earth and be satisfied to take the little that might be given him." After the untimely death of Valentin Heiser, the clergyman lamented that in order to gain "worldly wealth and a comfortable life," this young man "left his proper calling, gave up his farm, and rented a well-known tavern." Muhlenberg believed that many young people such as Heiser were "more concerned about visible, temporal goods" than they were "about invisible, eternal riches." He continued, "They do not consider how slippery and seductive the world and its sham wealth are, or how easily they take possession of the poor soul and entice it to the broad path which leads to damnation."[25]

Yet despite the perceived failings on the part of some Pennsylvanians Muhlenberg encountered, he praised others who earnestly sought to avoid the trap wrought by worldly goods. He told his superiors in Germany of Hans Michael Krumrein, who, early in his life, "was almost too fond of earthly things." Later, however, this man had come to see the error of his ways, tearfully confessed his "desire for earthly possessions," and prayed that God would free him from "this love and covetousness." Another of Muhlenberg's parishioners, Friedrich Marsteller, turned down chances for material gain in order to remain a part of the Augustus Lutheran congregation. According to the pastor, Marsteller "had opportunities to improve his material circumstances and to become wealthy by moving elsewhere, but he said he preferred to lose all his temporal possessions rather than exchange the Word of God and public worship for transitory riches."[26]

Among members of Reformed congregations, the desire to set boundaries regarding earthly possessions and behaviors—and instruct others to do the same—could be equally strong. Several of the illustrations Ludwig Denig, a member of Lancaster's Reformed church, produced in 1784 for his "Picture-Bible" addressed the issue of material prosperity. In the text accompanying an image entitled "The World with Its Diversions Leads to Nothing but Sorrow in the End," Denig began to explain his stand regarding wealth and the activities that normally accompanied it in the late eighteenth century. He wrote:

Yes, we see how the world acts in its way of life.
Each one sets his eyes upon luxury and money while he laughs in lust!
They eat, they drink without moderation, until nothing remains in pot and barrel. . . .
They contrive intrigues and think up infamies only to acquire riches.

The accompanying watercolor and ink drawing features two men who are caught up in the love of money and merriment that Denig describes (fig. 64). The two are seated at a table in a carefully landscaped garden setting. From the number of coins in front of them, they are engaged in either a business transaction or, more likely, a game of chance. One has just filled his glass from a bottle on the table and has raised it to drink. Nearby, another group of men stand pointing at the spectacle, and two women, or perhaps girls, sit neglected in the image's left foreground.

Returning to the text accompanying the image, Denig indicates that the activities in which the two central figures are engaged should be avoided. He writes, "if one wants to keep the eternal good, then he must shun all . . . social gatherings and pastimes of the world which urge them on in word and deed . . . against the glory of God." Pointing to biblical examples, he notes that the Holy Ghost defended those who desired to be protected from "the world with all its luxury." Queen Esther, he observes, although "outwardly adorned by means of the royal jewels . . . became full of humility in her heart"; David, "despite his great riches," grew "small in heart"; and Joseph, even "in the voluptuous house of his master . . . had a chaste heart." According to Denig, individuals who "relish[ed] in earthly, carnal things," like the two men in the illustration, would "remain inwardly hard and cold." Those who practiced "true contemplation of God" like Esther, David, and Joseph, on the other hand, would be shielded "from the luxury of the world."[27]

For Pennsylvania German sectarian groups, who left fewer written records than the Lutherans and Reformed, understanding how religious belief informed material manifestations of culture is more problematic. Unfortunately, there is little available information about the material culture of the eighteenth-century Amish, despite the group's prevalence in the popular image of "Plain" people today. Although outsiders had biases and could misinterpret what they were observing, the accounts they left provide some clues as to what made other "Plain" religious groups, most notably the Mennonites, distinct in eighteenth-century Pennsylvania.

As with the Quakers, clothing and language seem to have been the major tangible signifiers of membership in a Mennonite congregation. The author of *The American Geography* noted that Mennonites "all use[d] plainness of speech and dress." He added that some practitioners of the faith had even "been expelled from their society for wearing buckles in their shoes, and having pocket holes in their coats." When British ensign Thomas Hughes attended a Mennonite wedding in 1780, he further reported of the group that "they never wear buckles or metal buttons." In 1781, John Hunt, himself a member of the Society of Friends, retold the following story about Mennonite women's attire in his journal:

> A Friend A hatter Some years ago Took a parcel of women[']s hats to Lancaster to Sell & ye young menonist women were pleased with them & bought them but their Elders were not Easy with Any New fashion Coming amongst them & held a Conference Amongst the Elders & Concuded [sic] to and Accordingly Did Advise the friend the Nex [sic] time he Came with hats to Sell, not to be instrumental in introducing New fashion or Superfluity amongst them but in particular if he brought any more that way to Let them be plain & no Ribbon about them.

According to contemporary observers, including Quakers, Mennonites generally espoused plainness by avoiding unnecessary decorative embellishments on their clothing. Mennonite men avoided such flourishes as buckles and buttons made from metals, perhaps because of the shimmering quality of the material, and pocket holes, which were often embellished with trim. Mennonite women were obliged to forsake ornamental ribbons.[28]

Early Mennonites in Pennsylvania left less information about what they considered simple clothing until the late nineteenth century. A document offering a clear-cut interpretation of plain clothing was found in an eighteenth-century translation of the Bible belonging to the Mennonite Groffdale congregation in Earl Township, Lancaster County. It reads that "all sisters from now on, when they prepare anything woolen in clothing, shall make it turtle-dove-colored or, as is said, lead-colored, and all linen is to be white. . . . Cotton, when they make caps or aprons, is also to be white or light blue. What they make for stockings is also to be white or light blue." Unfortunately, the handwritten decree is undated, and the mention of cotton suggests it originated in the nineteenth century. According to John Landis Ruth, if this document does date to the earlier part of the century, it is unusual as it was not until the mid-1880s that an "older, informal attitude toward plain clothing would give way to a growing control of regulations spelled out by the bishops."[29]

While contemporary observers in the eighteenth century found Mennonite attire to be distinct in its plainness, it was much more diverse in cut, color, and material than the white gowns of Ephrata residents. Maria Wenger's 1773 will, for example, indicates that Mennonite dress could include expensive silk items as well as clothing of a wide variety of colors, not only earth tones and blues but also red. If Wenger's will is representative in its description of fabric types and hues, it indicates that Mennonites did not categorize improper attire in the eighteenth century in the same way they would later in the denomination's history. While Mennonites may have shown restraint in adorning their attire, they were not all wearing neutral-colored homespun woolens and linens.[30]

From a modern perspective, in the late eighteenth century Anabaptist religious groups such as the Mennonites adhered to more unmistakably "plain" aesthetics as they designed their worship spaces. Most religious groups in Pennsylvania met in members' houses rather than purpose-built church buildings during the early years of settlement. Among the Mennonites, Christian and Anna Herr's 1719 house was the location of a Mennonite meeting (see figs. 19–21). In 1744, according to a hymnbook that was donated by a member for use during services, the congregation was probably still meeting at the dwelling at that time. In London Derry Township at the present-day boundary between Lebanon and Dauphin Counties, 1798 Federal Direct Tax records indicate that even at the very close of the eighteenth century a portion of the upper story of Henry Landis's house was being used for religious services.[31]

While Amish groups continue to hold worship services in homes to this day, by the late 1740s and 1750s Mennonite congregations in Pennsylvania began to construct separate buildings for their religious meetings. Most of

COVENTRY CHESTER COUNTY, PA. — BUILT 1728

Fig. 65 Coventry Mennonite Meetinghouse, East Coventry Township, Chester County, Pennsylvania, 1798. The Mennonite meetinghouse in Coventry Township was no bigger than the largest houses in the area. The building was significantly altered in 1890, but originally congregants entered through two doors on one of its long walls. Inside, seating was arranged in an auditory plan. Image from Daniel K. Cassel, *History of the Mennonites* (Philadelphia: Daniel K. Cassel, 1888), between pp. 268 and 269.

Fig. 66 Interior, Pricetown Brethren Meetinghouse, Ruscombmanor Township, Berks County, Pennsylvania, c. 1777 or 1807. Seating within most eighteenth-century Anabaptist meetinghouses likely mirrored that at Pricetown. Backed benches faced a table (rather than a pulpit) located along one of the long walls of the building. This type of auditory plan, with the seats facing a long wall, was typical of religious meeting places in eighteenth-century Pennsylvania, although the type of seats, the use or nonuse of a pulpit, and the amount of decoration varied by denomination.

the earliest religious structures were small log, or occasionally stone, buildings. Like many Protestant groups in eighteenth-century Pennsylvania, when Mennonites built a discrete worship space, they did not refer to it as a church or *Kirche*.[32] Rather, they used the label *Gemeinhaus*. Literally translated as "congregation house" or "community house," English speakers referred to such structures as meeting places or meetinghouses. In Coventry Township, Chester County, for example, in 1751, a deed written in English reports that a Mennonite couple conveyed a small parcel of land to their meeting "for a Meetingplace &c." Although it is possible that a temporary structure was built on this property, by the end of the century the congregation had purchased another small tract on which it "erected a Meeting House." The one-story stone building, which was constructed in 1798 and measured approximately 28 by 39 feet, was no bigger than the largest houses in the township (fig. 65). The building apparently attracted little attention from outsiders when it was built. It was not even included on an early nineteenth-century map of the area, although nearby German Reformed, Dunkard, and Methodist meeting places were.[33]

The interior of the Coventry Mennonite meetinghouse was accessible though two doors on one of its long walls, and presumably its seating was oriented auditory-style toward the opposing wall. While the interior of the Coventry meetinghouse was significantly reworked in 1890, a Dunkard meetinghouse in Ruscombmanor Township in neighboring Berks County, which was built at roughly the same time, suggests how it may have been arranged (fig. 66). The main portion of the stone building includes benches oriented toward a table, rather than a pulpit, placed centrally along the long wall of the building opposite the entrance. An attached kitchen provided a place to prepare and store supplies for love feasts, symbolic religious meals in which members of Dunkard congregations and some other German sectarian groups in Pennsylvania partook.[34]

Like the Mennonites, Lutheran and Reformed congregations also began building discrete structures for worship in Pennsylvania in the first half of the eighteenth century. By 1736 there were five such buildings in the colony; in the decade between 1738 and 1748, at least another forty-four were erected. Although the first structures built by parishes were often "small" and built of "logs," some were more substantial. The Reformed minister Jacob Lischy, for example, reported in 1744 that both the congregation and the building at Seltenreich Reformed in Earl Township, Lancaster County, were "large." In Coventry Township, Chester County, that same year he described Brombach's (Brownback's) Reformed as a "pretty church."[35]

Reyer's Reformed Church, also known as Old Zion, near Brickerville in northern Lancaster County suggests the spatial arrangement of many of these worship spaces (figs. 67–68). Constructed in 1813, the present building replaced a log meetinghouse that dated to 1747. Despite its late date, the current structure was designed with an auditory seating plan. Pews were arranged on three sides of the building facing an elevated pulpit on the long northwest wall. A gallery above the pews provided additional seating.[36]

While the majority of Lutheran and Reformed worshipers listened to services from seats arranged auditory-style, just like Mennonites and Dunkers, some congregations utilized more atypical spatial arrangements that identified their buildings as distinct types of structures. In Philadelphia, the Reformed congregation chose to erect a six-sided building in the late 1740s, which was referred to in a patent deed of 1763 as "the Hexagon Church." Among the Lutherans, Heinrich Melchior Muhlenberg's arrival from Europe in 1742 sparked a wave of building that included Augustus Lutheran Church in Providence, or Trappe, in what is now Montgomery County (figs. 69–70). The box pews and benches on the main level and in the gallery of Augustus Lutheran Church were oriented toward a three-sided apse at one end of the building rather than toward one of the long walls. Not surprisingly, Augustus Lutheran was one of the few religious buildings on Nicholas Scull's 1759 map of the Pennsylvania countryside that was labeled as a church rather than a meetinghouse. Its axial configuration marked it as unique. Even from the outside, Augustus Lutheran's atypical apse end, like the Reformed church's hexagonal shape, marked it as a different kind of religious space.[37]

By the late eighteenth century, the church buildings constructed by Lutheran and Reformed congregations, especially in urban areas, were further demarcated by their size and exterior decorative elements. Benjamin Rush reported in 1789, for example, that many of the churches used by Lutheran and Reformed congregations were "large and splendid." In the years just before the American Revolution both denominations built new structures in Philadelphia. Of similar design, Zion Lutheran, which was dedicated in 1769, and the Reformed church building, which was consecrated five years later, both incorporated classical door pediments, engaged pilasters, and Palladian, compass-headed, and ocular windows (fig. 71). Referring to one of the two structures, reference books published in 1789 and 1795 described the "German church" as "one of the most elegant churches in America." In Lancaster, Trinity Lutheran Church, which was built between 1761 and 1766 and further improved from 1785 to 1794 with the addition of a tower and steeple, was similarly complimented (fig. 72). A European traveler concluded in the year the spire was completed that "the new German Lutheran church is very well built, of brick, and its steeple is the best built and the most elegant in the United States."[38]

Fig. 67 Reyer's Reformed (Old Zion), Elizabeth Township, Lancaster County, Pennsylvania, 1813. A fairly late example among the German Reformed of a meetinghouse utilizing the auditory plan, the exterior of Reyer's Reformed showed signs of the embrace of new models for religious spaces. It was constructed of brick, and its main door included a neoclassical fanlight and surround. Windows were compass-headed and topped with keystones.

Fig. 68 Interior, Reyer's Reformed (Old Zion). Congregants at Reyer's Reformed sat on either the first floor or in the balcony on backed benches oriented toward the raised pulpit on the long wall opposite the main door.

Fig. 69 Augustus Lutheran
Church, Trappe, Montgomery
County, Pennsylvania, 1743.
Served by newly arrived European
clergyman Heinrich Melchior
Muhlenberg, the congregation
at Augustus Lutheran attended
services at a building that looked
less like a meetinghouse and
more like a church. The latter
designation was in fact used to
refer to the building on a 1759
map of Pennsylvania. The gambrel
roof and particularly the polygonal
apse end distinguished Augustus
Lutheran from most other
religious structures in the early
Pennsylvania countryside.

Fig. 70 (*below left*)   Interior, Augustus Lutheran Church, Trappe. Inside Augustus Lutheran, the majority of the enclosed box pews and benches were arranged facing the apselike end. The raised pulpit was located to one side of the space. Photograph by Jack Boucher for the Historic American Buildings Survey, 1994. Library of Congress, Prints and Photographs Division, HABS, HABS-PA, 46-TRAP, 3–11.

Fig. 71   Engraving of Zion Lutheran, Philadelphia, Pennsylvania, from William Russell Birch, *The City of Philadelphia in the State of Pennsylvania, North America, as It Appeared in the Year 1800, Consisting of Twenty-eight Plates* (Springland Cot, Pa.: W. Birch, 1800), plate 6. By the second half of the eighteenth century, it was increasingly common for Lutheran and Reformed religious buildings to incorporate fashionable design elements. Birch's 1800 print reflects the appearance of Philadelphia's "New Lutheran Church" after rebuilding following a fire in 1794. Many of the classical features, including pilasters, a dentiled cornice, keystones over the windows, urns on the roof, and Palladian, compass-headed, and ocular windows, had probably appeared on the building when it was originally completed in 1769. Photograph courtesy of the New York State Historical Association Research Library.

Fig. 72 Trinity Lutheran, Lancaster, Pennsylvania, 1761–66; tower, 1785–94. Built in the same decade as Zion Lutheran and the Reformed church building in Philadelphia, the main block of Lancaster's Trinity Lutheran incorporated many similar classical design elements. The building was further improved in the latter decades of the eighteenth century with the addition of a steeple. A traveler called the new tower "the best built and the most elegant in the United States" (Théophile Cazenove, *Cazenove Journal, 1794: A Record of the Journey of Theophile Cazenove Through New Jersey and Pennsylvania,* ed. Rayner Wickersham Kelsey [Haverford, Pa.: The Pennsylvania History Press, 1922], 73).

By the end of the eighteenth century, the buildings erected by Lutheran and Reformed congregations for worship were visually distinct from those used by Mennonites and Dunkards. In the early part of the century, members of all four groups worshiped in spaces not specifically designed for that purpose. When they built their first meetinghouses in Pennsylvania, their buildings shared several common elements. Most were relatively small and constructed of logs, although occasionally masonry was used. Inside, seating was arranged auditory-style facing one of the long sides of the building. Augustus Lutheran, with its polygonal apselike end and axial plan, was unusual in design, perhaps because it served as the home church for newly arrived European clergyman Heinrich Melchior Muhlenberg. The building's gambrel roof, a feature also found on St. Michael's Lutheran Church constructed in Philadelphia in the 1740s and on Moravian buildings in Warwick, Oley, and Christiansbrunn, further distinguished it from many other religious structures. By the end of the century, however, while Mennonite and Dunkard meetinghouses continued to be house-like, an increasing number of Lutheran and Reformed religious buildings were built as churches with steeples and ornamental classical details.[39]

Houses for Clergy and Congregants

Given the state of church architecture in the second half of the eighteenth century, it is not surprising that many of the most prominent single-family two-story stone houses discussed in the last chapter were built by members of Lutheran and Reformed congregations. The Hottensteins, for example, were members of the Reformed group that met at St. John's Union Church in Kutztown, Berks County. Philip Erpff attended St. Luke's Lutheran Church in Schaefferstown, and Leonard Elmaker, whose family was Lutheran in background, went to St. John's Anglican (later Episcopal) Church in nearby Chester County. The latter congregation, although Anglican in name, was served by a German-speaking pastor named Traugott Friedrich Illing from the 1770s to the 1790s. The Reformed church in Worcester Township, in what is now Montgomery County, was actually built on land deeded by a member of Peter Wentz's family. And in Millbach, in present-day Lebanon County, it was George Müller who conveyed a small tract of land adjoining his own property to the Reformed church so that the congregation could "build a House of Worship." His son Michael Müller continued to affiliate himself with the church his family had helped found.[40]

Muhlenberg, because he served multiple Lutheran congregations after arriving in Pennsylvania, lived in several different houses over the course of his life. One of the first was a dwelling in Providence, which was located

Fig. 73   Heinrich Melchior and
Anna Maria Muhlenberg house
(formerly Jacob Schrack house),
Trappe, Montgomery County,
Pennsylvania, c. 1755. Upon
returning to Trappe in 1776, the
Muhlenbergs acquired a house
that was approximately twenty
years old, which had been built
for Jacob Schrack at about the
same time as the nearby Peter and
Rosina Margaretha Wentz house.
Like the Wentzes' residence, the
Schrack-Muhlenberg house was
two stories with a symmetrical
façade, constructed of coursed
stone, with a central door on both
the first and second floors.

Fig. 74   First-floor plan as
restored, Heinrich Melchior and
Anna Maria Muhlenberg house.
As restored in the 1990s, the first-
floor plan of the Muhlenbergs'
house incorporates a passage
that runs only half the width of
the house, terminating at an
enclosed staircase ascending to
the second floor. In addition to
this entryway, the first floor of the
Muhlenbergs' house includes a
stove room and kitchen with a
large hearth on the left side and
two more rooms, one heated by
a fireplace and the other by a
stove, on the right side. Entries in
Heinrich Melchior Muhlenberg's
diaries suggest that the latter two
rooms sometimes served as a
temporary dwelling for visitors or
those in need. Floor plan based
on plan by Tim Stuffle in Lisa M.
Minardi, "Of Massive Stones and
Durable Materials: Architecture
and Community in Eighteenth-
Century Trappe, Pennsylvania"
(M.A. thesis, Winterthur Program in
Early American Culture, University
of Delaware, 2006), 59.

near and built almost contemporaneously with Augustus Lutheran Church.[41] Although the construction of the edifice proved "burdensome," caused the clergyman "gray hairs," and put him "considerably in debt," apparently the pastor did not think it inappropriate. Throughout his life, Muhlenberg, while insisting that he was "content with the barest subsistence," continued to live in well-appointed houses.[42]

Muhlenberg's last earthly residence was also in Providence, where he returned in 1776 after spending several years serving congregations in Philadelphia. According to a real estate advertisement he summarized in his journal, the house he purchased was "a large two-story dwelling, built of massive stones, with four rooms on the lower and four on the upper floor." Although when he bought the building it was more than twenty years old and had been "allowed to get out of repair and go to ruin," Muhlenberg quickly made improvements to the structure, plastering walls and possibly ceilings, painting woodwork, improving the entrance with door posts and a stone threshold, adding stoves, and building an addition to provide space for tasks such as washing, baking, and processing agricultural products. The main portion of the house, which included on its first floor a kitchen, two stove rooms, and a fourth room with a sizable fireplace, also incorporated a passage, which as currently reconstructed runs from its front door about halfway through the building to an enclosed straight-run staircase leading to the second floor (figs. 73–74).[43]

In 1777, a representative of the colonial military visited the house with an aim to store provisions there. He had heard, reported Mühlenburg, "we had under our house, the largest and best cellar in this neighborhood." If word of the impressive size and quality of the cellar had spread, presumably the rest of the dwelling was well known and equally distinguished. Several years before purchasing the building, Muhlenberg had admired the new Lutheran parsonage in Tulpehocken, Pennsylvania, describing it as "laid out symmetrically according to the most approved architecture" as well as "very durable and conveniently arranged." His own house in Providence was equally agreeable in its symmetry, durable stone construction, convenient floor plan, and general use of "approved" architectural style.[44]

Lutheran and Reformed clergy and churchgoers were not alone in embracing new types of closed-plan houses in the second half of the eighteenth century. In eighteenth-century Conestoga Township, Lancaster County, 1798 Federal Direct Tax records allow for a comparison of houses owned and occupied by people affiliated with Mennonite and Lutheran congregations. Not surprisingly, in this area where early settlement was dominated by Mennonites, a Mennonite family owned the largest house, and Mennonites possessed the majority of highly valued houses. Not all Mennonites lived in grand residences, but not all lived in lowly houses either. Because the Mennonite

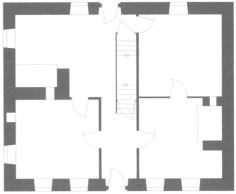

community had been established longer in Conestoga Township than the Lutheran congregation, its members had had more opportunity to acquire land and build houses and barns. While average house size, percentage of owner-occupied houses, and percentage of barns among householders were almost identical between the Mennonite and Lutheran populations, Mennonites more commonly owned and occupied buildings that represented the upper strata of the housing spectrum (table 1). One Mennonite family, headed by Benedict and Anna Eshleman, significantly influenced the highest-quality housing stock in the township.

Conestoga Township is located in the western part of Lancaster County, bordered to the west by the Susquehanna River, to the north by its tributary the Conestoga River, and to the south by another tributary of the Susquehanna, the Pequea Creek. Until 1853, when it was divided, Conestoga Township included the land that is now Pequea Township as well as Conestoga Township. During the eighteenth century, three Mennonite congregations were established in the area. Two, Byerland and New Danville, had built meetinghouses prior to 1755. The third, now known as River Corner, was granted land in 1773 and built a meetinghouse soon thereafter. The Lutherans and Reformed were latecomers to the area. In the 1790s, Lutheran clergy from Lancaster began ministering to a congregation in Conestoga, and in 1791 land was surveyed for both Lutheran and Reformed use. Through the first half of the nineteenth century Conestoga's Lutheran and Reformed shared a meetinghouse and cemetery.[45]

Table 1 **Conestoga Township Householders, 1798**

	All householders	Mennonites	Lutherans
	N = 135	N = 34	N = 14
Average square footage of house	1054	1158	1161
Average value of Schedule A property	$470	$526	$481
Percentage of houses owner-occupied	80%	85%	86%
Percentage of hewn or round log houses	69%	71%	64%
Percentage of two-story houses	24%	21%	29%
Percentage of houses with outbuildings	27%	30%	43%
Percentage of houses with tenant houses	22%	21%	50%
Percentage of houses with barns	70%	79%	79%
Average footprint of barn in square feet	1692	1869	1552
Average number of acres	109	134	88
Average value of Schedule B property	$2690	$3407	$2201

Note: Based on data recorded in the 1798 Federal Direct Tax Records, Conestoga Township, Lancaster County, Pennsylvania, Schedules A and B. "Householders" as defined in this study include all individuals listed on Schedule A and thus exclude those living in "tenant houses" valued under $100 and therefore listed on Schedule B.

Of the 135 householders who occupied houses worth more than $100 in Conestoga Township in 1798, 34 could be identified as Mennonite and 14 as Lutheran.[46] These 48 families likely represent the upper tiers of Conestoga society, as they left lasting records allowing them to be identified with a particular religious congregation such as a durable headstone in a church cemetery, an entry in communicant or baptismal records resulting from travel to Trinity Lutheran Church in Lancaster, or a tax record for having paid an extra impost rather than serve in the Revolutionary War, often because of pacifist religious convictions. In terms of material culture, householders in both groups occupied dwellings that averaged a higher assessed value and more square footage, were more likely to have outbuildings and barns associated with them, and were more likely to be owner-occupied than those held by other area residents.

At first glance, based on calculations from data recorded in the 1798 tax, the Mennonites in Conestoga might appear to be the stereotypical Pennsylvania German farmers to whom so many period writers referred. On average, Mennonites held more land than both Lutherans and the householding population as a whole. The average value of their land and productive buildings—such as barns, mills, craft shops, and tenant houses—was higher, and their barns averaged a larger size in terms of footprint. A greater percentage of Mennonites occupied one-story houses and houses built of log than other householders in the township.[47]

Yet despite the greater percentage of small houses and log houses, the dwellings of Conestoga Township Mennonites were not all of poor quality. In fact, the average value of property included on Schedule A of the 1798 return, which included the house, house lot, and domestic outbuildings, was significantly higher for Mennonites than for Lutherans or for all householders in the township. While some Mennonites lived in mean houses, others lived in very well-appointed two-story stone dwellings. In fact, of the five houses in Conestoga Township valued with their lots and associated outbuildings above $1,050 in 1798, three owners—Matthias Miller, John Burkholder, and John Good—were Mennonites; one, Richard Burk, married into a prominent Mennonite family; and only one, Tobias Stehman, was Lutheran.[48]

The highest-valued house in Conestoga Township in 1798 was owned and occupied by Tobias Stehman. It was a two-story stone structure measuring 45 by 39 feet. Its valuation at $1,400 included a 690-square-foot stone combination still and washhouse in addition to the main structure. Although the arrangement of rooms within the eighteenth-century Stehman house is unknown, Tobias's other financial investments suggest that he was near the pinnacle of wealth in Conestoga Township and may have chosen to live in a house using a closed plan. He owned over seventeen thousand acres of land, a limestone barn measuring 104 by 40 feet, a log barn, a smith shop, and a

Fig. 75 Benedict and Anna Eshleman house, Conestoga Township, Lancaster County, Pennsylvania, 1759. Mennonites Benedict and Anna (Stehman) Eshleman constructed multiple two-story stone houses for their family in the mid-eighteenth century. At approximately 46 by 35 feet, this building was the largest house in Conestoga Township in 1798, when it was owned by another Mennonite, Mathias Miller.

Fig. 76 Reconstructed first-floor plan, Benedict and Anna Eshleman house. Significantly remodeled in the 1890s, the first-floor plan of the Eshleman house originally included a center passage, a kitchen and stove room to the left of the passage, and two rooms heated by corner fireplaces to the right of the passage. The five-bay façade of the house was not quite symmetrical, reflecting the large size of the kitchen and stove room in comparison to the fireplace-heated rooms. Based on fieldwork by Sally McMurry, Diane Wenger, Kjirsten Gustavson, Eric Kernfeld, and Cynthia Falk.

Fig. 77 Barrel-vaulted cellar, Benedict and Anna Eshleman house. The cellar under the kitchen and stove room of the Eshleman house provided a large, cool storage area for provisions. It was accessed from the exterior at the front of the house and was lit by small windows with iron bars to keep out human and animal intruders. A staircase at the rear of the cellar provided a way to get to the first floor of the house without going outside. Photograph by Sally McMurry.

cider house as well as a second farmstead with a brick house, limestone barn, and cider house that were used by John Eshbach in 1798. He also owned three other tenant houses. Like so many of the Pennsylvania Germans who owned large, highly valued houses, Stehman invested in productive property as well as a grand dwelling. Based on what is known of the ownership of other such houses, it is not surprising that Tobias Stehman was Lutheran. According to records of Trinity Lutheran Church in Lancaster, Stehman was baptized at Trinity in 1783. What is unusual is that he was twenty-one years of age when the event took place, indicating that he converted to the faith rather than being born into it. Stehman's decision to join the Lutherans at twenty-one suggests that he hailed from an Anabaptist family that maintained a tradition of an adult profession of faith.[49]

Given previous interpretations of "Plain" Pennsylvania German religious groups, it would be easy to believe that Stehman's rejection of Anabaptist tenets and baptism into the Lutheran church facilitated his acquisition of vast holdings of property, including the well-appointed house where he lived. However, Mennonites in Conestoga Township—including Tobias's relatives— had already constructed some of the largest and most highly valued houses in the area, at least one of which was of a closed plan, prior to his conversion. Three of the other houses valued above $1,050 in 1798 were built by Mennonites Benedict Eshleman and his wife, Anna (Stehman) Eshleman, before Benedict's death in 1780. They were inherited by the Eshlemans' sons, John, Benedict, and David, who in turn sold them to a sister and brother-in-law, Mary and Richard Burk, and to fellow Mennonites Matthias Miller and John Good.[50]

The surviving two-story stone house, which was built by the Eshlemans in 1759 and owned by Mathias Miller in 1798, exemplifies the degree to which elite Mennonites in Conestoga Township embraced the move to grand closed-plan dwellings (figs. 75–81). The building, which measures more than 35 by 45 feet and was therefore the largest house in Conestoga Township in 1798, had a pent roof on all four sides and a plaster cove cornice. The façade was constructed of squared blocks of stone laid in even courses. It had five bays, which were not quite symmetrically spaced, and a central front door leading to a center passage. Although the building was significantly remodeled in the 1890s, particularly on the first floor, the original center-passage, double-pile floor plan is still discernible on the floor above. The first-floor rooms to the west of the passage included a kitchen to the rear and a stove room with a built-in corner cupboard to the front. The rooms to the opposite side of the passage were both heated by corner fireplaces. Below, a large vaulted cellar provided storage space under the kitchen and stove room. On the east side of the house, a separate cellar space existed under the front room.

The Eshlemans prominently labeled the house as their own with a date stone located on the façade of the building marked, "BENEDICT / ESCHLEMAN UND / SEINE HAUSFRAU / ANNA HABEN DE / SES HAUS GEBAU / ANNO 1759" (Benedict Eshleman and his wife Anna have built this house 1759). A second, equally visible date stone read, "WO GOTT / __UM HAUSZ / __CHT GIBT SEIN / __ST SO ARBEIT / __DERMAN UM= / SONST 1759." The latter saying appears to be a variation of Psalm 127:1a, "Except the Lord build the house, they labor in vain that build it."[51]

By embellishing the building with both of these inscribed stones, Mennonites Benedict and Anna Eshleman exhibited both their role and their divine Creator's role in erecting their new house. Rather than viewing the monumental building as being at odds with their Anabaptist faith, they saw the two as complementary. This is further evidenced by the fact that the Eshlemans,

Fig. 78 **Date stone, Benedict and Anna Eshleman house. The Eshlemans prominently labeled their house as their own with a date stone that read,** "BENEDICT / ESCHLEMAN UND / SEINE HAUSFRAU / ANNA HABEN DE / SES HAUS GEBAU / ANNO 1759" (Benedict Eshleman and his wife Anna have built this house 1759).

like so many elite Lutheran and Reformed church members, donated land adjacent to their grand house to their Mennonite meeting for the construction of a meetinghouse and burial ground in 1773. According to a history of the congregation, the new worship space was referred to as the Eshleman Meetinghouse in recognition of its prominent benefactor.[52]

Benedict Eshleman's possessions at the time of his death, like his family's house, illustrate a conflation of gentility, prosperity, and religious devotion. He owned "1 Clothes Press" and "1 Larch [large] Bible," both valued at £3, as well as clothing worth £25, "the House Clock" valued at £18, and a "Cyder Press & Mill" and "Still," each worth £10. During Benedict's lifetime, he purchased hundreds of acres of land and built multiple two-story stone houses, presumably as future residences for his children and their families. At the time of his death, he left each of his three sons significant holdings in land and buildings, and his five daughters each received £800. For Eshleman, being a Mennonite did not mean forsaking valuable textiles or the furniture in which to store them, a two-story stone house, or the equipment to process and enjoy the fruit of his agricultural labor. Subsequent Mennonite owners of the 1759 Benedict and Anna Eshleman house, including the Eshlemans' son David (who occupied the building even before his father's death) and Mathias Miller, likewise found the dwelling suitable to both their physical and spiritual needs. By the time of Miller's ownership, if not before, the house was part of a multifaceted landscape of affluence, which, not unlike Tobias Stehman's holdings, included a large limestone barn, still house, log stable, and log tenant house.[53]

Fig. 79 Date stone, Benedict and Anna Eshleman house. A second date stone reflected the Eshlemans' religious conviction. Its inscription, "WO GOTT / __UM HAUSZ / __CHT GIBT SEIN / __ST SO ARBEIT / __DERMAN UM= / SONST 1759," appears to be a variation of Psalm 127:1a, "Except the Lord build the house, they labor in vain that build it."

ARCHITECTURE AND ARTIFACTS OF THE PENNSYLVANIA GERMANS

In the eighteenth century, it was not a family's house that was most likely to express its religious affiliation. Among identified Lutherans in Conestoga Township, housing stock could range from one-story dwellings constructed from unhewn logs measuring 24 by 26 feet and valued at little more than $100 to Tobias Stehman's two-story masonry mansion. Furthermore, the built environments created by Stehman and his family and by the Mennonite Eshlemans and Millers were not all that different. The dictates of faith were more readily communicated through community buildings than through individual houses. At places like Ephrata, Bethlehem, and Lititz, this could include a vast number of structures that were used for worship, work, dining, and rest. Yet for most religious groups, the building most often associated with the covenanting community was its meetinghouse. The activities that went on in these spaces, including baptisms, communion, preaching, and the reading of scripture, represented the clear dogmatic differences that separated the sectarian Anabaptists from Lutheran and Reformed congregants.

Outside the meetinghouse or church, material differences between the groups were less clear. Pennsylvania German Protestants of all denominations were concerned about avoiding excess, although some went to different

Fig. 80 **Corner cupboard, first-floor stove room, Benedict and Anna Eshleman house. The Eshlemans' affiliation with the Mennonite faith did not preclude them from building a center-passage, double-pile house or displaying objects within the building. Built-in corner cupboards in two first-floor rooms provided a fashionable setting for the storage of household goods.**

Fig. 81 **Kitchen fireplace, Benedict and Anna Eshleman house. Fragments of black paint with white spots on the kitchen fireplace surround suggest that the Eshlemans, like the Wentzes and Hottensteins, may have opted for conspicuous painted decoration in their house.**

extremes than others. As with the Quakers, clothing seems to have been the primary means of material differentiation. Any group that wanted its members to be perceived as religiously distinct adopted a type of costume that diverged from the norm. At Ephrata, celibate Brothers and Sisters wore long white robes. Among Mennonites, outsiders remarked that the attire of both men and women was unusual, at least in its level of adornment. At Moravian Bethlehem, period accounts noted that the Single Brothers "all wore the same habit without distinction," and that the "dress of the sisterhood, though not quite uniform" was "very nearly so." Of particular interest to visitors were the women's unique "close tight linen caps, made with a peak in front, and tied under the chin with a piece of riband."[54] Visually distinctive clothing may have allowed some religious groups to avoid "extravagance" and "the follies of fashion."[55] More importantly, in an era when characterizations based on visual cues were readily accepted and often inflated, it created an identifiable outward appearance.

The focus on clothing, rather than houses, suggests that religious communities were concerned that their members be recognized when they went out into the world. Like the meetinghouse, clothing communicated religious identity on a public level. Houses, on the other hand, were viewed as more personal forms of expression.[56] Because they were geographically grounded and in most cases did not attract eighteenth-century tourists like the religious settlements at Ephrata and Bethlehem, houses were interpreted largely by the local community. There were limits to what was acceptable and unacceptable in single-family house design. However, these boundaries were governed more by general societal concepts of appropriateness than by tenets specific to any one denomination. These beliefs were biblically based, but they wove political, economic, and social theory of the period with theological concepts. As a result, the community primarily analyzed suitability based on the rank of the householder.

Vanity and Excess

The similarities and differences among the material culture of Mennonite and Lutheran and Reformed congregations and the relationship between all Pennsylvania German religious groups and the material world can be better understood by examining prevailing views in eighteenth-century Pennsylvania about proper material expressions. By the late eighteenth century, many authors began to condemn what they viewed as luxury. Even people like Benjamin Rush, who advocated the improvement of land, domestic accommodations, and manners, did so with an eye to avoiding excess. The ideas expressed by Rush and others demonstrate the interrelated nature of religion, property, and social organization in the discourse of the period. Pennsylvania German religious communities divided themselves one from another based on the material culture they fashioned, but they also did so in order to define themselves in opposition to the world by evading luxury.

Among late eighteenth-century Christians, the desire to limit material expressions of worldly wealth and status was biblically motivated. Religious condemnations of luxury predated the Protestant Reformation, but polemics against material excess pervaded the writings of Reformation-era continental European theologians such as Desiderius Erasmus and John Calvin.[57] In eighteenth-century Pennsylvania, period authors referred to the passage in the sixth chapter of Matthew which asserted that no one could serve as master both God and material wealth as evidence of a need for material restraint. A 1761 poem, *A Little Looking-Glass for the Times,* noted that many believers had recently begun to "Neglect the Cross" in favor of "*Mammon's* Altar." It gave specific examples of the types of possessions associated with the transgression, including "Luxurious Tables," "silken Robes," and "rich Attire," and called for reform in order to avoid "Calamity." Like many of his contemporaries, the poet found dining tables laden with sumptuous foods and elegant tableware, as well as clothing made of silk and other costly imported fabrics, to typify luxury and therefore be sinful.[58]

By the end of the century, the term "luxury" was used repeatedly by authors of diverse faiths to denote possessions and pastimes that were deemed inappropriate. Following the passage of the Stamp Act in 1765, the Townsend Acts in 1767, and the Coercive Acts in 1774, luxury took on political meaning and was tied to republican virtue as Americans limited their importation and consumption of British goods. In 1774, the first Continental Congress, meeting in Philadelphia, passed the "Association," which outlined a trade embargo and an accompanying moral code, prohibiting horse racing, cockfighting, gambling, theater, and elaborate funeral practices. While discussions of virtue carried political and economic connotations, their ability to influence behavior lay in the fact that they also incorporated widely held religious ideals. The concept of luxury conflated ideas about necessity, appropriateness based on rank and locale, and godliness.[59]

In the latter half of the eighteenth century, both American and European authors spent a good deal of energy defining just what the term "luxury" meant and what goods available to Pennsylvanians could be defined as luxuries. In general, they came to two conclusions: luxurious items were superfluous, and they were frequently at odds with the status of the individuals who owned them. In 1755, Benjamin Franklin invoked the first meaning of the term by equating the word "Luxuries" with "needless Manufactures." Several decades later, Jacques-Pierre Brissot agreed. He simply wrote, "Luxury begins where utility ends." According to Brissot, certain kinds of wearing apparel, furniture, food, drink, and even behaviors could be termed "luxuries." He explained that clothing made of the finest linen, for instance, had no "utility to the body."[60]

To clarify his point, Brissot enumerated for his readers several specific items he considered to be luxurious. One of these items was carpet, which he described as a sign of "vanity" and a "sacrifice [of] reason and utility to show." Particular types of attire also made his list. In addition to clothing of fine linen, Brissot also characterized clothing of silk as luxurious. He found women's fashions to be particularly influenced by luxury, or what he termed "prodigality." He observed that the women of Philadelphia wore "hats and caps almost as varied as those of Paris" and "bestow[ed] immense expenses on their toilet and head-dress."[61]

A French duke who visited Pennsylvania in the 1790s joined Brissot in his evaluation of female fashion in Philadelphia. He commented on the dresses of the women, calling them examples of "profusion and luxury," and noted that in "variety and richness" they "did not suffer in comparison with Europe." According to the duke, similar displays of luxury could be found more generally "at the tables of the wealthy" and "in their equipages." Both Brissot and the duke additionally equated luxury with certain behaviors. Brissot considered toasts following a meal to be examples of luxury, while the duke considered "frequent and sumptuous," or "great," dinners themselves to be luxurious. He also included tea parties, balls, and plays in this category.[62]

More detailed information about what specific household furnishings were considered luxuries comes from an Englishman who visited America in the last decade of the eighteenth century. He described both "pictures"—a term that could refer to either paintings or prints—and pier glasses (mirrors) as "articles of luxurious furniture."[63] And, like Brissot, he felt carpet to be a luxury. Furthermore, he noted that many luxurious items had to be imported to America. He directed those considering immigrating to the United States that there was "least opening for those, who have been used to [making] very fine and costly articles of luxury and shew." Appended to his account was an excerpt from a treatise written by Tench Coxe, assistant to the secretary of the treasury Alexander Hamilton, which stated that U.S. exports in the late eighteenth century consisted "chiefly of prime necessaries." Few articles of "comfort and utility" or "luxury" were exported from America, while imports consisted "in a great degree of article of comfortable accommodations, and in some degree of luxuries."[64]

In addition to defining certain types of objects as luxuries, people from a wide variety of backgrounds regularly condemned certain activities, which they associated with excess and impropriety. As early as 1744, one traveler reported that the "religious enthusiasm" that was stirred up in Philadelphia by Methodist minister George Whitefield's sermons had caused the population to rethink its attitude toward "assemblies of the gentry . . . for dancing or musick." According to this traveler, "an utter aversion" to "publick gay diversions" existed among residents of the city. Much to the regret of religious enthusiasts, that same spirit of denial was apparently not common in the late eighteenth century. An Anglican minister lamented of himself and fellow Philadelphians in 1772 that "we cannot bear to think, that our neighbour should dress better, entertain with more elegance and splendour, live in a better house, or keep up a more sumptuous equipage than ourselves."[65]

While some people who visited the commonwealth described self-indulgent activities, such as dancing and drinking, as merely "innocent amusements" that were "conducive to the improvement of politeness, good manners, and humanity," most religious folk thought otherwise. Dancing, for example, was considered a symbol of "excess" and, according to at least one author, was specifically described by the apostle Paul as a sinful behavior. Yet dancing, along with drinking and gambling, were apparently commonplace among many of the less pious residents of Pennsylvania during the second half of the eighteenth century. Muhlenberg, for example, noted in 1751 that "English laws forbid drinking, dancing, playing, etc., on Sunday. . . . But the idle, unconverted, so-called Christians must have some sort of pastime so they indulge in their sinful frivolities so much the more on weekdays and holidays." He later lamented that days specifically set aside to give thanks to God were observed in uninhibited, irreverent ways. In 1783, he reported, "the *mere* politicians of the gallant world would rather celebrate days of thanksgiving in the mode of refined taste in which healths and toasts are guzzled and fine dances held."[66]

The minister was particularly troubled by people within his own congregations who participated in such activities. He reported to his superiors in Europe that "as long as the preacher was present, everything was quite respectable and quiet. But as soon as he had turned his back, the people engaged in their calf-worship by dancing and other disorders." At the Lutheran church in Lancaster, Muhlenberg indicated that some members actually "had arranged a sleigh ride, had become drunk, and had danced and made fun of their preacher." In his own household, he found equally troubling behavior. In his journal he admonished his daughter-in-law Hanna for choreographing what he could only describe as a "sinful banquet." He wrote, "Today Mrs. Hanna had a first visit at her table from several neighboring women according to the prevailing fashion. They drink a glass of wine or a cup of tea and some cakes in the afternoon and evening and entertain one another with vain conversations. This fashion is not according to the counsel and command of our Lord and Savior."[67]

The pretentious, prideful activities that clergymen and their devout followers despised, like drinking, dancing, and even vain conversation around

the tea table, often took place either at taverns or at special gatherings, including those following weddings and funerals, which were often held in people's houses. At the festivities after one couple's wedding, for instance, Muhlenberg reported that "scoffers," despite several attempts on his part to admonish them, "seduced the young people [from his fellowship] into dancing." Such events were apparently common enough that at a conference for German and Swedish Lutheran ministers and lay leaders, the question of whether pastors should even attend "marriage feasts" was openly addressed. According to Muhlenberg, "The unanimous recommendation was that preachers ought not attend at all." However, the group further concluded that when a minister was "obliged to perform the marriage ceremony in a home," he could "eat a little and then depart, etc. without doing any harm."[68]

While clergy such as Muhlenberg might at least make an appearance at wedding feasts, they would be much less likely to frequent the taverns that dotted the Pennsylvania landscape in the late eighteenth century. Muhlenberg himself thought that the region was "being overrun with taverns and taverners," to which he attributed "physical and spiritual ruin." Ludwig Denig had equally strong feelings about the establishments. Denig included multiple watercolor and ink renderings of taverns in his 1784 "Picture-Bible."[69] In one image, entitled "O Man, How Can You Dance and Leap and Sing Wanton Songs?" the artist portrayed the interior of a tavern with two couples dancing and three musicians sitting around a table. The number of beverage containers communicates that sobriety is not a concern of the taverngoers (fig. 82). In the text accompanying the image, Denig wrote, "Making merry with the world has no place with Christ." He described "worldly honor, riches, and sensual pleasure" as things to be avoided and cautioned, "do not let the world seduce you with its diversions."[70]

Dancing and drinking, as well as gambling and other forms of gaming, were disreputable and irreverent. They could convert people's dwellings into dens of debauchery, and the establishments where they regularly took place—such as taverns—were interpreted as sources of vice and corruption. Yet if most Protestants considered these behaviors at odds with godliness, the problem for pious Christians in the late eighteenth century was determining where the line was between acceptable and unacceptable indulgences when it came to money and possessions. One Lutheran minister who turned down a guaranteed salary because he did not want to live "in the fleshly fashion of his predecessors" found that without it he "had to live in poverty."[71]

The definition of inappropriate belongings was not the same for all people in all places. What luxury items were available in the United States were not equally distributed across the country. Most commentators on life in late eighteenth-century America associated luxury with populous East Coast cities, such as New York and Philadelphia. As early as 1755, Benjamin Franklin observed, "Charges are greater in Cities, as Luxury is more common." At the close of the century, a French traveler remarked of American towns and particularly large cities, "Luxury is very high there, especially at New York and Philadelphia."[72]

According to period authors, luxury was fostered in large port cities in part because of the concentration of population and wealth in those locales. After visiting Philadelphia in 1788, Brissot explained of the city, which was home to roughly forty thousand residents, that "When towns acquire this degree of population, you must have hospitals, prisons, soldiers, police, spies, and all the sweeping train of luxury." Concerning the concentration of

Fig. 82 "O Man, How Can You Dance and Leap and Sing Wanton Songs?" Ludwig Denig (1755–1830), Lancaster, Pennsylvania, 1784. Watercolor and ink on paper. Private collection. Denig, as a result of his religious convictions, believed that taverns and the activities that went on inside them, like drinking and dancing, were to be avoided. Photograph courtesy of the American Folk Art Museum, Shirley K. Schlafer Library.

wealth in urban areas, Representative John Williams of New York reminded fellow members of the United States House of Representatives that many "moneyed men . . . lived in great cities." And even an English traveler, who heartily applauded the general lack of contrast between the rich and the poor in America, recognized some degree of material separation in large cities. Comparing his native England with the United States, he observed, "Temptations to unnecessary expence, owing to the numerous gradations of rank in England, are perpetual, and almost unconquerable. . . . Something like European manners, and something of the ill effect of inequality of riches, is to be found in the great towns of America."[73]

Luxury in cities was further advanced by the relative availability of imported, nonessential goods. A Frenchman observed that "there is no city of the United States where articles of consumption are to be found in such great abundance as at Philadelphia, even to almost all articles of luxury. Many shops are as well furnished as those of Paris or London." An English traveler came to a similar conclusion. Of Boston, New York, Philadelphia, and Baltimore, he wrote, "They are, in short, precisely what the larger and more opulent provincial towns of Great Britain are. Hence also you may easily conceive, that European comforts and conveniences are not scarce. In fact, you may find in Philadelphia or New York every article of that description usually kept in the shops of the English towns."[74]

Outside the large East Coast cities, particularly Philadelphia and New York, according to most visitors to America, luxury, and even comfort, was less common. A French duke, for example, remarked, "In the other towns, and especially in the country, luxury is less prevalent." Another traveler concurred, noting that an English "man of luxury" would not be content in most parts of the new United States. After comparing the Americans and the English, he observed of the United States, "in the interior of the country, things appear, at least, half a century behind them in point of comfort."[75]

Yet by the late eighteenth century, it was apparent to many travelers that the interior of America was changing. The duke noted that luxury, although not prevalent, was increasing outside East Coast cities. He wrote, "There is no point of the United States, however remote, even in the woods, in which one store, and frequently more, may not be found. There are established warehouses for foreign goods, which are emptied and filled again twice a year. . . . The home manufactures do not suffice alone to satisfy the taste for luxury." The duke noted that even in the "back-settlements," women and boys routinely attended church services wearing attire imported from Europe.[76]

The fact that luxurious, imported clothing had found its way to the "back-settlements" was particularly troubling to some authors. During the second half of the eighteenth century, while many people simply equated luxury with nonessentiality, a second definition of the term emphasized the relationship between a person's station in life and his or her possessions. The word "luxury" was used when a person's belongings were felt to be in excess of his or her wealth or rank. In a published letter to Benjamin Franklin, one author defined luxury as "a greater expense of subsistence than in prudence a man ought to consume." Writing to James Madison, the marquis de Chastellux stated that he considered luxury "only as an expence, abusive in its relations, whether with the fortune of individuals, or with their situation." In order to avoid any misunderstanding, he repeated several pages later that "luxury, as we have said, is often an abusive employ of riches, relatively, to the condition of him who possesses them." According to this decidedly negative definition, luxury meant excess either in relation to wealth or to station. While anyone could be guilty of it, it was most common among people of the lower or middling ranks, such as backcountry farmers, who were trying to rise above their station.[77]

In describing this type of luxury, which he equated with "dissipation," the marquis gave as an example a man who spent all "his property" on "flowers and shells." The marquis stated that "the sort of luxury into which he has fallen is only relative to his means, since his taste has led him further than his faculties would admit." Presumably, for a person of greater wealth and more exalted station, the purchase of the decorative items would not have been luxurious. Under different circumstances, the marquis' remarks suggest that such a procurement would actually have been in good taste. For the individual in question, however, the acquisition was a wasteful and foolish expenditure of precious resources.[78]

The marquis reminded his reader, James Madison, that the new United States was founded as a "republic" and that it lacked the "nobles" of England and France. For this reason, he believed that an individual must limit his or her consumption so that it remained "proportionable to his situation." He recognized that some individuals in the United States could afford to make extravagant purchases and gave as an illustration "a very wealthy citizen" who spent "only part of his fortune in building a noble palace." He noted, however, that the resulting edifice "shocks the public, in the same manner as proud and arrogant behaviour inspires estrangement and hatred." Even though the building's construction did not cause its owner financial ruin, it was still inappropriate for his station and locale. Although the structure may have been suitable as the residence of a noble family in Europe, it was not acceptable for even a wealthy citizen of the United States.[79]

For many people of elevated status living in late eighteenth-century Pennsylvania, the concept of luxury blended ideas about material affluence and appropriate restraint. Wealthy, educated individuals who worked to create material displays that corresponded with their social and economic status recognized that luxury items such as paintings, carpets, fashionable dresses, or sumptuous foods were generally associated with the elite. In the words of a French author, luxury was "the representation of riches," and for this reason it was often the rich who had access to articles of luxury. The procurement of luxury goods additionally demonstrated that purchasers had the knowledge to participate in the refined rituals associated with the upper class. Elaborate dinners and after-dinner toasts were indicators not only that these individuals had the extra money to purchase sumptuous cuisine but also that they knew what the right foods and drinks were as well as how they should be served and consumed.[80]

At the same time that luxury goods and activities served as indicators of elevated status, however, they were also to be avoided. Luxury came to be understood as unpatriotic and particularly unrepublican.[81] Residents of the new United States were to limit material displays so that they corresponded with their rank as well as their place of residence. Furthermore, they were to refrain from extravagant purchases and activities as an expression of their virtue. This was an era when ideas about social organization and property were regularly tied to morality and religion. In "An Account of the Progress of Population, Agriculture, Manners, And Government in Pennsylvania," Benjamin Rush, for example, noted that the third and highest "species" of settler, who avoided luxury by producing at home much of what he ate and wore, was also a good Christian. According to Rush, who was raised in a Presbyterian family, churches, which served as "the means of promoting order and happiness in society," garnered much of their support from this class of settler.[82]

Pennsylvania German Piety and Possessions

Among practitioners of diverse Protestant faiths, ideas about proper material displays and the appropriateness of refined activities, such as dancing at assemblies, caused some tangible variations among groups. Those who observed the Pennsylvania Germans certainly found reason to note differences of opinion on these subjects. Commentators thought the residents of Ephrata unusual because of their insistence on asceticism. They believed that Mennonites, like Quakers in British communities, visually and audibly distinguished themselves through their simplicity in dress and conversation. When tourists visited Moravian communities, on the other hand, they found adherents to that faith had different ideas, particularly about the built environment. Johann David Schöpf, for example, reported as he approached Bethlehem that the town made "the best impression" because of "its situation" and "the orderliness of its large houses."[83]

Yet despite the denominational variation, balancing religious convictions with the desire to convey elevated social and economic status remained a concern for most Pennsylvania Germans. Buildings that survive as part of the

Pennsylvania landscape suggest that erecting a two-story masonry closed-plan house was not at odds with the religious beliefs of all but the most extreme groups, such as the one at Ephrata. Yet writings and drawings left by Lutheran and Reformed churchgoers indicate that if the buildings themselves did not present a problem, the activities that could go on inside them brought some uneasiness. As new belongings—including closed-plan houses—and new behaviors came to be increasingly associated with refinement, luxury became a prevalent concern. While some activities were commonly considered superfluous and irreverent, when it came to belongings, appropriateness was usually measured based on rank, locale, and use.

Among Pennsylvanians of German descent, with the exception of the Moravians, who seem to have embraced genteel lifestyles with few reservations, members of most religious groups were troubled by the profusion of what they termed luxury, even among the upper class. Religious leaders

Fig. 83 **Michael Wenger house, Rapho Township, Lancaster County, Pennsylvania, before 1798.** The Wenger house, constructed for either Michael or his son Isaac, is believed to have served as both a meeting place for members of the Wengers' Anabaptist congregation as well as a dwelling. The corners of the building were highlighted with quoins and the first-floor windows were topped with jack-arch lintels, both created from carefully shaped stones in a contrasting color.

certainly recognized that some differentiation must exist among Pennsylvanians of various ranks. Ministers, for example, because of their "*education* and *constitution*," were expected to partake of a certain quality of food and live in a dwelling that met certain standards. However, by the end of the eighteenth century, some of the activities in which refined folk participated, such as dancing and drinking at assemblies, came in direct conflict with religious convictions. Perhaps for this reason, one visitor to Pennsylvania reported in the last decade of the eighteenth century, "few men go to church, at least few of the first class."[84]

Yet it would appear that however tenuous the balance, several prominent Pennsylvania Germans found ways to reconcile their desire to possess distinguished buildings and belongings with the scriptural commandments about simplicity that were upheld by their faith communities. Ludwig Denig, whose "Picture-Bible" indicates his concerns about inappropriate behaviors and belongings, resided in a large, highly valued masonry house. When Denig relocated from Lancaster to Chambersburg in Franklin County, he purchased property from Benjamin Chamber. He agreed as a condition of the 1789 sale that within two years he would erect "one good substantial dwelling House of the dimension of sixteen feet square at least with a good chimney of Brick or Stone." What Denig actually built, however, was a two-story brick dwelling, which measured 40 by 32 feet. The building was prominently located on Front Street (later Main Street) and had an adjoining brick kitchen building. In 1798, when other houses in the neighborhood were assessed as low as $125, Denig's residence was valued at an astounding $1,700. When Denig referred to the building in his will, he called it a mansion house. The men who valued his estate in 1837 used the same designation to refer to the residence.[85]

Members of Reformed and Lutheran churches were not alone in constructing large masonry closed-plan houses. So-called Plain folk also built houses of the best sort in the eighteenth century. In Rapho Township, Lancaster County, for example, members of the Mennonite Wenger family constructed a two-story stone house of roughly 30 by 40 feet (figs. 83–86). The building, which was assessed with its springhouse at $1,000 in 1798, may have served as a meeting place for their congregation as well as a dwelling house. On the first floor, four rooms—the two back heated by fireplaces and the two front by stoves—were arranged around the center passage. An open staircase led to the second floor, which in the eighteenth century may have been left undivided to accommodate large groups meeting for religious services.[86]

While it would be easy to suggest that the Wenger house was designed with a closed plan because it served both private family as well as community functions, similar houses, which do not seem to have been the regular site

Fig. 84 Center passage, Michael Wenger house. The Wengers chose a closed-plan house with a central passage. The prominent staircase provided access to the second floor, where religious meetings may have taken place. Entry to both formal rooms and workrooms on the first floor was also achieved from the passage.

Fig. 85 Corner cupboard in stove room, Michael Wenger house. Like the Mennonite Eshlemans, the Wenger family also utilized a built-in corner cupboard to store household objects. The wooden doors for the cupboard, which have since been removed, would have protected the contents from contamination and shielded them from view. The shaped shelves on the upper portion of the cupboard, however, suggest that the contents were meant to be seen, at least when the doors were open.

Fig. 86 Stove room, Michael Wenger house. Built after the invention of freestanding stoves, the first-floor front room on either side of the center passage at the Wenger house was heated by a six- or ten-plate stove vented into the chimney of the fireplace in the rear room. Holes for stove pipes remain as evidence of this heating arrangement.

of religious meetings, were also built by "Plain" folk. Mennonites Abraham and Anna Maria Landis, for example, built a large two-story stone structure in what is now East Lampeter Township, Lancaster County (figs. 87–88). The 1763 house included a passage that led from the front door about halfway through the building. Doors leading to the other spaces within the house were trimmed out with fashionable crosseted, or "eared," surrounds. By the time of Abraham Landis's death in 1790, the house was outfitted with stylish and valuable accouterments including a "great Cup-board," a "House Clock," "Table Cloths," a "Tea Kettle," and "Dutch and English Books." Abraham's wearing apparel was valued at over £5, and his five beds and bedsteads totaled £22.[87]

ARCHITECTURE AND ARTIFACTS OF THE PENNSYLVANIA GERMANS

Fig. 87　Abraham and Anna Maria Landis house, East Lampeter Township, Lancaster County, Pennsylvania, 1763. The Mennonite Landis family built a two-story stone closed-plan house labeled with two date stones as the property of "Abrabam [sic] Landes" and "Anna Maria Landesin." The addition of "-in" to Anna Maria's last name reflects the use of German grammar to create a feminine noun.

Fig. 88　Half-passage, Abraham and Anna Maria Landis house. The Landis residence included a central passage that ran about half the width of the building. The crosseted, or "eared," door surrounds reflect a familiarity with high-style patterns. The stair to the second floor was located in the space behind the passage.

Fig. 89 Martin Mylin house, Lancaster County, Pennsylvania. According to I. Daniel Rupp, Martin Mylin's 1740 house caused scandal within his Mennonite community due to its showiness. Unfortunately, the details of the incident were not recorded until more than one hundred years later, when Rupp published them, leaving many unanswered questions about why the building was considered inappropriate. Image from I. Daniel Rupp, *History of Lancaster County, to which is Prefixed a Brief Sketch of the Early History of Pennsylvania* (1844; reprint, Spartanburg, S.C.: Reprint Company for the Pennsylvania Reprint Society and Southwest Pennsylvania Genealogical Services, 1984), plate between pp. 286 and 287.

While highly valued, well-provisioned masonry houses were acceptable for Reformed churchgoers like Denig as well as for Lutherans and even Mennonites such as the Wengers and the Landises, the range of material expressions pious Pennsylvania Germans could choose from was not boundless. It was limited by popular perceptions about what was appropriate for people of certain ranks and residents of certain locales. When Heinrich Melchior Muhlenberg was serving his country congregation in Providence, for example, he reported humbly wearing clothing that his wife had made for him. When he traveled to New York City to minister there, he had to change his attire to suit the more cosmopolitan atmosphere of the city. While religious belief motivated him to "live with meekness," the attitudes of contemporaries—both devout Christians and irreverent scoffers—also affected his choices about his possessions. The community in which he was serving determined the standard to which he subscribed.[88]

Many pious elite Pennsylvanians like Muhlenberg found themselves faced with a dilemma in the second half of the eighteenth century. As Philadelphia grew to be the largest city in British North America and the Pennsylvania countryside was rapidly being settled by Europeans, new types of goods and new types of behaviors began to distinguish those who had the knowledge and money to participate in the culture of refinement. Possessions such as two-story masonry houses and ritualistic activities such as dining at well-provisioned tables could be viewed as symbols of improvement and therefore Christian piety. However, the lines between appropriateness and ostentation were not always clear.

Telling the story of two fictional travelers who toured Luzerne County in the northeastern part of Pennsylvania in 1789, Michel-Guillaume Jean de Crèvecoeur described the duo's reaction to "one of the most pleasing meals" they had beheld since they left Carlisle in the more cultured part of the state. One of the characters remarked to his Polish hostess, "What luxury for new colonists!" The woman responded, "Why do you call it that . . . when it is only the enjoyment of the fruits of our labor? The tea comes from China, it is true; but we pay for it with ginseng from our woods. The shad, the ham, the beef, the honeycombs, the preserves, and the sugar; everything is our own." While Crèvecoeur's story clearly exaggerates the self-sufficiency of Pennsylvania's late eighteenth-century settlers, within the context of debates about the meaning of luxury, the tale demonstrates how widespread concern about inappropriate expenditures had become. Crèvecoeur indicated that recognizing excess, and therefore impiety, was a matter of interpretation. Yet, despite varying definitions, luxury had begun to take on increasingly negative connotations. Immoderation and superfluity were certainly to be avoided.[89]

Among Pennsylvania Germans, ideas related to luxury served to both unite and divide the population. On one level, as people of German descent fashioned identities through material goods, they sometimes chose to physically express their religious convictions. Building a place to hold worship services was one way for a congregation to create a public identity. Adopting distinct clothing was another way by which members of specific groups came to differentiate themselves. The practice allowed congregants to make visual statements as they went out into the world, both about their affiliation and about their detachment from worldly fashion. Some groups chose to go still further by creating closed communities where faith dictated a distinct aesthetic.

Over time, as new generations of Pennsylvanians have taken up the task of interpreting the relationship between religious belief and material culture, particularly among Pennsylvania German Anabaptist groups, they have often chosen to emphasize instances of extreme simplicity. In 1844, for example, Israel Daniel Rupp, in his *History of Lancaster County,* focused on the inappropriateness of a large two-story house built by Mennonites Martin and Anna Mylin in 1740 in Lampeter Township, Lancaster County. According to Rupp, contemporaries referred to the couple's new dwelling as a "palace." An illustration of the building, produced for the 1844 history, indicates that the house, which had a central chimney and a front door located to one side of its façade, was probably of the entry-kitchen variety (fig. 89). Measuring more than 30 by 30 feet, it was similar in appearance, and presumably floor plan, to the house George and Maria Caterina Müller constructed in Millbach some twelve years later (see figs. 27–29). The building had a cellar, first and second floors, and two attic stories underneath its gambrel roof. The Mylins' house was additionally distinguished because the limestone blocks that composed its front façade were uniformly shaped and laid in even courses.[90]

Rupp reported that the Mylin residence began to attract negative attention from members of their Mennonite meeting soon after its construction. Religious leaders, he said, considered the building "too showy for a Mennonite." Although Martin Mylin insisted that he had taken "only his comfort" into consideration when constructing the dwelling, fellow Mennonites debated the proper response to his action. In the end, Mylin was only reprimanded. He was allowed to remain an active member of his congregation and to continue living in his new palace-like house.[91]

Unfortunately, Rupp's history and local tradition are the only sources that shed any light on the incident. John Landis Ruth, a modern scholar of the Mennonites in Lancaster County, believes the incident to have been spurred by mid-eighteenth-century antipacifist and anti-German sentiment that forced Mennonite communities in Pennsylvania to avoid anything that might evoke jealousy or added attention. It is just as likely that Rupp and the oral histories that informed his work were influenced by the climate of the early nineteenth century when the Mennonite faith saw division, leading to the creation of the River Brethren (Brethren in Christ) and Reformed Mennonites, in part due to issues relating to worldliness. It is telling that the illustration of the building included with Rupp's history reveals two date stones, one labeled 1740 and the other 1823, suggesting a rebuilding or significant remodeling at the later date.[92]

Of course it could be that Lancaster County Mennonites truly did find the building, as originally constructed, inappropriate. Perhaps the churchly gambrel roof was simply unacceptable, although Mennonite preacher Dielman Kolb had built a stone house with a gambrel roof in what is now Lower Salford Township, Montgomery County, at about the same time.[93] Maybe, at only twenty-five years of age,[94] Martin Mylin had not yet achieved enough stature in the community to be considered worthy of the type of house he erected. What may be most significant is that in the retelling of the story, the Mylins were not forced to leave their faith community. While there may have been some disagreement about the appropriateness of their house, the conflict was not momentous enough to cause a permanent rift in the congregation. In fact, the incident was not even recorded in writing until more than one hundred years later.[95]

A recent study of eighteenth-century Quaker houses in Pennsylvania and New Jersey concludes that the interpretation of plainness in Quaker domestic architecture reflects values of the late nineteenth century that persist to the present day. The houses built by the region's early leading Quakers were designed, like those of other Pennsylvanians, to emphasize "wealth, display, authority, and monumentality."[96] The same could be said of the dwellings erected by leading Mennonites in Pennsylvania in the eighteenth century. In Conestoga Township, where Mennonites constituted a large percentage of the population, they occupied a range of house types that varied from small one-room log dwellings owned by others to owner-occupied, two-story, closed-plan masonry mansions clearly labeled on date stones as the property of their residents. Those built by Benedict and Anna Eshleman dispel any suggestion of Mennonite aversion to sizable, highly valued, and visible houses.

Although the material environment could reflect religious difference among Pennsylvania German faith communities, the degree of divergence should not be overstated. Most Pennsylvania Germans, like most Pennsylvanians from other ethnic groups, were Protestant in background. During the second half of the eighteenth century, they were increasingly concerned about the relationship between certain behaviors and piety. The availability of luxury items and the growing popularity of pastimes such as dancing sounded an alarm. Affluent Pennsylvania Germans were particularly affected by contemporary debates about luxury. Like prosperous individuals from other ethnic groups, their choices were influenced by popular conceptions about propriety and religiosity.

The delicate balance an educated person like Heinrich Melchior Muhlenberg fashioned allowed the clergyman to express both his status as a professional and his religious convictions. Muhlenberg spent the last years of his life in a closed-plan house. Inside that dwelling, his journals suggest that he tried to live meekly and avoid the trap wrought by worldly goods and particularly worldly behaviors. As a member of the clergy, he set an example for his congregants, but he also had to reconcile his personal convictions with what was acceptable within his community. Like so many of his contemporaries, Muhlenberg's decisions regarding his house, household furnishings, and the activities they made possible reflected real concerns over the relationship between identity based on social and economic status and that based on religious belief. While a certain degree of refinement among the upper class was expected and appreciated, ungodly, and unrepublican, excess could lead to earthly scorn and eternal damnation.

Peter Ranck

Dressing table

Changes and Choices

Authors who observed the diverse Pennsylvania population during the eighteenth century often remarked on several defining personal characteristics. In categorizing and classifying individuals, they might specifically note a person's ethnic background, social and economic status, religious affiliation, or some combination of the three. One midcentury traveler, for example, remarked on the "very mixed company of different nations and religions" he encountered in a Philadelphia tavern. According to his recollection, of the twenty-five people seated around a table, "there were Scots, English, Dutch, Germans, and Irish." In addition to ethnic differences, he also noted that the group—despite religious admonitions to avoid taverns—was composed of people representing a wide variety of faiths, including "Roman Catholicks, Churchmen, Presbyterians, Quakers, Newlightmen, Methodists, Seventhdaymen, Moravians, Anabaptists, and one Jew."[1]

Depending on their personal views and the context of their comments, the weight individual authors placed on various distinguishing attributes could fluctuate considerably. Some, like the above commentator, found ethnic background and religious belief to be two of the most notable components of personal identity. Others, however, came to very different conclusions. A late eighteenth-century French traveler believed that personal distinction in Pennsylvania was largely based on "fortune, and the nature of professions." He divided the population into three distinct groups, which he defined according to occupation, and added that "in balls, concerts, and public amusements, these classes do not mix."[2]

By the end of the eighteenth century, comments like this that empha-sized the divisive nature of wealth and work became increasingly common.[3] Differences based on ethnic background particularly began to be overshad-owed by those grounded in social and economic status. This is not to say that national origin no longer mattered either to outside commentators or to the individuals in question. Instead, issues related to social and economic status simply began to take on greater significance. In the intellectual landscape of late eighteenth-century Pennsylvania, it was more important to determine how someone fit within the social and economic structure of the new republic of the United States than to determine where they or their ancestors had fit within the national boundaries of Europe.

Religious belief, too, created less fragmentation in eighteenth-century Pennsylvania than modern Lancaster County tourist attractions would have the twenty-first-century traveler believe. While certain religious groups created closed communities where unusual doctrines and rituals were prac-ticed within very distinctive built environments, most Pennsylvania Germans were Protestants whose beliefs were similar enough to foster some degree of accord. By the late eighteenth century, Christian dictates regarding sim-plicity became intertwined with ideas about virtue, republicanism, and excess. They were a subject of concern for Pennsylvania Germans from Lutherans to Mennonites, and more generally for every citizen who wanted to avoid impropriety and superfluity. For most, luxury came to be tied to issues of rank, locale, and appropriate use of one's wealth. The elite, regardless of religious affiliation, were expected to occupy different types of houses, own differ-ent types of goods, and behave differently from their social and economic inferiors.

As the contours of difference began to be redefined, increasingly focus-ing on class rather than ethnic background or religious affiliation, material culture became one means by which to understand cleavages. Buildings and belongings continued to be described in ethnic terms, but often comments were designed to cognitively place people of a certain nationality within a specific social and economic group. What became paramount was how peo-ple's possessions fit within the rubric of improvement, a concept that came to embody ideas about the interrelated nature of rank, property, and moral-ity. Did a house and the furnishings within it symbolize uncivilized, unrefined displays of poverty or ostentatious, impious exhibitions of luxury? Or did they belong within the slippery but esteemed category of appropriateness and restrained gentility?

In the case of the Pennsylvania Germans, many authors used descrip-tions of the built environment to portray members of the group specifically as farmers. Depending on their opinion of those who worked the land, this characterization could be viewed as a positive or a negative attribute. Some authors, particularly members of the European aristocratic or professional classes, typified Pennsylvanians of German descent as hardworking but frugal and ignorant. They used portrayals of the group's poor, sparsely furnished houses to support their claims. In their minds, among Euro-Americans, Pennsylvania Germans occupied the low end on the spectrum of improvement. Rather than attribute their modest domestic accommodations to virtuous attempts to limit luxury, they credited them to incivility.[4]

Another group of commentators, principally composed of supporters of egalitarianism, agriculture, and increasingly democratic government, came to very different conclusions. Relying in large measure on the same descriptions, they determined that people of German descent were among America's most noble citizens. They presented their houses as evidence of propriety, and their frugality, or economy, as a manifestation of virtuous restraint. It is not surprising that in addition to noting the lack of luxury in Pennsylvania German dwellings, these authors also emphasized Germans' temperance, particularly when it came to strong liquors such as rum. While not focusing on the members of any particular denomination, they generally depicted people of German descent as examples of popular contemporary principles of virtue achieved through appropriate moderation.[5]

Most authors who recorded what made the houses occupied by people of German descent distinct were not interested in creating authentic, unbiased representations. Rather, they used their descriptions to support their opinions about the nature of farmers and farming in American society. They sometimes happened to note what seem to be genuine ethnic preferences regarding such topics as heating sources and foodways. However, their observations were typified by exaggerated stereotypes. Because they were most interested in determining where agriculturalists fell within the spectrum of cultural and therefore physical improvement, their remarks about the Pennsylvania Germans cannot routinely be taken at face value.

Those who were physically engaged in fashioning their own self-image through objects sometimes expressed as little concern about tangible ethnic characteristics as the late eighteenth-century authors. Throughout this work, the term "Pennsylvania German" has been used to refer to all people of German descent living in the commonwealth. However, shared national origin did not necessarily lead to a collective sense of ethnic identity. Nor did a lack of German lineage always preclude membership in the Pennsylvania German community. A 1721 tax list, for example, divides the population of the Conestoga region of what would become Lancaster County into two groups: the English and the Palatines. Yet some individuals with British surnames, such as Edmund Cartlidge, are included in the Palatine section of the list. The reason for Cartlidge's identification as a German may have been clear at the time, but has become lost to historians.[6] Maybe his name had been

Fig. 90 Flagon, basin, and plate, Reformed Church of Pikes [Pikeland] Township, Chester County, Pennsylvania, c. 1757. This congregation's ecclesiastical pewter included objects crafted in Cologne, London, and Philadelphia. Photograph, Philadelphia Museum of Art. Courtesy of the East Vincent United Church of Christ, Spring City, Pennsylvania.

anglicized, or though British perhaps he had spent time among continental Europeans before coming to the New World, or his wife might have been of German descent, or perhaps he simply adopted German ways. For whatever reason, the tax assessors considered him "Palatine," and it is possible that he defined himself that way as well.

Ethnicity, according to social scientists, is a subjective quality, and if it is to be used as a means to differentiate, it requires ethnic self-consciousness.[7] In eighteenth-century Pennsylvania, the level of self-awareness that leads to self-definition was grounded in a number of personal attributes, only one of which was ethnic background. Patronage of craftsmen, for example, did not need to be based on shared national origin. Relationships could be formed as a result of other real or perceived mutual qualities such as political views, professional allegiances, familial connections, economic interests, or membership in religious or social groups.

In 1757, for instance, the German Reformed congregation in Pikeland Township in northern Chester County undertook the task of assembling a three-piece ecclesiastical pewter set (fig. 90). The objects acquired were all crafted in a similar contemporary style, though they came from three completely different locales and were made by members of three distinct ethnic groups. The flagon was made in the German city of Cologne, the basin by London pewterer John Townsend, and the plate by Cornelius Bradford, a New York artisan who had recently relocated to Philadelphia. Once the set was complete, all three pieces were decorated with similar line engraving, two pieces were embellished with verses from the book of Matthew, and all were inscribed, "VOR DIE REFORMIRTE GEMEINE DER KRCH IN PEICKS TOWN SHIP 1757" (For the Reformed congregation of the church in Pikes Township, 1757). While members of the congregation chose to have all the text on these pewter vessels printed in the German language, it apparently mattered little to them that the individual pieces had been produced by residents of Cologne, London, and Philadelphia.[8]

Surviving objects from Jonestown, in what is now Lebanon County, demonstrate the ease with which Pennsylvania German craftsmen, like the members of the German Reformed congregation in Pikeland, bridged the now seemingly insurmountable gap between German and English tastes. In the late eighteenth and early nineteenth centuries, members of the Seltzer and Ranck families of Jonestown were responsible for making a large number of visually distinct painted chests (fig. 91). The chests they produced usually incorporated two or three painted panels across their fronts, which were filled with stylized flowers protruding from vases. Often the artisan responsible for a chest would scratch his name and sometimes the date into the body of one or more of the vases before the paint dried. In at least two cases, Christian Seltzer and his son John Seltzer signed the same chest twice, once using the German form of their names written in German script and once using the English form of their names printed in English roman characters.[9] Rather than suggest that these two men were entangled in a period of schizophrenic crisis regarding their ethnic identities, it seems more logical to postulate from the two signatures that the Seltzers lived in a community and served clients who wrote and spoke both German and English. They identified themselves as chest joiners and decorators in a way that all literate members of their bilingual, multiethnic society could understand.[10]

As people living hundreds of years later have become more interested in the role of ethnic background in late eighteenth-century Pennsylvania, it has been easy for them to be swayed by the remarks made by firsthand observers centuries earlier. Perhaps for this reason, debates about the differences and similarities between Pennsylvanians of German and British descent have dominated much literature, particularly on Pennsylvania German material culture. Questions about the degree to which people of German descent chose or were forced to adopt English ways have commanded attention and dictated the terms of numerous studies. In comparing Pennsylvania's English and German populations, emphasis is placed on change among the Germans and continuity, at least from an ethnic standpoint, among the English.[11]

It must be remembered, however, that everyone who lived in Pennsylvania during the second half of the eighteenth century was living in a period of rapid transition. During the time in question, thirteen of the British North American colonies broke from their parent country and formed a new independent nation. The transformation was political in nature, but it also encompassed numerous social, economic, and cultural changes.[12] When an Englishman visited the new United States in the 1790s, he noted a divergence between English and American ways of life. He wrote in his published travel account that "although American manners and society approach nearer to English than any other, they are not quite English." The United States and its residents were becoming, according to this traveler, noticeably distinct from Europe and Europeans. A Pennsylvanian, writing his recollections of the Revolutionary War period, recorded what may have been common practice when it came to identifying the national origin of the American-born populace. Of the soldiers fighting in the Pennsylvania line he reported, "I find there were twenty from Ireland, four from England, two from Scotland, two from Germany, and the remaining forty-five were Americans." Presumably, this chronicler classified people who were not born in Europe as American regardless of from where their ancestors had emigrated. Whether they were of British or German descent, in his mind they had exchanged the European identities of their ancestors for their own American identities.[13]

As the eighteenth century progressed and the residents of Pennsylvania became more noticeably American, other changes were taking place among certain members of the group as well. In the early part of the century, wealthy, prominent settlers had often distinguished themselves materially by building houses that were larger and constructed of more durable materials than those of their neighbors. They may have additionally embellished their dwellings with certain decorative details and purchased a greater number of household implements. However, their belongings rarely varied in form from those possessed by their social and economic inferiors. By midcentury, this had begun to change. Increasingly, a select group of area residents built different kinds of houses and purchased new types of household accouterments.[14] On the exterior, their buildings were distinguished because the openings for windows and doors were arranged symmetrically, and the façade was frequently constructed of courses of regularly shaped stones or bricks. It might also have been embellished with decorative quoins at its corners or jack-arch lintels over its windows (see figs. 34, 36, 48, 53, 83, 94,

95, and 100). More important, however, were changes on the inside. The new buildings were often of a closed rather than an open plan. They had center or side passages that served as intermediary spaces between the outside world and more formal spaces for entertaining and more private bedrooms inside.

Unlike most open-plan houses, new center-passage houses usually had four rooms on their first floor in addition to the passage, and an equal number of second-floor chambers. Side-passage houses, while not quite as large, also incorporated increasingly specialized spaces. Because of larger windows, the rooms inside these houses were better lit than those in more humble dwellings. They also tended to have plastered ceilings, and their walls were usually plastered or paneled. In new types of rooms designed specifically for dining, individual drinking vessels and eating utensils were becoming more common, as were matched sets of chairs and tableware. In other rooms, tables that served specific functions, such as tea tables or card tables, were appearing with increasing regularity. Household goods such as textiles, glassware, and ceramics were often imported from Europe or far-off Asia.[15]

Such houses and the objects inside them contrasted notably with older dwellings and more modest contemporary buildings occupied by people of both British and German descent. Among the British, more humble houses often had only one or two rooms on their first floor. If of the two-room variety,

Fig. 91 **Chest, Johannes Ranck, 1790.** Members of the Seltzer and Ranck families of Jonestown, Lebanon County, Pennsylvania, were responsible for the creation of a number of painted chests like this one. Their designs usually included two or three rectangular or arched painted panels filled with floral forms protruding from vases. In this case, Johannes Ranck marked the vase in the center panel with his name, "Johannes Ranck," and the date 1790. Inscriptions in the vases on the left and right are no longer readable, so we can only guess as to whether Ranck, like the Seltzers, might have signed his name on the same chest in two different languages. Courtesy of Winterthur Museum.

they were generally of the hall-and-parlor plan. German houses may have had as many as four first-floor rooms, but often had fewer. Such buildings, which were usually of the entry-kitchen variety, shared several characteristics with hall-and-parlor houses. Primarily, both types of buildings utilized an open plan in which one passed through the front door into a principal space that often incorporated work functions. Furthermore, the vast majority of both types of houses were built of wood—in Pennsylvania, usually log—and were only one story in height.

Fig. 92 **Desk and bookcase, attributed to Michael Lind, c. 1780–1800. Made for Michael Withers of Strasburg Township, Lancaster County, this desk and bookcase was designed in the rococo style with ogee bracket feet, carved corner columns, document drawers with shell motifs, and a scroll-top pediment with flame finials and rosettes. Originally it was stained to simulate mahogany. Courtesy of Winterthur Museum.**

Fig. 93 **Sugar bowl, Christian Wiltberger, c. 1793–1819. Philadelphia silversmith Christian Wiltberger produced serving pieces such as this one in the neoclassical style. Courtesy of Winterthur Museum.**

As travelers observed this varied Pennsylvania landscape marked at its extremes by small, open-plan, wooden houses at one end and large, closed-plan, masonry houses at the other, ethnicity was not their primary concern. Rather, they were interested in interpreting how buildings and the objects inside them represented contemporary ideas about improvement. As they toured the Pennsylvania countryside, they perceived a gradual progression from huts or cottages constructed quickly from felled trees to more finished but still small houses of hewed logs to larger masonry dwellings that were well furnished and proved both "comfortable" and "convenient." Commentators correlated the transition with the wealth, occupation, education, and even virtue of the buildings' male and female inhabitants. They were quick to point out the general relationship between houses, furnishings, and social and economic status. They were also likely to point out breaches in the pattern. Anyone who overstepped the bounds of acceptability brought cause for alarm.

Fig. 94 Henry and Susanna Fisher house, Oley Township, Berks County, Pennsylvania, 1799–1801. Contrasted with the nearby Lesher house (see figs. 44–47), which was built in the mid-eighteenth century, the Fisher house shows the increased formalism of many houses built at the close of the 1700s. The Fishers chose a five-bay symmetrical façade of coursed stone with jack-arch lintels over the windows, a fanlight over the central front door, and a carved wooden cornice. Both buildings had a center-passage, double-pile floor plan, but at the Fisher house it was packaged within a more stylish, and standard, exterior.

Pennsylvanians of German descent, like their English neighbors, occupied each perceived stage in the three-part evolution. German immigrants and their descendants did not all always live in small, poorly furnished houses, nor did they always operate outside dominant eighteenth-century styles. Members of the group built center- and side-passage houses and furnished them with stylish accouterments associated with refined living. Rococo desks and bookcases stained to simulate mahogany and neoclassical silver serving pieces were both made and used by people of German descent (figs. 92–93). Early glassmaking in the United States was dominated by German entrepreneurs such as Caspar and Richard Wistar, John Frederick Amelung, and Henry William Stiegel. In 1771, members of the American Philosophical Society, likely in an effort to encourage the consumption of domestic rather than imported goods, determined that glass manufactured at Stiegel's Lancaster County glasshouse was "equal in beauty and quality to the generality of Flint Glass, imported from England." It would seem, then, that people of German and non-German descent were not always as divided in their aesthetic preferences as is sometimes assumed.[16]

Furthermore, there was great cultural diversity among the German population in Pennsylvania. People of German descent were separated by their occupations, wealth, religions, regions of origin in Europe, and years of residency in America. Even contemporary travelers found that some people of German descent, such as scientist David Rittenhouse, physician Adam Simon Kuhn, and clergyman-botanist Gotthilf Henry Ernest Muhlenberg, were "respectable for their knowledge," or, in the case of Lancaster merchant Paul Zantzinger, were "very obliging to strangers."[17] Even a cursory study of the dwellings inhabited by Pennsylvania Germans demonstrates the variety of experiences among German immigrants and their descendants. In the late eighteenth century, Pennsylvania Germans lived in small wooden houses of log construction as well as larger masonry structures built from stone or brick. Additionally, some Pennsylvania Germans resided not in single-family dwellings but in structures designed to house larger groups of people with similar religious beliefs at communities such as Ephrata or Bethlehem, Nazareth, or Lititz.

Yet despite this diversity of expression in domestic architecture, researchers have often pointed to only one type of house—the entry-kitchen house—as truly "German." They have chosen to emphasize the differences rather than the similarities between German and English houses in Pennsylvania and have ignored the fact that the entry-kitchen house was associated by period commentators with certain types of people, namely, poor farmers.[18] By examining surviving buildings it becomes clear that entry-kitchen houses were not the only kinds of dwellings being built and occupied by Pennsylvania Germans. As early as the 1740s, Moravians began using closed plans with through-passages when building large community buildings. In the 1750s, prosperous Pennsylvania Germans, such as Peter and Rosina Margaretha Wentz, built center-passage, double-pile houses (see figs. 30–33). Typically students of eighteenth-century domestic architecture have called this type of center-passage house "Georgian" and associated its introduction in America with elite people of British descent. However, Britons were not the only ones to build houses that used so-called Georgian floor plans. German immigrant Johannes Lesher built an early center-passage, double-pile house at Oley Forge in Berks County in the mid-eighteenth century (see figs. 44–47). Nearby, German-Americans Henry and Susanna Fisher began work on a similar, if somewhat more developed, house form as the century came to a close (fig. 94).[19]

The Georgian houses that Pennsylvania Germans built sometimes gave away the ethnic background of their builders. Roofs, for example, could be

Fig. 95 **John and Maria Pfeiffer house, Manheim Township, Lancaster County, Pennsylvania, 1799.** The Pfeiffers built their late eighteenth-century house in brick. Its five symmetrical bays, central door, belt courses, jack-arch lintels, and Flemish bond brickwork contributed to its refined exterior appearance.

framed differently from those on houses built by English carpenters. Or the flooring between the cellar and the first story might be better insulated or the cellar ceiling vaulted. In addition to these often hidden elements, some of the Georgian buildings Pennsylvania Germans constructed incorporated other, more noticeable ethnic features. Prominently placed German-language date stones advertised the national origin of a house's original owners. Inside, a five-plate stove fed from the kitchen fireplace, like that at the Peter and Rosina Margaretha Wentz house, or a freestanding six- or ten-plate stove could also serve as an expression of ethnic background. In many cases, as Pennsylvanians of German descent began to adopt the Georgian house type, they did so in distinct ways. They found ways to combine particularly German attributes within new forms known throughout the Western world.

When the Vernacular Architecture Forum, a group of individuals committed to the study and preservation of everyday buildings, met in Pennsylvania in 2004, its guidebook referred to houses such as the Wentzes' in German as *Durchgangigen,* or through-passage, houses and traced elements of the form to continental Europe. The publication distinguished these "hybrid" houses from other Georgian houses built by Pennsylvania Germans, which did not include a stove-heated room. Readers were told that these buildings, as well as similar structures with a passage running only half the width of the house, had a distinct public/private split with the exterior representing "dominant post-renaissance (or politically 'English') formal styles" and the interior "retaining Germanic formats and behaviors." Yet this description of a "split personality" fails to take into account several factors. On the exterior, the date stones that embellished and labeled all varieties of Pennsylvania German closed-plan houses often included German language phrases in addition to a construction date and male and female householders' names.

Fig. 96 Date stones, John and Maria Pfeiffer house. Two date stones on the Pfeiffer house reflected the Pfeiffers' German heritage and religious devotion. They read, "Er Bauer Von John Pfeiffer Und Maria Pfeiffer 1799" (Built by John Pfeiffer and Maria Pfeiffer 1799) and "Gott Segene Diesen Bau Und Haus und Was da Gehes Ern Und 17 Auf 99" (God bless this building and house and whatever there solemnly rises 1799).

These stones clearly identified the owners of houses such as John and Maria Pfeiffer's 1799 dwelling, which had a very formal, symmetrical façade executed in Flemish bond brickwork with two belt courses between the first and second floors and jack-arch lintels over the windows, as German speakers (figs. 95–96). The surviving 1783 building contract between Christian Hagenbuch and Jacob Kratzer suggests that inside closed-plan houses, Pennsylvania Germans did not necessarily think about or use the spaces differently just because they sometimes opted for fireplace-heated rather than stove-heated rooms. In some cases, a *Stube* could still be a *Stube* without a stove.[20]

In a world that was changing at a rapid pace, the houses that elite Pennsylvania Germans erected reflected the options available to them. One could hire house builders trained in continental Europe or England or America and expect the construction techniques they used to reflect that distinction. One could heat with fireplaces or stoves or a combination of the two. One could design the façade with one date stone, or two date stones, or no date stone. One could even opt for a Georgian house with a façade that included three or four, rather than five, bays across its front. What was required of a "good" house was a closed plan with a distinct entrance and sequestered work space. But even the location of that work space varied. One could situate the kitchen toward the rear of the house, on a lower level, or in a distinct attached or detached building. For this reason, center- and side-passage houses built by Pennsylvanians of German descent in the eighteenth century vary from one to the other. The men and women who desired them were experimenting with a new transatlantic form and adapting it in ways that suited their personal and local needs. There were key spatial elements that had to be included, and others—such as visual symmetry—that were highly desirable, but just how these were put together in a final package was still somewhat variable in the late eighteenth century.

Because these houses combined elements from a variety of sources in innovative ways, the term "creole" is not an improper designation.[21] However, it must be appropriately defined and applied. In the study of communication, the adjective "creole" is used to describe a language that has been derived from another, usually European, language. Often the term is applied to the tongues used by "Creoles," or people of European descent born and raised in a colonial environment. Because of its derivative nature, a creole language is often perceived as marginal or even inferior to its parent language. In the study of architecture, the term "creole" has likewise been applied to derivative structures, especially in colonial Louisiana. There the term has additionally come to symbolize a mixture of various European, African, and Native American traditions.[22]

To apply to the houses erected by affluent Pennsylvania Germans, the term "creole" must be stripped of its derivative, and assimilative, connotations

Fig. 97 **Ten-plate stove, Henry William Stiegel, Elizabeth Furnace, Elizabeth Township, Lancaster County, Pennsylvania, 1769.** The front plate of this stove included, within a rococo surround, the image from Aesop's fable of a dog admiring his reflection in the water. The Steigel stove is in the collection of the Hershey Museum.

and be understood to refer to a new regional style that is widely accepted by people belonging to a number of different groups. Ira Berlin, in a study of the lives of Africans and African Americans before slavery became an institution in the American South, has used the phrase "Atlantic creole" to refer to people who bridged the continents of Africa, Europe, and the Americas with fluency in commerce, multiple languages, cultures, and traditions. In Berlin's words, "they were cosmopolitan in the fullest sense of the word."[23] In Pennsylvania, that same kind of cosmopolitan, or creole, culture developed in the late eighteenth century among people from various European backgrounds, who from the beginning shared more culture traditions than Berlin's subjects.

The Pennsylvania barn is but one example of a form that resulted from a mixing of multiple ethnic influences. Robert Ensminger has convincingly

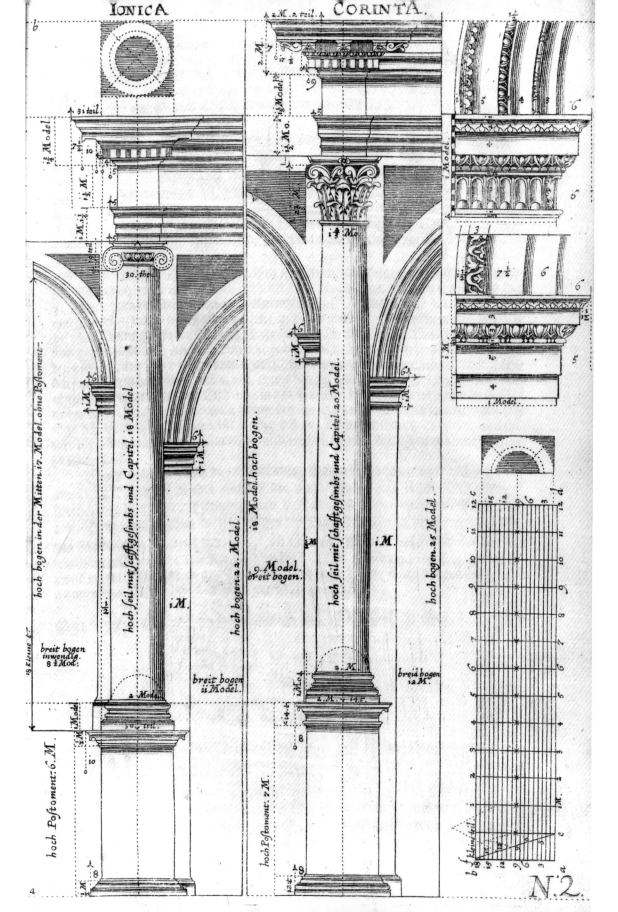

IONICA   CORINTA.

N.2

demonstrated that the two-story bank barn form with an overhanging forebay on the long downhill side developed on the continent, specifically in Switzerland, but also had roots in the Lake District of northwestern England. Hence, in Pennsylvania, it appeared in various permutations in areas where German speakers lived and in areas where people of English descent resided. While period commentators like Rush associated multiuse bank barns specifically with Pennsylvanian Germans, new forms were already evolving by the close of the eighteenth century that brought together elements derived from both continental and English building traditions. While some new barns continued to resemble Swiss models and others more closely reflected English prototypes, several barn types came to represent "the fusion of English and Pennsylvania-German barn forms."[24]

European settlers in Pennsylvania developed building types that could be easily understood and appreciated by one another. In barn design, with an increase in commercial farming, Pennsylvanians of all ethnic backgrounds adopted and adapted multistory, multiuse barns that provided more storage and stabling space.[25] In their houses, as distinct entries, separate work spaces, symmetrical façades, and areas for display and entertaining became desirable among elite Pennsylvanians, a suitable house form emerged. The resulting center- and side-passage houses were understood to be symbols of social and economic status regardless of whether they were heated by stoves or fireplaces or embellished with date stones in the German or English language. They were creole buildings in that as a group they responded to the needs of the multiethnic stratified society of eighteenth-century Pennsylvania. While some may have been more "English" and others more "German" in orientation, they had enough elements in common to be recognizable across ethnic boundaries.

The term "German-Georgian" can also be used to describe a center- or side-passage house fashioned by a Pennsylvania German. Such buildings did fuse certain ethnic characteristics that were found in more traditional German and German-American house forms with Georgian features such as symmetrical façades, center or side passages, formal rooms specifically designed for entertainment purposes, and more secluded work spaces such as kitchens. However, the term "Georgian" should not be understood as a synonym for English or British. Instead of signifying the assimilation of German immigrants and their descendants, the construction of a Georgian house primarily served as a means to express elite social and economic status. In terms of ethnic attributes, many of the Georgian houses built by Pennsylvania Germans were undeniably German. They were "German-Georgian" in the same way that center- and side-passage houses built by people of English descent were "English-Georgian." The buildings simultaneously served as symbols of both affluence and ethnic background.

Fig. 99 **House owned by Abraham Brower and occupied by Philip Seltzer in 1798, East Coventry Township, Chester County, Pennsylvania, before 1798. Like many late eighteenth-century dwellings, this one-story log house was assessed in 1798 at less than $200. Photograph courtesy of Thomas Batchelor.**

Moving from architecture to objects, the same type of experimentation with new cosmopolitan styles associated with elevated status as well as more traditional ethnic aesthetics is also apparent. Stoves made in the second half of the eighteenth century, for instance, which were still used principally by people of German descent, were often decorated with designs that conformed to the popular styles of the period in which they were made. A ten-plate stove that was cast at Henry William Stiegel's Elizabeth Furnace in Lancaster County in 1769 or shortly thereafter included scrolling acanthus leaves, undulating ribbons, and, amidst a fanciful rococo cartouche, a scene from Aesop's fables (fig. 97). Unlike many earlier stoves, which were decorated with Biblical scenes or stylized flowers and other emblems familiar to students of Pennsylvania folk art, this stove and others like it were influenced by sophisticated, academic aesthetics. Because of its function, the object was uniquely ethnic—that is Pennsylvania German—but in its decoration it was overwhelmingly cosmopolitan in design.[26]

The decision to build a Georgian house or use a stove embellished with rococo motifs did not necessarily represent a desire on the part of German immigrants to adopt English aesthetics. In Europe, Germans had long been influenced by the same aesthetic trends in architecture and household furnishings as people living in the British Isles. A seventeenth-century architectural pattern book published in Nuremberg, for instance, demonstrated for German-reading craftsmen the correct uses and proportions for stylish features such as Doric, Ionic, Tuscan, Corinthian, and composite columns (fig. 98). Like English architectural pattern books, the designs in the German example were expressions of a classical revival that had begun in Renaissance Italy.[27] Clearly, not everyone living in the German principalities of Europe had access to the ideas presented in such books or propagated by the artisans who read them. However, the same was true in the British Isles and in the new United States.

Fig. 100 **John Hiester house, East Coventry Township, Chester County, Pennsylvania, c. 1775.** The Hiester house was constructed according to a side-passage, double-pile plan. On the exterior, the dwelling was additionally distinguished by the use of coursed stonework and jack-arch lintels on the façade. In 1798, the house was valued at $1,000, the highest assessment in Coventry Township.

Fig. 101 Plaster ceiling, originally from the George and Magdalena Elizabeth Hehn house (later the residence of Captain Conrad Kershner), Heidelberg Township, Berks County, Pennsylvania, now installed at the Winterthur Museum, 1755. The stove room at the entry-kitchen house built for the Hehns included plastered ceiling designs on both the first and the second floor. The use of such decoration indicates a familiarity with and preference for high-style baroque elements even within an open-plan house. Courtesy of Winterthur Museum.

Just as differences in wealth and status could affect one's knowledge of and desire for classical column designs, they could also affect the very type of house a person chose to inhabit. Most people who lived in Coventry Township in northern Chester County in 1798, for example, lived in small, often one-room log houses, which were valued by tax assessors at $200 or less (fig. 99). On the other hand, a select group of people lived in much larger buildings, which were generally of the side-passage, double-pile variety and assessed in 1798 as high as $1,000 (see figs. 34–35, 100). Their decision to construct Georgian houses, and perhaps purchase certain kinds of stylish household furniture, was one way they could communicate their elevated standing in their community.[28]

Clearly not everyone who achieved a certain level of economic success or social prominence embraced new cosmopolitan aesthetics. Besides social and economic status, other personal attributes clearly affected the choices

people made about the goods they purchased. Inside closed religious communities, most notably Ephrata, members were willing to place limits on material expressions of prosperity. They gave up their personal property and agreed to live a life of austerity, dressing, eating, and living according to the dictates of the community. Outside of these unusual settlements, leaders and members of Anabaptist, Lutheran, and Reformed congregations issued warnings about material excess. By the late eighteenth century, widely accepted Protestant beliefs concerning the value of simplicity, mingled with political and economic condemnations of luxury, caused many Pennsylvanians to reconsider the appropriateness and virtuousness of material display and, more importantly, the behaviors that went with it.

How ethnic background, social and economic status, and religious belief all worked together to influence the kinds of goods a person acquired is hard to determine. Like their twenty-first-century counterparts, the men

Fig. 102 **Clock case, Peter Ranck or Daniel Arnd, before 1817. In addition to the chests for which the Ranck and Seltzer families are known, Peter Ranck was also familiar with more cosmopolitan forms, as this drawing of a case for a tall case clock in his account book demonstrates. Courtesy of the Winterthur Library, Joseph Downs Collection of Manuscripts and Printed Ephemera.**

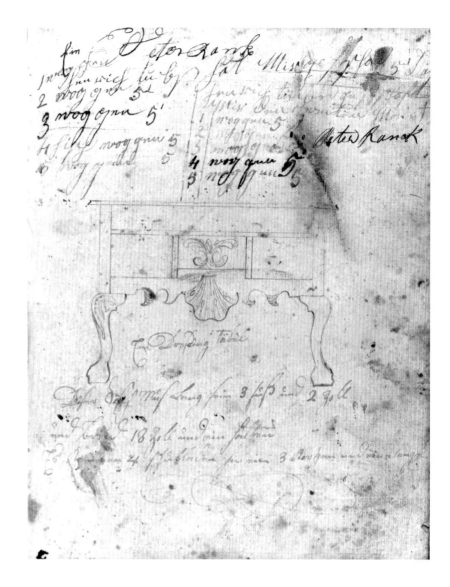

and women who resided in late eighteenth-century Pennsylvania rarely recorded the thought process they went through when making a purchase. What is clear is that by the close of the eighteenth century, Pennsylvania Germans were faced with significant choices when it came to their houses and their household furnishings. The choice between traditional forms and decorative schemes and more cosmopolitan aesthetics was not an either/or proposition.

In 1755, in Heidelberg Township, Berks County, for example, George and Magdalena Elizabeth Hehn built an entry-kitchen house, which on the interior included multiple baroque raised plaster ceilings (fig. 101). Other ceilings embellished with raised plaster decoration were found at the homes of prominent Philadelphia residents such as colonial governor James Hamilton and lawyer William Peters.[29] In South Carolina, a ceiling of similar overall design still exists at plantation owner John Drayton's country estate, Drayton Hall. From a modern perspective, it is surprising that the Hehns incorporated such a high-style element within their presumably ethnic entry-kitchen house. The Hehns, however, apparently did not think the ceiling and the dwelling it was in were inconsistent with one another.

Perhaps the best example of the equivocal nature of aesthetic tastes among Pennsylvania Germans is evidenced by furniture maker Peter Ranck. Ranck was part of the group of Jonestown chest makers and decorators that included Christian and John Seltzer. Peter is unique among members of the group because his account book, which details his business transactions from 1794 to 1817, survives. The ledger indicates that Peter made sixty chests during this period. It also demonstrates that this artisan was familiar with more cosmopolitan furniture styles as well. Either he or a craftsman who owned the book before him filled it with working drawings for tall case clocks, dressing tables, wardrobes, and chests of drawers, which were adorned with carved leaves and shells as well as corner columns, ogee bracket feet, and flame finials (figs. 102–3). While Peter Ranck may be best known today for the brightly painted chests that he inscribed with his name, his knowledge of contemporary furniture styles was much more comprehensive. His account book indicates that his clients could purchase a wide variety of case furniture from him, including desks, corner cupboards, and chests of drawers.[30]

A close study of Pennsylvania German buildings and furnishings reveals the difficulty in definitively assigning objects to categories based on ethnic characteristics. Ethnic cleavages in the late eighteenth-century landscape were rarely as clear-cut as period commentators indicated. Instead, people of German descent, who were faced with multiple choices in regard to their material surroundings, often opted for items or assemblages of items that reflected multiple aspects of their personal identity. While in some cases they selected objects that because of their function and German-language decoration were a direct reflection of their ethnic background, this was not always the case.

By the second half of the eighteenth century, some people of German descent, like some of their non-German neighbors, had begun to turn to new cosmopolitan models for houses and household furnishings. They erected so-called Georgian houses and purchased stylish rococo or neoclassical furnishings as a reflection of their elevated positions within their communities. Their choices did not necessarily signal a rejection of German culture. When people of German descent built houses with symmetrical façades and center passages, they often continued to use both ethnic construction techniques and ethnic heating devices. At some houses they even incorporated date stones written in the German language and decorated with ethnic design elements and color schemes.

Surviving material culture makes it clear that not all Pennsylvanians of German descent lived in the small, poorly furnished houses that period commentators reported seeing as they toured the region's countryside. However, it also indicates that not all rushed to embrace new models either. Some may have been more comfortable with traditional forms, some may have been limited by their financial resources, and still others may have been influenced by religious exhortations against extravagance. The variety of material expressions Pennsylvania Germans chose for themselves and their families suggests the diversity of this ethnic community. Its members had emigrated from numerous central European principalities and spoke several distinct German-based dialects. They were divided by their religious beliefs as well as by their personal piety. They practiced different trades and, in their new homeland, achieved different levels of social and economic prominence. It is therefore not surprising that members of the group opted for objects that varied in design.

In the late eighteenth century, period commentators clearly defined only one segment of this population as "German." Perhaps the Pennsylvania Germans themselves would have come to a similar conclusion. It is more likely, however, that in defining themselves, people of German descent thought about identity on several different levels based on a variety of factors. Eighteenth-century Pennsylvania Germans, like all people, existed as individuals, functioning within multiple communities, which were regularly observed by outsiders. While this work has primarily considered religious identity as created by communities, social and economic identity as fashioned by individuals, and ethnic identity as perceived by outsiders, each was in fact interwoven. Religious communities took into account an individual's status, individuals expressed their ethnic background, and outsiders commented on religious practices and material culture. Still other factors, such as age, gender, familial relationships, skills, livelihood, and length of settlement, also affected the way Pennsylvania Germans defined themselves and were defined by others.

As people of German descent built the closed-plan Georgian houses with which this study has been primarily concerned, they were expressing their place in the world. As individuals, they fit within several communities, defined by such factors as geography, background, belief, and wealth, and they were regularly observed by people who were not like them either because they were of a different class, different faith, different heritage, or different place. The material environments they fashioned had to take all these layers of identity into account. Houses and household goods represented choices that men and women made as they decided how to portray themselves within their communities and to the wider world.

In recent years, we have acquired a greater understanding of difference among the eighteenth-century residents of what would become the United States. We more fully appreciate communities defined by race, ethnicity, class, gender, and religious belief. Yet this project suggests that in studying personal identity and constructions of otherness, researchers need to be careful not to create categories that are too rigid. In the case of the Pennsylvania Germans, an uncritical acceptance of evidence produced by late eighteenth-century authors, coupled with an emphasis on certain kinds of traditional houses and folk furnishings, has led to a skewed interpretation.

Like eighteenth-century travelers, modern visitors to Pennsylvania bring their own ideas and agendas to the destinations they visit. In the Pennsylvania German countryside, heritage tourism, built around the continued traditional practices of the Old Order Amish, dominates. Travelers come to the area to experience temporarily a "simple" way of life, free from modern technologies and filled with hearty food and handmade goods.[31] Sightseers can take in the "Amish Village," ride in a buggy, eat at numerous smorgasbords, or visit the amusement park Dutch Wonderland, which until recently included the Discover Lancaster County History Museum, featuring an animated Amish barn-raising presentation.[32]

Those modern sightseers who want to learn more about the culture and material culture of German immigrants and their descendants in Pennsylvania might extend their visit to include another museum. However, even at the most prestigious and professional institutions, interpretations of Pennsylvania German life are limited. Historic sites and museum galleries are filled with the types of objects that demonstrate the Pennsylvania Germans' uniqueness among other early American settlers. Some, particularly art museums, treat the material culture of German immigrants and their descendants as folk art. The Philadelphia Museum of Art, which began its Pennsylvania German collection in 1891 with a sgraffito-decorated redware plate, epitomizes this trend in the interpretation of Pennsylvania German material culture.[33] Objects are artistically arranged in galleries and in period-room settings. A catalogue of the collection explains, "The pragmatism and piety of objects made by and for the Pennsylvania German community shine through their overlay of color and wit, setting them apart from the objects produced by and for their Anglo-American neighbors in rural Pennsylvania." In many museums, Pennsylvania German objects are presented as artistic yet utilitarian, fanciful yet reverent, and always ethnically distinct.[34]

Other museums call attention to specific, often numerically small and culturally atypical, segments of the Pennsylvania German population. In Lancaster County the modern museumgoer might choose to visit Ephrata Cloister, one of the best-known Pennsylvania Historical and Museum Commission sites. The former religious community has been attracting curious travelers since its founding in the 1730s. At Ephrata today, visitors can learn about German immigrant Conrad Beissel, the religious community he founded, and the ascetic lifestyle he advocated. At Ephrata, despite staff efforts to make Beissel and his followers relevant to modern museum audiences, their strict dietary regime, distinct clothing, regimented sleep and worship schedule, communal living patterns, and celibate lifestyle seem odd to visitors. This is not surprising, since contemporaries also found the religious practices of Ephrata residents peculiar. In 1772, one clergyman from Philadelphia reported that the "principles and manners" of the Ephrata community were "very singular."[35]

Museums that interpret German-Georgian houses, and other less traditional or culturally distinct objects, have a more difficult time conveying their message to visitors, who often come to the region looking for something unique or outside their own everyday experience. If their message is that these types of objects symbolize the process of giving up ethnic identity, the institutions' difficulty connecting with the public is no wonder, because assimilation is a hard sell in an era that values pluralism. However, if they emphasize how these objects represent choices and balancing various aspects of personal identity, there is more potential for engaging their audience.[36]

It is places like the Peter Wentz Farmstead Historic Site, a property of the Montgomery County Parks and Heritage Services Department; the Henry Melchior Muhlenberg House, a Historical Society of Trappe, Collegeville, Perkiomen Valley, Inc., museum; and the Troxell-Steckel House, a Lehigh County Historical Society historic site, that have the opportunity to connect with the public—not by creating an experience that is divorced from that of the twenty-first-century museumgoer, but by emphasizing the fundamental connections between people of the past and people living today. The idea of simultaneously balancing family, job, and community affiliations is not new. In the late eighteenth century, people of German descent in Pennsylvania also managed multiple roles based on factors including their heritage, their status, and their faith. They communicated their personal identities to those around them and continue to communicate with us today through the material world they constructed.

The late eighteenth century was a period of transition in Pennsylvania and the other British colonies that were becoming the United States. European allegiances were failing, and decisions about the political and cultural nature of the new nation were regularly debated both by residents and outsiders. Amid all the changes, Americans were faced with numerous choices, including those about how to represent themselves outwardly through their material culture. In a region with exceptional ethnic and religious diversity and distinct New World economic and social conditions, Pennsylvanians of German descent used their personal property to align themselves with certain groups and distance themselves from others. Rather than being one-dimensional, Pennsylvania German material culture communicated statements about multiple aspects of personal identity tied to the past, present, and future. It is this dynamic story.about cultural continuity and change that many of the late eighteenth-century buildings and belongings made and used by German immigrants and their descendants best convey to those who encounter them today.

Appendix A

An Account of the Manners of the German Inhabitants of Pennsylvania (1789)

Benjamin Rush

Benjamin Rush's essay "An Account of the Manners of the German Inhabitants of Pennsylvania" has attracted the attention of people interested in the everyday life of German immigrants and their descendants in Pennsylvania since it was written in the late eighteenth century. In 1875, Israel Daniel Rupp reprinted the essay along with his own preface on Benjamin Rush's life, an appendix rebutting a newspaper article criticizing the character of the Pennsylvania Germans, and numerous notes on the content of Rush's account.[1] While Rupp made only minor changes to the text of Rush's work—generally only updating spelling and punctuation, fixing verb tenses, and correcting printing errors—it is sometimes difficult to tell where Rush's voice ends and Rupp's starts.

Rupp's version of "An Account of the German Inhabitants of Pennsylvania" has been reprinted several times, including in 1910 by the Pennsylvania German Society in the nineteenth volume of its *Proceedings and Addresses.* That reprinting provides important information about interpretations of Pennsylvania German life in both the latter part of nineteenth century, as well as in 1789. This transcription returns to Rush's version of the text, published in the January 1789 edition of the *Columbian Magazine,* before Rupp added his notes and annotations. While the modern letter "s" is used in place of Rush's "*f,*" other spellings, usages, and even typographical errors are left as in the original.

An Account of the Manners of the German Inhabitants of Pennsylvania

THE state of Pennsylvania is so much indebted for her prosperity and reputation, to the German part of her citizens, that a short account of their manners may, perhaps, be useful and agreeable to their fellow citizens in every part of the United States.

The aged Germans, and the ancestors of those who are young, migrated chiefly from the Palatinate; from Alsace, Swabia, Saxony, and Switzerland; but natives of every principality and dukedom, in Germany, are to be found in different parts of the state. They brought but little property with them. A few pieces of gold or silver coin, a chest filled with clothes, a bible, and a prayer or an hymn book, constituted the whole stock of most of them. Many of them bound themselves, or one or more of their children, to masters, after their arrival, for four, five, or seven years, in order to pay for their passages across the ocean. A clergyman always accompanied them when they came in large bodies.

The principal part of them were farmers; but there were many mechanics, who brought with them a knowledge of those arts which are necessary and useful in all countries. These mechanics were chiefly weavers, taylors, tanners, shoe-makers, comb-makers, smiths of all kinds, butchers, bakera, paper-makers, watch makers, and sugar-bakers. I shall begin this account of the German inhabitants of Pennsylvania, by describing the manners of the German farmers.

This body of citizens are not only industrious and frugal, but skilful cultivators of the earth. I shall enumerate a few particulars, in which they differ from most of the other farmers of Pennsylvania.

1st. In settling a tract of land, they always provide large and suitable accommodations for their horses and cattle, before they lay out much money in building a house for themselves. The barn and the stables are generally under one roof, and contrived in such a manner as to enable them to feed their horses and cattle, and to remove their dung, with as little trouble as possible. The first dwelling house upon this farm is small, and built of logs. It generally lasts the life time of the first settler of a tract of land; and hence they have a saying, that "a son should always begin his improvements where his father left off,"—that is, by building a large and convenient stone house.

2d. They always prefer good land, or that land on which there is a large quantity of meadow ground. From an attention to the cultivation of grass, they often double the value of an old farm in a few years, and grow rich on farms, on which their predecessors of whom they purchased them, have nearly starved. They prefer purchasing farms with some improvements, to settling on a new tract of land.

3d. In clearing new land, they do not girdle the trees simply, and leave them to perish in the ground, as is the custom of their English or Irish neighbours; but they generally cut them down and burn them. In destroying underwood and bushes, they generally grub them out of the ground; by which means a field is as fit for cultivation the second year after it is cleared, as it is in twenty years afterwards. The advantages of this mode of clearing, consist in the immediate product of the field, and in the greater facility with which it is ploughed harrowed and reaped. The expense of repairing a plough, which is often broken two or three times in a year by small stumps concealed in the ground, is often greater than the extraordinary expense of grubbing the same field completely, in clearing it.

4th. They feed their horses and cows, of which they keep only a small number, in such a manner, that the former perform twice the labour of those horses, and the latter yield twice the quantity of milk of those cows, that are less plentifully fed. There is great economy in this practice, especially in a country where so much of the labour of a farmer is necessary to support his domestic animals. A German horse is known in every part of the state: indeed he seems to "feel with his lord, the pleasure and the pride" of his extraordinary size or fat.

5th. The fences of a German farm are generally high, and well built; so that his fields seldom suffer from the inroads of his own, or his neighbours, horses, cattle, hogs, or sheep.

6th. The German farmers are great economists of their *wood*. Hence they burn it only in stoves, in which they consume but a 4th. or 5th. part of what is commonly burnt in ordinary open fire places: Besides, their horses are saved, by means of this economy, from that immense labour, in hauling wood in the middle of winter, which frequently unfits the horses of their neighbours for the toils of the ensuing spring. Their houses are, moreover, rendered so comfortable, at all times, by large close stoves, that twice the business is done by every branch of the family, in knitting, spinning, and mending farming utensils, that is done in houses where every member of the family crouds near to a common fire-place, or shivers at a distance from it,—with hands and fingers that move, by reason of the cold, with only half their usual quickness.

They discover economy in the preservation and increase of their wood in several other ways. They sometimes defend it, by high fences, from their cattle; by which means the young forest trees are suffered to grow, to replace those that are cut down for the necessary use of the farm. But where this cannot be conveniently done, they surround the stump of that tree which is most useful for fences, viz. the chestnut, with a small triangular fence. From this stump a number of suckers shoot out in a few years, two or three of which, in the course of five and twenty years, grow into trees of the same size as the tree from whose roots they derived their origin.

7th. They keep their horses and cattle as warm as possible in winter, by which means they save a great deal of their hay and grain; for those animals, when cold, eat much more than when they are in a more comfortable situation.

8th. The German farmers live frugally in their families, with respect to diet, furniture and apparel. They sell their most profitable grain, which is wheat; and eat that which is less profitable, but more nourishing, that is rye or Indian corn. The profit to a farmer, from this single article of economy, is equal, in the course of a life time, to the price of a farm for one of his children. They eat sparingly of *boiled* animal food, with large quantities of vegetables, particularly with sallad, turneps, onions, and cabbage, the last of which they make into *sour crout*. They likewise use a large quantity of milk and cheese in their diet. Perhaps the Germans do not proportion the quantity of their animal food, to the degrees of their labour; hence it has been thought, by some people, that they decline in strength sooner than their English or Irish neighbours. Very few of them ever use distilled spirits in their families: their common drinks are cyder, beer, wine, and simple water. The furniture of their house is plain and useful. They cover themselves in winter with light feather beds instead of blankets: in this contrivance there is both convenience and economy, for the beds are warmer than blankets, and they are made by themselves. The apparel of the German farmers is usually *homespun*. When they use European articles of dress, they prefer those which are of the best quality, and of the highest price. They are afraid of debt, and seldom purchase any thing without paying cash for it.

9th. The German farmers have large or profitable gardens near their houses. These contain little else but useful vegetables. Pennsylvania is indebted to the Germans for the principal part of her knowledge in horticulture. There was a time when turneps and cabbage were the principal vegetables that were used in diet by the citizens of Philadelphia. This will not surprize those persons, who know that the first English settlers in Pennsylvania, left England while horticulture was in its infancy in that country. It was not 'till the reign of William III. that this useful and agreeable art was cultivated by the English nation. Since the settlement of a number of German gardeners in the neighbourhood of Philadelphia, the tables of all classes of citizens have been covered with a variety of vegetables, in every season of the year; and to the use of these vegetables, in diet, may be ascribed the general exemption of the citizens of Philadelphia from diseases of the skin.

10th. The Germans seldom *hire* men to work upon their farms. The feebleness of that authority which masters possess over hired servants, is such that their wages are seldom procured from their labour, except in harvest, when they work in the presence of their masters. The wives and daughters of the German farmers frequently forsake, for a while, their dairy and spinning-wheel, and join their husbands and brothers in the labour of cutting down, collecting and bringing home the fruits of the fields and orchards. The work of the gardens is generally done by the women of the family.

11th. A large and strong waggon, covered with linen cloth, is an essential part of the furniture of a German farm. In this waggon, drawn by four or five large horses of a peculiar breed, they convey to market over the roughest roads, between 2 or 3 thousand pounds weight of the produce of their farms. In the months of september and october, it is no uncommon thing, on the Lancaster and Reading roads, to meet in one day from fifty to an hundred of these waggons, on their way to Philadelphia, most of which belong to German farmers.

12th. The favourable influence of agriculture, as conducted by the Germans in extending human happiness, is manifested by the joy they express upon the birth of a child. No dread of poverty, nor distrust of providence from an encreasing family, depress the spirits of these industrious and frugal people. Upon the birth of a son, they exult in the gift of a ploughman or a waggoner; and upon the birth of a daughter, they rejoice in the addition of another spinster, or milk-maid, to their family. Happy state of human society! what blessings can civilization confer, that can atone for the extinction of the ancient and patriarchal pleasure of raising up a numerous and healthy family of children, to labour for their parents, for themselves, and for their country; and finally to partake of the knowledge and happiness which are annexed to existence! The joy of parents upon the birth of a child, is the grateful echo of creating goodness. May the mountains of Pennsylvania be for ever vocal, with songs of joy upon these occasions! They will be the infallible signs of innocence, industry, wealth and happiness in the state.

15th. The Germans take great pains to produce, in their children, not only *habits* of labour, but a *love* of it. In this they submit to the irreversible sentence inflicted upon man, in such a manner, as to convert the wrath of heaven into a private and public happiness. "To fear God, and to love work," are the first lessons they teach their children. They prefer industrious habits to money itself; hence, when a young man asks the consent of his father to marry the girl of his choice, he does not enquire so much whether she be rich or poor? or whether she possess any personal or mental accomplishments—as whether she be industrious, and acquainted with the duties of a good house-wife?

14th. The Germans set a great value upon patrimonial property. This useful principle in human nature prevents much folly and vice in young people. It moreover leads to lasting and extensive advantages, in the improvement of a farm; for what inducement can be stronger in a parent to plant an orchard, to preserve forest-trees, or to build a commodious and durable house, than the idea, that they will all be possessed by a succession of generations, who shall inherit his blood and name.

15th. The German farmers are very much influenced in planting and pruning trees, also in sowing and reaping, by the age and appearances of the moon. This attention to the state of the moon has been ascribed to superstition; but if the facts related by mr. Wilson in his observations upon climates are true, part of their success in agriculture must be ascribed to their being so much influenced by it.

16th. From the history that has been given of the German agriculture, it will hardly be necessary to add, that a German farm may be distinguished from the farms of the other citizens of the state, by the superior size of their barns; the plain, but compact form of their houses; the height of their enclosures; the extent of their orchards; the fertility of their fields; the luxuriance of their meadows, and a general appearance of plenty and neatness in every thing that belonged to them.

The German mechanic possesses some of the traits of the character that has been drawn of the German farmer. His first object is to become a freeholder; and hence we find few of them live in rented houses. The highest compliment that can be paid to them on entering their houses, is to ask them, 'is this house your own?' They are industrious, frugal, punctual and just. Since their settlement in Pennsylvania, many of them have acquired a knowledge of those mechanical arts, which are more immediately necessary and useful in a new country; while they continue at the same time, to carry on the arts they imported from Germany, with vigour and success.

But the genius of the Germans of Pennsylvania is not confined to agriculture and the mechanical arts. Many of them have acquired great wealth by foreign and domestic commerce. As merchants they are candid and punctual. The bank of North America has witnessed, from its first institution, their fidelity to all their pecuniary engagements.

Thus far have I described the *individual* character of several orders of the German citizens of Pennsylvania. I shall now take notice of some of their manners in a collective capacity.

All the different sects among them are particularly attentive to the religious education of their children, and to the establishment and support of the christian religion. For this purpose they settle as much as possible together—and make the erection of a school house and a place of worship the first objects of their care. They commit the education and instruction of their children in a peculiar manner to the ministers and officers of their churches;—hence they grow up with prejudices in favour of public worship, and of the obligations of christianity. Such has been the influence of a pious education among the Germans lutherans in Pennsylvania, that in the course of nineteen years, only one of them has ever been brought to a place of public shame or punishment.

As members of civil government, the Germans are peaceable,—and exact in the payment of their taxes. Since they have participated in the power of the state, many of them have become sensible and enlightened in the science of legislation. Pennsylvania has had the speaker's chair of her assembly, and the vice-president's office of her council, filled with dignity by gentlemen of German families. The same gentlemen have since been advanced to seats in the house of representatives, under the new constitution of the United States. In the great controversy about the national government, a large majority of the Germans in Pennsylvania decided in favor of its adoption, notwithstanding the most popular arts were used to prejudice them against it.

The Germans are but little addicted to convivial pleasures.

They seldom meet for the simple purpose of eating and drinking in what are justly called 'feeding parties'; but they are not strangers to the virtue of hospitality.—The hungry or benighted traveller is always sure to find a hearty welcome under their roofs. A gentleman of Irish extraction, who lost his way in travelling through Lancaster county, called late at night at the door of a German farmer: he was kindly received and entertained with the best of everything the house afforded. The next morning, he offered to pay his host for his lodging, and other accommodations: 'No' said the friendly German, in broken English—'I will take nothing from you. I was once lost, and entertained, as you have been, at the house of a stranger who would take no pay from me for his trouble. I am therefore now only discharging that debt:—do you pay your debt to me in the same way to somebody else.'—

They are extremely kind and friendly as neighbours. They often assist each other by loans of money for a short time, without interest—when the purchase of a plantation makes a larger sum necessary than is commonly possessed by a single farmer. To secure their confidence, it is necessary to be punctual. They never lend money a second time, to a man who has once disappointed them in paying what he had borrowed agreeably to his promise or obligation. It was remarked, during the late war, that there were very few instances of any of them discharging a bond, or a debt, with depreciated paper money.

It has been said, that the Germans are deficient in learning; and that in consequence of their want of more general and extensive education, they are much addicted to superstition, and are frequently imposed upon in the management of their affairs. Many of them have lost valuable estates, by being unacquainted with the common forms of law, in the most simple transactions; and many more of them have lost their lives, by applying to quacks in sickness: But this objection to the Germans will soon cease to have any foundation in Pennsylvania. Several young men, born of German parents, have been educated in law, physic and divinity, who have demonstrated by their abilities and knowledge, that the German genius for literature has not depreciated in America. A college has lately been founded by the state in

Lancaster,* and committed chiefly to the care of the Germans of all sects, for the purpose of diffusing learning among their children. In this college they are to be taught the German and English languages, and all those branches of literature which are usually taught in the colleges of Europe and America. The principal of this college is a native of Pennsylvania, of German parentage. His extensive knowledge and taste in the arts and sciences, joined with his industry in the discharge of the duties of his station, have afforded to the friends of learning in Pennsylvania, the most flattering prospects of the future importance and usefulness of this institution.

Both sexes of the Germans discover a strong propensity to vocal and instrumental music. They excel, in psalmody, all the other religious societies in the state.

The freedom and toleration of the government has produced a great variety of sects, among the Germans in Pennsylvania. The Lutherans compose a great proportion of the German citizens of the state. Many of their churches are large and splendid. The German Presbyterians are the next to them in numbers. Their churches are likewise large, and furnished, in many places, with organs. The clergy, belonging to these churches, have moderate salaries, but they are punctually and justly paid. In the country they have glebes, which are stocked and occasionally worked by their congregations. The extra expences of their ministers, in all their excursions to their ecclesiastical meetings, are borne by their respective congregations: by this means the discipline and the general interests of their churches are preserved and promoted. The German Lutherans and Presbyterians live in great harmony with each other; insomuch that they often preach in each other's churches, and, in some instances, unite in building a church, in which they both worship at different times. This harmony between two sects, once so much opposed to each other, is owing to the relaxation of the Presbyterians in some of the peculiar doctrines of Calvinism. I have called them Presbyterians, because most of them object to being designated by the name of Calvinists. The Menonists, the Moravians, the Swingfielders, and the Catholics, compose the other sects of the German inhabitants of Pennsylvania. The Menonists hold war and oaths to be unlawful. They admit the sacraments of baptism, by *sprinkling,* and the supper. From them a sect has arisen, who hold, with the above principles and ceremonies, the necessity of *immersion* in baptism; hence they are called *Dunkers,* or Baptists. Previously to their partaking of the sacrament of the supper, they wash each other's feet, and set down to a love-feast. They practise these ceremonies of their religion with great humility and solemnity. They, moreover, hold the doctrine of universal salvation. From this sect there

* This college is called after dr. FRANKLIN, who was president of the state at the time it was founded, and who contributed very liberally to its funds.

have been several seceders, one of whom devoted themselves to perpetual celibacy. They have exhibited, for many years, a curious spectacle of pious mortification, at a village called Ephrata, in Lancaster county. They are at present reduced to fourteen or fifteen members. The *Separatists,* who likewise dissented from the Dunkers, reject the ordinances of baptism and the sacrament; and hold the doctrine of the *Friends,* concerning the internal revelation of the gospel. They hold, with the Dunkers, the doctrine of universal salvation. The singular piety and exemplary morality of these sects, have been urged, by the advocates for the salvation of all mankind, as a proof that the belief of that doctrine is not so unfriendly to morals, and the order of society, as has been supposed. The Dunkers and Separatists agree in taking no interest upon money, and in not applying to law to recover their debts.

The German Moravians are a numerous and respectable body of christians in Pennsylvania. In their village of Bethlehem, there are two large stone buildings, in which the different sexes are educated in habits of industry in useful manufactures. The sisters (for by that epithet the women are called) all sleep in two large and neat apartments. Two of them watch over the rest, in turns, every night, to afford relief from those sudden indispositions which sometimes occur, in the most healthy persons, in the hours of sleep. It is impossible to record this fact, without pausing a moment to do homage to that religion, which produces so much union and kindness in human souls. The number of women who belong to this sequestered female society, amounts sometimes to 120, and seldom to less than 100. It is remarkable that notwithstanding they lead a sedentary life, and sit constantly in close stove-rooms in winter, that not more than one of them, upon an average, dies in a year. The disease which generally produces this annual death, is the consumption. The conditions and ages of the women of the village, as well as of the society that has been mentioned, are distinguished by ribbands of a peculiar kind which they wear on their caps: the widows, by white; the married women, by blue; the single women, above 18 years of age, by pink; and those under that age, by a ribband of a cinnamon colour. Formerly this body of Moravians held all their property in common, in imitation of the primitive christians; but, in the year 1760, a division of the whole of it took place, except a tavern, a tan-yard, 2000 acres of land near Bethlehem, and 5000 acres near Nazareth, a village in the neighbourhood of Bethlehem. The profits of these estates are appropriated to the support and propagation of the gospel. There are many valuable manufactures carried on at Bethlehem. The inhabitants possess a gentleness in their manners, which is peculiarly agreeable to strangers. They inure their children, of five and six years old, to habits of early industry. By this means they are not only taught those kinds of labour which are suited to their strength and capacities, but are preserved from many of the hurtful vices and accidents to which children are exposed.

The Swingfielders are a small society. They hold the same principles as the Friends, but they differ from them in using psalmody in their worship.

The German Catholics are numerous in Philadelphia, and have several small chapels in other parts of the state.

There is an incorporated charitable society of Germans in Philadelphia, whose objects are their poor or distressed countrymen.

There is likewise a German society of labourers and journeymen mechanics, who contribute 2s. 6d. eight times a year, towards a fund, out of which they allow 30s. a week to each other's families, when the head of it is unable to work; and 7l. 10s. to his widow, as soon as he is taken from his family by death.

The Germans of Pennsylvania, including all the sects that have been mentioned, compose nearly one third part of the whole inhabitants of the state.

The intercourse of the Germans with each other, is kept up chiefly in their own language; but most of their men, who visit the capital, and the trading or county towns of the state, speak the English language. A certain number of the laws of the state are now printed in German, for the benefit of those of them who cannot read English. A large number of German newspapers are likewise circulated through the state; by which knowledge and intelligence have been diffused, much to the advantage of the government. There is scarcely an instance of a German, of either sex, in Pennsylvania, that cannot read; but many of the wives and daughters of the German farmers cannot write. The present state of society among them renders this accomplishment of little consequence to their improvement or happiness.

If it were possible to determine the amount of all the property brought into Pennsylvania by the present German inhabitants of the state, and their ancestors, and then compare it with the present amount of their property, the contrast would form such a monument of human INDUSTRY and ECONOMY as has seldom been contemplated in any age or country.

I have been informed that there was an ancient prophecy which foretold, that 'God would bless the Germans 'in foreign countries.' This prediction has been faithfully verified in Pennsylvania. They enjoy here every blessing that liberty, toleration, independence, affluence, virtue and reputation, can confer upon them.

How different is their situation here, from what it was in Germany! Could the subjects of the princes of Germany, who now groan away their lives in slavery and unprofitable labour, view from an eminence, in the month of June, the German settlements of Stratsburg, or Manheim in Lancaster county, or of Lebanon or Bethlehem in the counties of Dauphin and Northampton; could they be accompanied on this eminence by a venerable German farmer, and be told by him that many of those extensive fields of grain, full-fed herds, luxuriant meadows, orchards promising loads of fruit, together with the spacious barns and commodious stone-dwelling houses, which compose the prospects that have been mentioned, were all the product of the labour of a single family, and of *one* generation; and that they were all secured to the owners of them by *certain* laws; I am persuaded that no chains would be but able to detain them from sharing in the freedom of their Pennsylvania friends and former fellow-subjects. 'We will assert our dignity'—(would be their language)—'we will be men—we will be free—we will enjoy the fruits of our own labours—we will no longer be bought and sold to fight battles in which we have neither interest nor resentment—we will inherit a portion of that blessing which God has promised to the Germans in foreign countries— we will be Pennsylvanians'.

I shall conclude this account of the manners of the German inhabitants of Pennsylvania by remarking that if I have failed in doing them justice, it has not been the fault of my subject. The German character once employed the pen of one of the first historians of antiquity.—I mean the elegant and enlightened Tacitus. It is very remarkable that the Germans in Pennsylvania retain in a great degree all the virtues which this author ascribes to their ancestors in his treatise '*de moribus Germanorum.*'—They inherit their integrity—fidelity—and chastity—but christianity has banished from them, their drunkenness, idleness, and love of military glory. There is a singular trait in the features of the German character in Pennsylvania, which shews how long the most trifling custom may exist among a people who have not been mixed with other nations. Tacitus describes the manner in which the ancient Germans built their villages, in the following words. '*Suam quisque domum spatiis circumdat sive adversus casus ignis remedium, sive inscitia ædificandi.*' Many of the German villages in Pennsylvania are constructed in the same manner: the small houses are composed of a mixture, of wood, brick and clay, neatly united together; the large houses are built of stone, and many of them after the English fashion. Very few of the houses in Germantown are connected together.—Where the Germans connect their houses in their villages, they appear to have deviated from one of the customs they imported from Germany.

CITIZENS of the United States! learn from the account that has been given of the German inhabitants of Pennsylvania, to prize knowledge and industry in agriculture and manufactures, as the basis of domestic happiness and national prosperity.

LEGISLATORS of the United-States! learn from the wealth, and independence of the German inhabitants of Pennsylvania, to encourage by your example and laws the republican virtues of industry and economy.—They are the only pillars which can support the present constitution of the United States.

LEGISLATORS of Pennsylvania! learn from the history of your German fellow citizens that you possess an inexhaustible treasure in the bosom of the state, in their manners and arts. Continue to patronize their newly established seminary of learning, and spare no expense in supporting their public free-schools. The vices which follow the want of religious instruction, among the children of poor people, lay the foundation of most of the jails, and places of public punishment in the state. Do not contend with their prejudices in favour of their language: it will be the channel through which the knowledge and discoveries of one of the wisest nations in Europe, may be conveyed into our country. In proportion as they are instructed and enlightened in their own language, they will become acquainted with the language of the United States. Invite them to share in the power and offices of government: it will be the means of producing an union in principle and conduct between them, and those of their enlightened fellow-citizens who are descended from other nations. Above all, cherish with peculiar tenderness, those sects among them who hold war to be unlawful.—Relieve them from the oppression of absurd and unnecessary militia laws. Protect them as the repositories of a truth of the gospel, which has existed in every age of the church, and which must spread hereafter over every part of the world.

The opinions respecting the commerce and slavery of the Africans, which have nearly produced a revolution in their favour, in some of the European governments, were transplanted from a sect of christians in Pennsylvania. Perhaps those German sects of christians among us, who refuse to bear arms for the purpose of shedding human blood, may be preserved by divine providence, as the centre of a circle, which shall gradually embrace all the nationa of the earth in a perpetual treaty of friendship and peace.

Appendix B

Progress of Cultivation in Pennsylvania (1792)

Jacques-Pierre Brissot de Warville

In November 1786, Benjamin Rush published an essay entitled "An Account of the Progress of Population, Agriculture, Manners, and Government in Pennsylvania" in the *Columbian Magazine*. Jacques-Pierre Brissot de Warville was one of several authors who printed later versions of the essay. Brissot's first appeared as letter 28 in the Paris edition of his work *Nouveau Voyage dans les États-Unis de L'Amérique Septentrionale, Fait en 1788*. The transcription below is taken from letter 26 of the English-language edition published in Dublin in 1792.[1] The notes by the original translator are included with the text.

Brissot's interpretation differs from Rush's in that it states that the third and highest class of settlers in Pennsylvania was largely composed of Germans. Rush had made no mention of the European heritage of the various classes. Brissot also added to Rush's essay by ending the 1791 French edition of his letter with advice to Frenchmen who planned to immigrate to the United States. That portion of the text was eliminated from the Dublin edition, and so the text ends abruptly with a brief discussion of taxes in Pennsylvania.

Progress of Cultivation in Pennsylvania

HITHERTO, my friend, we have spoken only of farms already in good culture, and in the neighbourhood of towns. We must now penetrate farther, descend into the midst of the wilderness, and observe the man, detached from society, with his axe in his hand, felling the venerable oak, that had been respected by the savage, and supplying its place with the humble spire of corn. We must follow this man in his progress, observe the changes that his cabin undergoes, when it becomes the center of twenty other cabins which rise successively round it. An American farmer has communicated to me the principal traits of the rural picture which I am going to lay before you. The first planter,* or he who begins a settlement in the woods, is generally a man who has lost his fortune and his credit in the cultivated part of the state. He emigrates in the month of April. His first work is to build a little cabin for himself and family; the roof is of rough hewn wood, the floor of earth. It is lighted by the door, or sometimes by a little window with oiled paper. A more wretched building adjoining it gives shelter to a cow and two miserable horses. This done, he attacks the trees that surround his cabin. To extirpate them by the root, would require too much labour. He contents himself by cutting them at two or three feet from the ground. The space thus cleared is then plowed, and planted with Indian corn. The soil, being new, requires little culture; in the month of October it yields a harvest of forty or fifty bushels the acre. Even from the month of September, this corn furnishes a plentiful and agreeable nourishment to his family. Hunting and fishing, with a little grain, suffice, during the winter, for the subsistence of his family; while the cow and horses of our planter feed on the poor wild grass, or the buds of trees. During the first year, he suffers much from cold and hunger; but he endures it without repining. Being near the savages, he adopts their manners; his fatigue is violent, but it is suspended by long intervals of repose: his pleasures consist in fishing and hunting; he loves spirituous liquors; he eats, drinks, and sleeps in the filth of his little cabin.

Thus roll away the first three years of our planter in laziness, independence, the variation of pleasure, and of labour. But population augments in

---

* As the translator recollects to have seen this fanciful description many times published in America, he was less anxious in re-translating it, to flatter the original author, by retaining all his ideas, than he was to save the credit of M. de Warville, by abridging the piece. Credulity is indeed a less fault in a traveller than prejudice; but it ought, however, to be corrected. Accounts like this put one in mind of Dr. Franklin's romance of *Mary Baker,* so religiously believed and copied by the Abbé Raynal, in his History of the Two Indies.

his neighbourhood, and then his troubles begin. His cattle could before run at large; but now his neighbours force him to retain them within his little farm. Formerly the wild beasts gave subsistence to his family; they now fly a country which begins to be peopled by men, and consequently by enemies. An increasing society brings regulations, taxes, and the parade of laws; and nothing is so terrible to our independent planter as all these shackles. He will not consent to sacrifice a single natural right for all the benefits of government; he abandons then his little establishment, and goes to seek a second retreat in the wilderness, where he can recommence his labours, and prepare a farm for cultivation. Such are the charms of independence, that many men have begun the clearing of farms four times in different parts of this State.

It has been remarked, that the preaching of the Gospel always drives off men of this class. And it is not surprising if we consider how much its precepts are opposed to the licentiousness of their manner of life. But the labour bestowed by the first planter gives some value to the farm, which now comes to be occupied by a man of the second class of planters. He begins by adding to his cabin a house. A saw-mill in the neighbouring settlement, furnishes him with boards. His house is covered with shingles, and is two stories high. He makes a little meadow, plants an orchard of two or three hundred apple-trees. His stable is enlarged; he builds a spacious barn of wood, and covers it with rye-straw. Instead of planting only Indian corn, he cultivates wheat and rye; the last is destined to make whisky. But this planter manages ill; his fields are badly plowed, never manured, and give but small crops. His cattle break through his fences, destroy his crops, and often cut off the hopes of the year. His horses are ill fed, and feeble; his cattle often die with hunger in the Spring; his house and his farm give equal proofs of the want of industry; the glass of his windows has given place to old hats and rags. This man is fond of company; he drinks to excess; passes much of his time in disputing about politics. Thus he contracts debts, and is forced, after some years, to sell his plantation to a planter of the third and last class.

This is ordinarily a man of property, and of a cultivated mind. His first object is to convert into meadow all his land, on which he can conduct water. He then builds a barn of stone, sometimes a hundred feet in length, and forty in breadth. This defends his cattle from cold, and they eat less when kept warm, than when exposed to the frost. To spare the consumption of fuel, he makes use of economical stoves, and by this he saves immense labour in cutting and carting wood. He multiplies the objects of culture; besides corn, wheat, and rye, he cultivates oats and buck-wheat. Near his house he forms a garden of one or two acres, which gives him quantities of cabbage, potatoes, and turnips. Near the spring which furnishes him with water, he builds a dairy-house. He augments the number, and improves the quality of his fruit-trees. His sons are always at work by his side; his wife and daughter quit their wheels for the labour of the harvest. The last object of industry is to build a house for his own use. This building is generally of stone; it is vast, well distributed, and well furnished. His horses and cattle, by their good appearance, their strength, and fecundity, prove that they are well fed, and well attended. His table abounds with delicate and various dishes. His kitchen flows with milk and honey. The ordinary drink of his family, is beer, cyder, and wine; his wife and daughters manufacture their cloathing. In proportion as he grows rich, he perceives the value of the protection of the laws; he pays his taxes with punctuality; he contributes to the support of churches and schools, as the only means of insuring order and tranquillity.

Two-thirds of the farmers of Pennsylvania belong to this third class. It is to them that the State owes its ancient reputation and importance. If they have less of cunning than their neighbours of the South, who cultivate their lands by slaves, they have more of the republican virtues. It was from their farms that the American and French armies were principally supplied during the last war; it was from their produce that came those millions of dollars brought from the Havanna after the year 1780—millions which laid the foundation of the bank of North-America, and supported the American army till the peace.

This is a feeble sketch of the happiness of a Pennsylvania farmer; a happiness to which this State calls men of all countries and of all religions. It offers not the pleasures of the Arcadia of the poets, or those of the great towns of Europe; but it promises you independence, plenty, and happiness— in return for patience, industry, and labour. The moderate price of lands, the credit that may be obtained, and the perfect security that the courts of justice give to every species of property, place these advantages within the reach of every condition of men.

I do not pretend here to give the history of all the settlements of Pennsylvania. It often happens, that the same man, or the same family, holds the place of the first and second, and sometimes of the third class of planters above described. In the counties near Philadelphia, you see vast houses of brick, and farms well cultivated, in the possession of the descendants, in the second or third degree, of the companions of William Penn.

This passion for emigration, of which I have spoken, will appear to you unaccountable:—that a man should voluntarily abandon the country that gave him birth, the church where he was consecrated to God, the tombs of his ancestors, the companions and friends of his youth, and all the pleasures of polished society—to expose himself to the dangers and difficulties of conquering savage nature, is, in the eyes of a European philosopher, a phenomenon which contradicts the ordinary progress and principles of the actions of men. But such is the fact; and this passion contributes to increase the population of America, not only in the new settlements, but in the old states; for, when the number of farmers is augmented in any canton beyond the number of convenient farms, the population languishes, the price of lands rise to such a degree as to diminish the profits of agriculture, encourage idleness, or turn the attention to less honourable pursuits. The best preventative of these evils is the emigration of part of the inhabitants. This part generally consists of the most idle and dissipated, who necessarily become industrious in their new settlement; while the departure augments the means of subsistence and population to those left behind; as pruning increases the size of the tree, and the quantity of its fruit.

The third class of cultivators which I have described, is chiefly composed of Germans. They make a great part of the population of Pennsylvania. It is more than a century since the first Germans were established here. They are regarded as the most honest, the most industrious and œconomical of the farmers. They never contract debts; they are, of all the Americans, the least attached to the use of rum and other ardent spirits. Thus their families are the most numerous. It is very common to see them have twelve or fourteen children.[†] It is said, they have not so much information as the other Americans; and information is the soul of a Republican Government: but yet you find many men respectable for their knowledge and understanding amongst them, such as Rittenhouse, Kuhn, Mulhenberg, &c.

A principal cause of emigration in the back parts of Pennsylvania, is the hope of escaping taxes; yet the land-tax is very light, as it does not exceed a penny in the pound of the estimation; and the estimation is much under the value of the lands.

There is much irregularity in the land-tax, as likewise in the capitation or poll-tax; but I see with pleasure, that bachelors pay more than married men.

[†] According to M. Moheau, one family of 25,000 in France has thirteen children; two have twelve.

Notes

Introduction

1. François Alexandre-Frédéric, duc de La Rochefoucauld Liancourt, *Travels Through the United States of North America, the Country of the Iroquois, and Upper Canada, in the Years 1795, 1796, and 1797; With an Authentic Account of Lower Canada* (London: R. Phillips, 1799), 2:395.

2. Many scholars of material culture have built on the premise that objects are endowed with meaning. For just a few examples, see Henry Glassie, "Meaningful Things and Appropriate Myths: The Artifact's Place in American Studies," in *Material Life in America, 1600–1860,* ed. Robert Blair St. George (Boston: Northeastern University Press, 1988), 63–92, especially 83–84, 85–86; Jules David Prown, "Mind in Matter: An Introduction to Material Culture Theory and Method," in *Material Life in America, 1600–1860,* 19–20; Mihaly Csikszentmihalyi, "Why We Need Things," in *History from Things: Essays on Material Culture,* ed. Steven Lubar and W. David Kingery (Washington, D.C.: Smithsonian Institution Press, 1993), 23–28.

3. Nancy Dunlap Bercaw, "Solid Objects/Mutable Meanings: Fancywork and the Construction of Bourgeois Culture, 1840–1880," *Winterthur Portfolio* 26, no. 4 (Winter 1991): 239–40, 246–47; Bernard L. Herman, *The Stolen House* (Charlottesville: University Press of Virginia, 1992), 4–5.

4. Don Yoder describes the underlying problems in studying ethnicity among the Pennsylvania Germans, one of which is the wide variety of ethnic or regional identities within the group itself ("The Pennsylvania Germans: Three Centuries of Identity Crisis," in *America and the Germans: An Assessment of a Three-Hundred-Year History,* ed. Frank Trommler and Joseph McVeigh [Philadelphia: University of Pennsylvania Press, 1985], 1:42–45).

5. T. H. Breen, *The Marketplace of the Revolution: How Consumer Politics Shaped American Independence* (New York: Oxford University Press, 2004), quotation from p. xv.

6. Laurel Thatcher Ulrich, *The Age of Homespun: Objects and Stories in the Creation of an American Myth* (New York: Alfred A. Knopf, 2001). Chapters 4 to 7 directly relate to the second half of the eighteenth century.

7. Farley Grubb, "German Immigration to Pennsylvania, 1709–1820," *Journal of Interdisciplinary History* 20, no. 3 (Winter 1990): 419, 422, 429, 431–32; Marianne S. Wokeck, *Trade in Strangers: The Beginnings of Mass Migration to North America* (University Park: Pennsylvania State University Press, 1999), 38, 44, 47, 50, 52; Mark Haberlein, "German Migrants in Colonial Pennsylvania: Resources, Opportunities, and Experience," *William and Mary Quarterly,* 3rd series, 50, no. 3 (July 1993): 559–61, 574. The figures on wealth that Haberlein supplies are based on a limited group of emigrants from Baden-Durlach between 1732 and 1745.

8. Grubb, "German Immigration to Pennsylvania," 436; Wokeck, *Trade in Strangers,* 81, 151; Haberlein, "German Migrants in Colonial Pennsylvania," 574; Aaron Spencer Fogleman, *Hopeful Journeys: German Immigration, Settlement, and Political Culture in Colonial America, 1717–1775* (Philadelphia: University of Pennsylvania Press, 1996), 73, 78, 85; James T. Lemon, *The Best Poor Man's Country: A Geographical Study of Early Southeastern Pennsylvania* (Baltimore: Johns Hopkins University Press, 1972), 50; Cynthia G. Falk, "Symbols of Assimilation or Status? The Meanings of Eighteenth-Century Houses in Coventry Township, Chester County, Pennsylvania," *Winterthur Portfolio* 33, nos. 2/3 (Summer/Autumn 1998): 109–13.

9. For a recent analysis of this contradiction, see Gabrielle M. Lanier, *The Delaware Valley in the Early Republic: Architecture, Landscape, and Regional Identity* (Baltimore: Johns Hopkins University Press, 2005), 21–69.

10. Benjamin Rush, "An Account of the Manners of the German Inhabitants of Pennsylvania," *Columbian Magazine,* January 1789, 22–30. Rush summarizes these differences on p. 25, writing that "a German farm may be distinguished from the farms of the other citizens of the state" by "the superior size of their barns; the plain, but compact form of their houses; the height of their enclosures; the extent of their orchards; the fertility of their fields; the luxuriance of their meadows, and the general appearance of plenty and neatness in everything that belongs to them." A complete transcription of Rush's essay is included as an appendix to this work.

11. Scott T. Swank, "Proxemic Patterns," in *Arts of the Pennsylvania Germans,* ed. Scott T. Swank et al. (New York: W. W. Norton for the Henry Francis du Pont Winterthur Museum, 1983), 47, 55–56.

12. On personal identity as self-description, see Greg Dening, "Reflections on Defining Self," in *Through a Glass Darkly: Reflections on Personal Identity in Early America,* ed. Ronald Hoffman, Mechal Sobel, and Fredrika J. Teute (Chapel Hill: University of North Carolina Press, 1997), 344–45. On the role of material culture as a "signature" or "text" of self, see Greg Dening, "Introduction: In Search of a Metaphor," and Greg Dening, "Texts of Self," in *Through a Glass Darkly,* 6, 159.

13. On the ownership of property, see Marylynn Salmon, *Women and the Law of Property in Early America* (Chapel Hill: University of North Carolina Press, 1986), especially 24–28, and Ulrich, *The Age of Homespun,* 129–31. On domesticity and separate spheres, see Nancy F. Cott, *The Bonds of Womanhood: "Woman's Sphere" in New England, 1780–1835* (New Haven: Yale University Press, 1977); Ann Douglas, *The Feminization of American Culture* (New York: Alfred A. Knopf, 1977), 44–79; Mary P. Ryan, *Cradle of the Middle Class: The Family in Oneida County, New York, 1790–1865* (New York: Cambridge University Press, 1981), 191–98; Angel Kwolek-Folland, "Gender as a Category of Analysis in Vernacular Architecture Studies," in *Gender, Class, and Shelter,* ed. Elizabeth Collins Cromley and Carter L. Hudgins, Perspectives in Vernacular Architecture 5 (Knoxville: University of Tennessee Press, 1995), 4. In her classic work, *The Bonds of Womanhood,* Nancy F. Cott finds that it was not until the 1830s that "the concept of domesticity crystallized" (8).

14. On otherness, see Mechal Sobel, "The Revolution in Selves: Black and White Inner Aliens," in *Through a Glass Darkly,* 170–71. Sobel takes her interpretive framework from Stephen Greenblatt, *Renaissance Self-Fashioning: From More to Shakespeare* (Chicago: University of Chicago Press, 1980), 9.

15. Scholars have recognized the need to use both documentary

sources and actual objects in the study of material culture. See Herman, *Stolen House,* 11–12, and Ann Smart Martin and J. Ritchie Garrison, "Shaping the Field: The Multidisciplinary Perspectives of Material Culture," in *American Material Culture: The Shape of the Field,* ed. Ann Smart Martin and J. Ritchie Garrison (Winterthur, Del.: Henry Francis du Pont Winterthur Museum, distributed by University of Tennessee Press, 1997), 16, 20.

16. Robert F. Berkhoffer Jr., *The White Man's Indian: Images of the American Indian From Columbus to the Present* (New York: Alfred A. Knopf, 1978), 3, 24–25.

17. Richard L. Bushman, *The Refinement of America: Persons, Houses, Cities* (New York: Alfred A. Knopf, 1992), 3–9, 100–122; Kevin M. Sweeney, "High-Style Vernacular: Lifestyles of the Colonial Elite," in *Of Consuming Interests: The Style of Life in the Eighteenth Century,* ed. Cary Carson, Ronald Hoffman, and Peter J. Albert (Charlottesville: University Press of Virginia for the United States Capitol Historical Society, 1994), 11–24; Kevin M. Sweeney, "Mansion People: Kinship, Class, and Architecture in Western Massachusetts in the Mid-Eighteenth Century," *Winterthur Portfolio* 19, no. 4 (Winter 1984): 231–55.

18. Don Yoder, "Sects and Religious Movements of German Origin," in *Encyclopedia of the American Religious Experience: Studies of Traditions and Movements,* ed. Charles H. Lippy and Peter W. Williams (New York: Charles Scribner's Sons, 1988), 1:615, 616; A. G. Roeber, *Palatines, Liberty, and Property: German Lutherans in Colonial British America* (Baltimore: Johns Hopkins University Press, 1993), ix.

19. On Mennonite and Amish material culture, see Steve Friesen, *A Modest Mennonite Home: The Story of the 1719 Hans Herr House, an Early Colonial Landmark* (Intercourse, Pa.: Good Books, 1990), 49, 71; Henry Glassie, *Pattern in the Material Folk Culture of the Eastern United States* (Philadelphia: University of Pennsylvania Press, 1968), 62–64; Scott T. Swank, "Proxemic Patterns," 35–38. On the effects of tourism and popular culture on the image of the Amish, see David Walbert, *Garden Spot: Lancaster County, the Old Order Amish, and the Selling of Rural America* (Oxford: Oxford University Press, 2002), and David Weaver-Zercher, *The Amish in the American Imagination* (Baltimore: Johns Hopkins University Press, 2001).

Chapter 1

1. Henry Glassie may have been the first to use a variation of the term "German-Georgian" in print when he referred to a building as "Georgian-Germanic" in a figure caption in his 1972 article "Eighteenth-Century Cultural Process in Delaware Valley Folk Building," *Winterthur Portfolio* 7 (1972): 43, fig. 13. The use of the term has become pervasive in recent years. When the Vernacular Architecture Forum met in Harrisburg, Pennsylvania, in 2004, a published introduction to the conference referred to "hybrid 'German-Georgian' buildings" (*Vernacular Architecture Newsletter* 99 [Spring 2004]: 1).

2. Michael Kammen, *Empire and Interests: The American Colonies and the Politics of Mercantilism* (Philadelphia: J. B. Lippincott, 1970), 23–25; T. H. Breen, "'Baubles of Britain': The American and

Consumer Revolutions of the Eighteenth Century," in *Of Consuming Interests: The Style of Life in the Eighteenth Century,* ed. Cary Carson, Ronald Hoffman, and Peter J. Albert (Charlottesville: University Press of Virginia for the United States Capitol Historical Society, 1994), 458.

3. Beatrice Garvan, *The Pennsylvania German Collection* (Philadelphia: Philadelphia Museum of Art, 1982), 18–25, 175–76, 179, 184–86, 193, 199–200, 202, 214–15, 294, 296–300; Patricia J. Keller-Conner, "Workmanship, Form, and Cultural Identity: The Black-Unicorn Paint-Decorated Chests of Berks County, Pennsylvania" (M.A. thesis, University of Delaware, 1984); Monroe H. Fabian, *The Pennsylvania-German Decorated Chest* (New York: Universe Books, 1978); Scott T. Swank et al., *Arts of the Pennsylvania Germans* (New York: W. W. Norton for the Henry Francis du Pont Winterthur Museum, 1983), 136–48, 187–95, 230–34, 236–37, 239–41, 243–44, 247, 249, 252–56, 258–61, 263–64, plates 12–29.

4. H. K. Landis, "Abbreviated Inscriptions in German Pennsylvania," *The Magazine Antiques* 32, no. 3 (September 1937): 122–23; Stephanie Grauman Wolf, *Urban Village: Population, Community, and Family Structure in Germantown, Pennsylvania, 1683–1800* (Princeton: Princeton University Press, 1976), 142.

5. Henry Glassie, *Pattern in the Material Folk Culture of the Eastern United States* (Philadelphia: University of Pennsylvania Press, 1968), 5.

6. Three of the most comprehensive monographs on Pennsylvania German material culture were produced in the 1980s by Winterthur Museum and the Philadelphia Museum of Art as catalogues of their collections. All three emphasize the differences between English and German objects and to some degree offer accounts of German assimilation. See Garvan, *The Pennsylvania German Collection,* xiii; Beatrice Garvan and Charles Hummel, *The Pennsylvania Germans: A Celebration of Their Arts, 1683–1850* (Philadelphia: Philadelphia Museum of Art, 1982), 103–11, captions for plates 74, 75, 78, and 80, and Swank et al., *Arts of the Pennsylvania Germans,* 34, 126, 207–8, 220, 304.

7. Gottlieb Mittelberger, *Journey to Pennsylvania,* ed. and trans. Oscar Handlin and John Clive (Cambridge, Mass.: Harvard University Press, 1960), 83; François Alexandre-Frédéric, duc de La Rochefoucauld Liancourt, *Travels Through the United States of North America, the Country of the Iroquois, and Upper Canada, in the Years 1795, 1796, and 1797; With an Authentic Account of Lower Canada* (London: R. Phillips, 1799), 1:24, 35; 2:673. On forgetting the German language, see also Henry Melchior Muhlenberg, *The Journals of Henry Melchior Muhlenberg,* trans. Theodore G. Tappert and John W. Doberstein (Philadelphia: Evangelical Lutheran Ministerium of Pennsylvania and Adjacent States and the Muhlenberg Press, 1942), 1:473, 491. On retaining German, see J[ohn] F. D. Smyth, *A Tour in the United States of America: Containing an Account of the Present Situation of That Country* (London: Printed for G. Robinson, 1784), 2:258.

8. Mittelberger, *Journey to Pennsylvania,* 88; La Rochefoucauld Liancourt, *Travels Through the United States,* 1:47; 2:392, 584, 673.

9. Call for the Convention of April 15, 1891, for the formation of the Pennsylvania German Society, *The Pennsylvania German Society: Proceedings and Addresses* 1 (1891): 10–11, reprinted in Homer Tope

Rosenberger, *The Pennsylvania Germans, 1891–1965* (Lancaster: Pennsylvania German Society, 1966), 80; Sections 1 and 2 of Article 3 of the Constitution of the Pennsylvania German Society, *The Pennsylvania German Society: Proceedings and Addresses* 1 (1891): 84–85, reprinted in Rosenberger, *The Pennsylvania Germans,* 85; Don Yoder, "The Pennsylvania Germans: Three Centuries of Identity Crisis," in *America and the Germans: An Assessment of a Three-Hundred-Year History,* ed. Frank Trommler and Joseph McVeigh (Philadelphia: University of Pennsylvania Press, 1985), 1:51, 53, 61.

10. Simon J. Bronner, *Following Tradition: Folklore in the Discourse of American Culture* (Logan: Utah State University Press, 1998), 292–98. The Shoemaker quotation is from Alfred L. Shoemaker, "Stop Sneering," *Pennsylvania Dutchman* (5 May 1949): 3. *The Pennsylvania Dutchman* was retitled *Pennsylvania Folklife* in 1957; the Pennsylvania Dutch Folklore Center became the Pennsylvania Folklife Society; and the Pennsylvania Dutch Folk Festival was renamed the Kutztown Folk Festival.

11. For other interpretations of Pennsylvania German distinctiveness and/or eventual assimilation (aside from the three museum catalogues *The Pennsylvania German Collection, The Pennsylvania Germans,* and *Arts of the Pennsylvania Germans*), see Morrison H. Heckscher and Leslie Greene Bowman, *American Rococo, 1750–1775: Elegance in Ornament* (New York: Metropolitan Museum of Art), 59, 227, and William J. Murtagh, *Moravian Architecture and Town Planning: Bethlehem, Pennsylvania, and Other Eighteenth-Century American Settlements* (Chapel Hill: University of North Carolina Press, 1967), vii–viii, 42; and Wolf, *Urban Village,* 127–53.

12. James T. Lemon, *The Best Poor Man's Country: A Geographical Study of Early Southeastern Pennsylvania* (Baltimore: Johns Hopkins University Press, 1972), 4, 14–17.

13. Stephanie Grauman Wolf, "Hyphenated America: The Creation of an Eighteenth-Century German-American Culture," in *America and the Germans: An Assessment of a Three-Hundred-Year History,* 1:66–84; Aaron Spencer Fogleman, *Hopeful Journeys: German Immigration, Settlement, and Political Culture in Colonial America, 1717–1775* (Philadelphia: University of Pennsylvania Press, 1996), 12, 152–53; Philip E. Pendleton, *Oley Valley Heritage: The Colonial Years, 1700–1775* (Birdsboro, Pa.: Pennsylvania German Society; Oley, Pa.: Oley Valley Heritage Association, 1994), 149; Steven M. Nolt, *Foreigners in Their Own Land: Pennsylvania Germans in the Early Republic* (University Park: Pennsylvania State University Press, 2002), 3. For another three-part model of cultural change, see Yoder, "The Pennsylvania Germans," 1:41–65. For an early reference to the "Americanization" of a Pennsylvania German community, see Gillian Lindt Gollin, *Moravians in Two Worlds: A Study of Changing Communities* (New York: Columbia University Press, 1967).

14. Scott T. Swank, "The Germanic Fragment," in *Arts of the Pennsylvania Germans,* 4–5.

15. G. Edwin Brumbaugh, "Colonial Architecture of the Pennsylvania Germans," *Pennsylvania German Society Proceedings* 41 (1933): 8–9 and 39.

16. Robert C. Bucher, "The Continental Log House," *Pennsylvania Folklife* 12, no. 4 (Summer 1962): 14–19; Henry Glassie, "A Central

Chimney Continental Log House from Cumberland County," *Pennsylvania Folklife* 18, no. 2 (Winter 1968–69): 32–39. By 1986, Edward Chappell noted that the form was "now occasionally called a *Flurküchenhaus.*" See Edward Chappell, "Germans and Swiss," in *America's Architectural Roots: Ethnic Groups that Built America,* ed. Dell Upton (Washington, D.C.: Preservation Press, 1986), 68. The use of the term "continental plan" by Bucher and Glassie was preceded by Alfred Shoemaker's reference to the "Continental type house." See Alfred Shoemaker, *The Pennsylvania Dutch Country* (Lancaster: Pennsylvania Dutch Folklore Center, Franklin and Marshall College, 1954), n.p.

17. It is impossible to determine exactly what percentage of eighteenth-century Pennsylvania German houses were constructed with a three-room entry-kitchen plan, but many surviving entry-kitchen houses seem to be of this variety. It is likely that smaller one- or two-room structures were replaced or expanded long before the twenty-first century.

18. On the derivation of the word *Stube* and its relationship with stove heat, see William Woys Weaver, "The Pennsylvania German House: European Antecedents and New World Forms," *Winterthur Portfolio* 21, no. 4 (Winter 1986): 257.

19. Weaver, "The Pennsylvania German House," 244, 253, 257–58, 264.

20. Charles Bergengren, "The Cycle of Transformations in the Houses of Schaefferstown, Pennsylvania" (Ph.D. diss., University of Pennsylvania, 1988), 74–96. Bergengren continues his discussion of these house types in his "Pennsylvania German House Forms," in *Guidebook for the Vernacular Architecture Forum Annual Conference: Architecture and Landscape of the Pennsylvania Germans, May 12–16, 2004, Harrisburg, Pennsylvania* (n.p.: Vernacular Architecture Forum, 2004).

21. Scott T. Swank, "The Architectural Landscape," in *Arts of the Pennsylvania Germans,* 34; Scott T. Swank, "Proxemic Patterns," in *Arts of the Pennsylvania Germans,* 43; Edward A. Chappell, "Acculturation in the Shenandoah Valley: Rhenish Houses of the Massanutten Settlement," in *Common Places: Readings in American Vernacular Architecture,* ed. Dell Upton and John Michael Vlach (Athens: University of Georgia Press, 1986), 28, 42–43.

22. Cary Carson, "English," in *America's Architectural Roots,* 57; Cary Carson, "The Consumer Revolution in Colonial British America: Why Demand?" in *Of Consuming Interests,* 672.

23. Several recent studies suggest that German immigrants maintained more contact with people who remained in continental Europe than was previously thought. See, for example, Fogleman, *Hopeful Journeys,* 75–80; A. G. Roeber, *Palatines, Liberty, and Property: German Lutherans in Colonial British America* (Baltimore: Johns Hopkins University Press, 1993), 96. On Moravian communication networks, see Murtagh, *Moravian Architecture,* 9. On the Single Brothers' house, see Garth H. Howland, "Reconstructional Problems Associated with the Moravian Buildings in Bethlehem," *Transactions of the Moravian Historical Society* 13, nos. 3/4 (1944): 203–9, and Murtagh, *Moravian Architecture,* 36–39. The best, most accurate, information on the original floor plan of the structure comes from a 1766 map of Bethlehem reproduced in Ralph Grayson

Schwarz, *Bethlehem on the Lehigh* (Bethlehem: Bethlehem Area Foundation, n.d.), 18, and floor plans of the *Gemeinhaus* and related buildings in Bethlehem from the collection of the Moravian Archives, Herrnhut, Germany, dating to 1751 (TS Mp.216.15).

24. Christian Hagenbuch, Building Contract, November 18, 1783, Joseph Downs Collection of Manuscripts and Printed Ephemera, Doc. 250, Winterthur Museum, Garden and Library, Winterthur, Del., Doc. 250. For additional information on the Hagenbuch house as actually constructed, see 1798 Federal Direct Tax Records for Allen Township, Northampton County, Pennsylvania, Schedule A, National Archives, Washington, D.C. (microfilm, Center for Historic Architecture and Design, University of Delaware, Newark, Del.).

25. For an example, see Pendleton, *Oley Valley Heritage,* 77.

26. Chappell, "Acculturation in the Shenandoah Valley," 29–30; Weaver, "The Pennsylvania German House," 258.

27. Richard White, "'Although I Am Dead, I Am Not Entirely Dead. I Have Left a Second of Myself': Constructing Self and Persons on the Middle Ground of Early America," in *Through a Glass Darkly: Reflections on Personal Identity in Early America,* ed. Ronald Hoffman, Mechal Sobel, and Fredrika J. Teute (Chapel Hill: University of North Carolina Press, 1997), 418.

28. Scott Swank writes, "The forging of Pennsylvania German identity out of such diverse elements was no slight task, but over time a distinct Pennsylvania German culture did emerge" ("The Germanic Fragment," in *Arts of the Pennsylvania Germans,* 4). For a discussion of the formation of German identity among diverse German immigrants to England and then New York, see also Philip Otterness, *Becoming German: The 1709 Palatine Migration to New York* (Ithaca: Cornell University Press, 2004), especially 1–4, 55–56, 65–66.

29. Nolt, *Foreigners in Their Own Land,* 71–74, 120–21, 134–38; Yoder, "The Pennsylvania Germans," 1:50–51, 53–51, 60–61; Simon J. Bronner, "Elaborating Tradition: A Pennsylvania-German Folk Artist Ministers to His Community," in *Creativity and Tradition in Folklore: New Directions,* ed. Simon J. Bronner (Logan: Utah State University Press, 1992), 281; Donald Scott McPherson, "The Fight Against Free Schools in Pennsylvania: Popular Opposition to the Common School System, 1834–1874" (Ph.D. diss., University of Pittsburgh, 1977), 179–85, 204–6, 214–32; Don Yoder and Thomas E. Graves, *Hex Signs: Pennsylvania Dutch Barn Symbols and Their Meaning,* 2nd ed. (Mechanicsburg, Pa.: Stackpole Books, 2000), 7, 19, 21. Hex signs, or barn stars, first appeared on the gable ends of stone barns in the late eighteenth century. However, the more familiar painted decoration on wooden barn cladding burgeoned later in the nineteenth century. Robert W. Reynolds, "From Barn Stars to Hex Signs and Back Again" (paper presented at the Cooperstown Graduate Association Folk Art conference, Cooperstown, N.Y., October 28, 2006).

30. Nolt, *Foreigners in Their Own Land,* 4. The emphasis on culture appears in Nolt's work.

Chapter 2

1. On the rise of European nationalism, see Benedict Anderson, *Imagined Communities: Reflections on the Origin and Spread of Nationalism* (London: Verso, 1983). For descriptions of the Swiss, Swedes, Dutch, and Spanish, see *The Modern Dictionary of Arts and Sciences; or, Complete System of Literature* (London, 1774), s.v. "Holland" (vol. 2) and s.vv. "Switzerland," "Sweden," and "Spain" (vol. 4).

2. The fifteen European travelers and short-term residents include: Israel Acrelius; Thomas Anburey; Jacques-Pierre Brissot de Warville; Théophile Cazenove; the marquis de Chastellux; Thomas Cooper; John Fransham; Peter Kalm; François Alexandre-Frédéric, duc de La Rochefoucauld Liancourt; Gottlieb Mittelberger; Johann David Schöpf; John F. D. Symth; Sir Benjamin Thompson (Count Rumford); Henry Wansey; and Isaac Weld. American authors include: Jacob Duché; Lewis Evans; Benjamin Franklin; Alexander Graydon; Alexander Hamilton (1712–1756); and Benjamin Rush. The other reference sources include: *Carey's American Pocket Atlas,* Jedidiah Morse's *The American Geography, The North-American and the West-Indian Gazetteer,* Joseph Scott's *The United States Gazetteer,* and William Winterbotham's *An Historical, Geographical, Commercial, and Philosophical View of the American United States, and of the European Settlements in America and the West-Indies.*

3. Drew R. McCoy, *The Elusive Republic: Political Economy in Jeffersonian America* (Chapel Hill: University of North Carolina Press for the Institute of Early American History and Culture, 1980), 17–47; Ronald L. Meek, *Social Science and the Ignoble Savage* (New York: Cambridge University Press, 1976), 2, 64; Daniel Richter, "'Believing that Many of the Red People Suffer Much for the Want of Food': Hunting, Agriculture, and a Quaker Construction of Indianness in the Early Republic" (paper presented at the McNeil Center for Early American Studies Seminar Series, Library Company of Philadelphia, Philadelphia, Pa., October 8, 1999).

4. Benjamin Rush, "An Account of the Manners of the German Inhabitants of Pennsylvania," *Columbian Magazine,* January 1789, 22; A. F. M. Willich and James Mease, *The Domestic Encyclopædia; or, A Dictionary of Facts and Useful Knowledge* (Philadelphia: William Young Birch and Abraham Small, 1804), 2:484, 486–87; Don Yoder, "The 'Domestic Encyclopedia' of 1803–1804," *Pennsylvania Folklife* 14, no. 3 (Spring 1965): 15, 20–21; Chester County Deed Book R2, p. 249, and Deed Book S2, p. 64, Chester County Archives, West Chester, Pennsylvania. For a description of the English practice of using separate structures for storing grain and housing animals, see Robert Blair St. George, "'Set Thine House in Order': The Domestication of the Yeomanry in Seventeenth Century New England," in *Common Places: Readings in American Vernacular Architecture,* ed. Dell Upton and John Michael Vlach (Athens: University of Georgia Press, 1986), 337.

5. Johann David Schöpf, *Travels in the Confederation, 1783–1784,* trans. and ed. Alfred J. Morrison (Philadelphia: William J. Campbell, 1911), 1:125.

6. The entry-kitchen house form is discussed in some detail in chapter 1. See also Robert C. Bucher, "The Continental Log House," *Pennsylvania Folklife* 12, no. 4 (Summer 1962): 14–19; Henry Glassie,

"A Central Chimney Continental Log House from Cumberland County," *Pennsylvania Folklife* 18, no. 2 (Winter 1968–69): 32–39; Steve Friesen, *A Modest Mennonite Home: The Story of the 1719 Hans Herr House, an Early Colonial Landmark* (Intercourse, Pa.: Good Books, 1990), 71–74, 82; Edward Chappell, "Germans and Swiss," in *America's Architectural Roots: Ethnic Groups that Built America,* ed. Dell Upton (Washington, D.C.: Preservation Press, 1986), 68. For additional information on the Bertolet-Herbein house, see: Philip E. Pendleton, *Oley Valley Heritage: The Colonial Years, 1700–1775* (Birdsboro, Pa.: Pennsylvania German Society; Oley, Pa.: Oley Valley Heritage Association, 1994), 57, 71–72, and Pendleton, "Oley Valley Tour," in *Guidebook for the Vernacular Architecture Forum Annual Conference: Architecture and Landscape of the Pennsylvania Germans, May 12–16, 2004, Harrisburg, Pennsylvania* (n.p.: Vernacular Architecture Forum, 2004), 81.

7. Théophile Cazenove, *Cazenove Journal, 1794: A Record of the Journey of Theophile Cazenove Through New Jersey and Pennsylvania,* ed. Rayner Wickersham Kelsey (Haverford, Pa.: The Pennsylvania History Press, 1922), 84. On the identification of coal-burning fireplaces with the English, wood-burning fireplaces with the French, and stoves with the Germans, see Benjamin Franklin, *Observations on Smoky Chimneys, Their Causes and Cure; With Considerations on Fuel and Stoves* (London: I. and J. Taylor, 1793), 28.

8. Franklin, *Observations on Smoky Chimneys,* 28; Benjamin Franklin, "An Account of the Newly Invented Pennsylvanian Fire-Places," in *The Papers of Benjamin Franklin,* ed. Leonard W. Labaree (New Haven: Yale University Press, 1959–), 2:429; Rush, "An Account of the Manners of the German Inhabitants of Pennsylvania," 23, 28; David Seibt to his brother, December 20, 1734, in *The Journals and Papers of David Schultze,* trans. and ed. Andrew S. Berky (Pennsburg, Pa.: Schwenkfelder Library, 1952), 1:55; Sir Benjamin Thompson, Count Rumford, *Essay IV: Of Chimney Fire-places, With Proposals for Improving Them, to Save Fuel, to Render Dwelling-houses More Comfortable and Salubrious, and, Effectually to Prevent Chimnies from Smoking* (London: Printed for T. Cadell and W. Davies, 1796), 304.

9. David Schultze, *The Journals of David Schultze,* 2:206; Henry Melchior Muhlenberg, *The Journals of Henry Melchior Muhlenberg,* trans. Theodore G. Tappert and John W. Doberstein (Philadelphia: Evangelical Lutheran Ministerium of Pennsylvania and Adjacent States and the Muhlenberg Press, 1942), 3:106; Schöpf, *Travels in the Confederation,* 1:60. For the definition of tin-plate, see Donald L. Fennimore, "Metalwork," in *Arts of the Pennsylvania Germans,* ed. Scott T. Swank et al. (New York: W. W. Norton for the Henry Francis du Pont Winterthur Museum, 1983), 213.

10. Rumford, *Essay IV,* 303–4; Cazenove, *Cazenove Journal,* 26.

11. Schöpf, *Travels in the Confederation,* 2:6; Rush, "An Account of the Manners of the German Inhabitants of Pennsylvania," 23. See also Franklin, *Observations on Smoky Chimneys,* 48–49. Heinrich Melchior Muhlenberg made a similar observation about the inadequacies of the heat provided by fireplaces. On February 15, 1769, he recorded in his journal, "Very few families [in New Germantown, New Jersey] are supplied with stoves. Most of them have poor houses and, at best, open fireplaces which freeze a person on one side and broil him on the other. Like the sun, which warms only one side of our dark planet, these fireplaces heat only one side of our bodies unless we turn continuously on our own axis like a roast on a spit" (*The Journals of Henry Melchior Muhlenberg,* 2:379).

12. Gottlieb Mittelberger, *Journey to Pennsylvania,* ed. and trans. Oscar Handlin and John Clive (Cambridge, Mass.: Harvard University Press, 1960), 91; David Seibt to his brother, in *The Journals of David Schultze,* 1:55.

13. Schöpf, *Travels in the Confederation,* 1:208; 2:24; Mittelberger, *Journey to Pennsylvania,* 49; Cazenove, *Cazenove Journal,* 83.

14. Rush, "An Account of the Manners of the German Inhabitants of Pennsylvania," 23–24; Levi Hollingsworth Correspondence, May 17, 1774, Hollingsworth Collection, Historical Society of Pennsylvania, Philadelphia, Pa. I am indebted to Brooke Hunter for pointing out this source.

15. Mittelberger, *Journey to Pennsylvania,* 51; Cazenove, *Cazenove Journal,* 83.

16. Schöpf, *Travels in the Confederation,* 1:104; F. J. Chastellux, *Travels in North-America, in the Years 1780, 1781, and 1782* (London: G. G. J. and J. Robinson, 1787), 2:327; Probate Inventory of Michael Roth (1795), #4456, Chester County Archives, West Chester, Pennsylvania. Roth's familiarity with the German language is evidenced by his will, which is written in German. The will is also found in probate file #4456, Chester County Archives, West Chester, Pennsylvania.

17. Oxford English Dictionary, online edition, s.v. "Dutch"; David Weaver-Zercher, *The Amish in the American Imagination* (Baltimore: Johns Hopkins University Press, 2001), 203n9; Aaron Spencer Fogleman, *Hopeful Journeys: German Immigration, Settlement, and Political Culture in Colonial America, 1717–1775* (Philadelphia: University of Pennsylvania Press, 1996), 197. Weaver-Zercher writes, "Contrary to popular thought, the ethnic label 'Dutch' was not a mistranslation of the German word *Deutsche,* but rather it was the established eighteenth-century English word for the Rhine Valley immigrants" (203).

18. Beatrice Garvan and Charles Hummel, *The Pennsylvania Germans: A Celebration of Their Arts, 1683–1850* (Philadelphia: Philadelphia Museum of Art, 1982), 155.

19. Schöpf, *Travels in the Confederation,* 1:104; 2:23.

20. Muhlenberg, *The Journals of Henry Melchior Muhlenberg,* 1:343; Cazenove, *Cazenove Journal,* 45; Schöpf, *Travels in the Confederation,* 1:106. On straw hats as German, see also Mittelberger, *Journey to Pennsylvania,* 88–89. The description of "blue stockings" may have indicated something about the class of the "old German country-man," as the terms "blue apron" and "blue collar" have both been used to designate manual laborers at various points in history.

21. Franklin, *Observations on Smoky Chimneys,* 48; Cazenove, *Cazenove Journal,* 83.

22. Rush, "An Account of the Manners of the German Inhabitants of Pennsylvania," 22–24.

23. Schöpf, *Travels in the Confederation,* 1:105–6.

24. *A New and Complete Dictionary of Arts and Sciences; Comprehending all the Branches of Useful Knowledge* (London: W.

Owen, 1754), 2:1423; Adrien Faucher-Magnan, *The Small German Courts in the Eighteenth Century,* trans. Mervyn Savill (Paris, 1947; reprint, London: Methuen, 1958), 17–29; Rudolf Vierhaus, *Germany in the Age of Absolutism,* trans. Jonathan B. Knudsen (Cambridge: Cambridge University Press, 1988), 90–103.

25. *Encyclopedia; or, A Dictionary of Arts, Sciences, and Miscellaneous Literature* (Philadelphia: Printed by Thomas Dobson, 1798), 7:710, 711, 712; John G. Gagliardo, *Germany Under the Old Regime, 1600–1790* (London: Longman, 1991), 123–25; Wolfgang Michael, *England Under George I: The Beginnings of the Hanoverian Dynasty* (London, 1936; reprint, Westport, Conn.: Greenwood Press, 1981), 77–78; "The Blessings Attending George's Accession and Coronation" and [William Shippen], "Pasquin to the Queen's Statue at St. Paul's, During the Procession, January 20, 1714," in *Anthology of Poems on Affairs of State: Augustan Satirical Verse, 1660–1714,* ed. George deForest Lord (New Haven: Yale University Press, 1975), 752, 753n40. For additional analysis of the decidedly negative eighteenth-century views of the "ancient Germans," see Meek, *Social Science and the Ignoble Savage,* 134–35, 138–40, 142, 166.

26. *Encyclopedia; or, A Dictionary of Arts, Sciences, and Miscellaneous Literature,* 7:712; Chastellux, *Travels in North-America,* 2:362.

27. Schöpf, *Travels in the Confederation,* 1:102; La Rochefoucauld Liancourt, *Travels Through the United States,* 1:70; Cazenove, *Cazenove Journal,* 44.

28. Cazenove, *Cazenove Journal,* 30; Rush, "An Account of the Manners of the German Inhabitants of Pennsylvania," 23, 24.

29. Schöpf, *Travels in the Confederation,* 1:103; Cazenove, *Cazenove Journal,* 44; La Rochefoucauld Liancourt, *Travels Through the United States,* 1:35, 46.

30. La Rochefoucauld Liancourt, *Travels Through the United States,* 1:35, 46; Chastellux, *Travels in North-America,* 2:233; Schöpf, *Travels in the Confederation,* 1:104; Cazenove, *Cazenove Journal,* 42, 83, 84.

31. Rush, "An Account of the Manners of the German Inhabitants of Pennsylvania," 22; La Rochefoucauld Liancourt, *Travels Through the United States,* 1:35, 46.

32. Cazenove, *Cazenove Journal,* 83, 84.

33. Cazenove, *Cazenove Journal,* 84–85.

34. Schöpf, *Travels in the Confederation,* 1:104. The bold typeface is found in the published translation.

35. Cazenove, *Cazenove Journal,* 104–5.

36. Schöpf, *Travels in the Confederation,* 1:169; Jedidiah Morse, *The American Geography; or, a View of the Present Situation of the United States of America* (Elizabethtown, [N.J.]: Shepard Kollock, 1789), 313. The practice of using salt to keep away witches, break spells, or bring good luck has been well documented and was by no means limited to Pennsylvanians of German descent. See, for example, Newman Ivey White, ed., *The Frank Brown Collection of North Carolina Folklore* (Durham: Duke University Press, 1952–64), 6:382 (no. 2949), 663 (no. 4864); 7:106 (no. 5562), 125 (nos. 5641 and 5642).

37. Rush, "An Account of the Manners of the German Inhabitants of Pennsylvania," 26; W[illiam] Winterbotham, *An Historical,*

Geographical, Commercial, and Philosophical View of the American United States, and of the European Settlements in America and the West-Indies (London, 1795), 2:439–40.

38. J[ohn] F. D. Smyth, *A Tour in the United States of America: Containing an Account of the Present Situation of That Country* (London: Printed for G. Robinson, 1784), 2:258; Cazenove, *Cazenove Journal,* 34; Schöpf, *Travels in the Confederation,* 1:103–4.

39. Cazenove, *Cazenove Journal,* 76.

40. In order to make accurate comparisons between the holdings of people of German and British descent, I chose Pennsylvania townships that included both German and British settlement. In these places, the same assessor reviewed all properties, and any idiosyncrasies in his recording method were applied to all the data. In Coventry Township, Chester County, of householders whose surnames could be identified as either German or British, 71 percent were German and 29 percent were British. Conestoga Township, Lancaster County, had a similar breakdown with 69 percent German and 31 percent non-German householders. In Hempfield Township, Lancaster County, the proportion of Germans was slightly higher at 79 percent. Cynthia Falk, "Symbols of Assimilation or Status? The Meanings of Eighteenth-Century Houses in Coventry Township, Chester County, Pennsylvania," *Winterthur Portfolio* 33, nos. 2/3 (Summer/Autumn 1998): 130; Gabrielle M. Lanier, *The Delaware Valley in the Early Republic: Architecture, Landscape, and Regional Identity* (Baltimore: Johns Hopkins University Press, 2005), 182–83.

41. On the inadequacies of the 1798 federal direct tax, Gabrielle Lanier notes, "Despite its comprehensiveness and precision, then, the 1798 tax record is ultimately—and paradoxically—an abstraction of the built world, a text that is seductive in its thoroughness but fundamentally devoid of texture, a landscape narrative that heightens our awareness of objects that have since vanished from the countryside but that, in the end, reduces the sense of place" (*The Delaware Valley in the Early Republic,* 69).

42. The area that was Coventry Township in 1798 includes North, South, and East Coventry townships today.

43. Schöpf, *Travels in the Confederation,* 1:104; 1798 Federal Direct Tax Records for Coventry Township, Chester County, Pennsylvania, Schedule A, National Archives, Washington, D.C. (microfilm, Center for Historic Architecture and Design, University of Delaware, Newark, Del.); Falk, "Symbols of Assimilation or Status?" 107–34. Square footage figures account for space on the first floor and the second floor if one existed.

44. Lanier, *The Delaware Valley in the Early Republic,* 40, 182–83. Conestoga Township in 1798 included what are now Conestoga and Pequea townships in Lancaster County. What was Hempfield township in 1798 is now East and West Hempfield townships, the boroughs of Columbia and Mountville, and part of the borough of East Petersburg.

45. For examples of large, highly valued German houses in a more western county, see Nancy Van Dolsen, *Cumberland County: An Architectural Survey* (Carlisle, Pa.: Cumberland County Historical Society, 1990), 13–18, 149–50.

46. Lanier, *The Delaware Valley in the Early Republic,* 36–43, 181–83; 1798 Federal Direct Tax Records for Coventry Township,

Chester County, Pennsylvania, Schedule B.

47. Thirty-four of the barns enumerated on the 1798 tax returns for Coventry Township have no dimensions listed; twenty-two of these are described as "small," "old," "rotten," or "bad," or are described as "unfinished." Only one is described as "good."

48. 1798 Federal Direct Tax Records for Coventry Township, Chester County, Pennsylvania, Schedule B; Lanier, *The Delaware Valley in the Early Republic,* 39, 40–41, 43, 181–83.

49. 1798 Federal Direct Tax Records for Coventry Township, Chester County, Pennsylvania, Schedules A and B.

50. Gabrielle Lanier comes to a similar conclusion when comparing traveler's accounts and the Lancaster County landscape in tax records from 1798 and 1815 (*The Delaware Valley in the Early Republic,* 50–51).

51. Only eleven householders with German surnames held property that included a house with less than 450 feet of interior space and a barn that measured more than 20 by 36 feet. 1798 Federal Direct Tax Records for Coventry Township, Chester County, Pennsylvania, Schedules A and B.

52. McCoy, *The Elusive Republic,* 19; Meek, *Social Science and the Ignoble Savage,* 35–36, 177.

53. La Rochefoucauld Liancourt, *Travels Through the United States,* 1:70; Cazenove, *Cazenove Journal,* 44.

54. Thomas Jefferson, *The Papers of Thomas Jefferson,* ed. Julian P. Boyd (Princeton: Princeton University Press, 1950–), 12:6; 14:492.

55. Benjamin Rush, *Letters of Benjamin Rush,* ed. L. H. Butterfield (Princeton: Princeton University Press for the American Philosophical Society, 1951), 1:367.

56. Rush, *Letters of Benjamin Rush,* 1:366–68. For a contradictory view about the compatibility of farming and education, see Cazenove, *Cazenove Journal,* 34.

57. Rush, *Letters of Benjamin Rush,* 1:365, 426; Rush, "An Account of the Manners of the German Inhabitants of Pennsylvania," 22, 23, 25, 26, 29. For Rush's opinions of David Rittenhouse, see Benjamin Rush, *An Eulogium, Intended to Perpetuate the Memory of David Rittenhouse, Late President of the American Philosophical Society* (Philadelphia: J. Ormrod, n.d.).

58. Rush, "An Account of the Manners of the German Inhabitants of Pennsylvania," 24.

59. Durand Echeverria and Mara Soceanu Vamos, introduction to *New Travels in the United States of America, 1788,* by Jacques-Pierre Brissot de Warville (Cambridge, Mass.: Harvard University Press, 1964), ix; Brissot, *New Travels in the United States of America Performed in 1788* (Dublin: W. Corbet, 1792), xvii, xix, 334–35, 338. Specifically on the disuse of strong liquors, see Rush, "An Account of the Manners of the German Inhabitants of Pennsylvania," 24, and Brissot, *New Travels in the United States of America Performed in 1788,* 338. A complete transcription of Brissot's "Progress of Cultivation in Pennsylvania," which amends an essay written by Rush to focus more specifically on the German population of Pennsylvania, is included as an appendix to this work.

60. Franklin, *The Papers of Benjamin Franklin,* 4:120, 234, 483; 5:201, 159–60; 6:40.

61. Franklin, *The Papers of Benjamin Franklin,* 4:485; 11:375, 382,

385, 397; Charles Coleman Sellers, *Benjamin Franklin in Portraiture* (New Haven: Yale University Press, 1962), 381–82, plate 7; John B. Frantz, "Franklin and the Pennsylvania Germans," *Pennsylvania History* 65, no. 1 (Winter 1998): 21–34; Glenn Weaver, "Benjamin Franklin and the Pennsylvania Germans," *William and Mary Quarterly,* 3rd series, 14, no. 4 (October 1975): 536–59.

62. McCoy, *The Elusive Republic,* 52–60; Franklin, *The Papers of Benjamin Franklin,* 20:443.

63. Franklin, *The Papers of Benjamin Franklin,* 4:120, 485.

64. Benjamin Franklin, *The Complete Works of Benjamin Franklin,* comp. and ed. John Biglow (New York: G. P. Putnam's Sons, 1888), 9:229, 246. See also Franklin, *Observations on Smoky Chimneys,* 28, 48–49.

65. Uriah Tracy to Oliver Wolcott, August 7, 1800, in George Gibbs, *Memoirs of the Administration of Washington and John Adams, Edited from the Papers of Oliver Wolcott, Secretary of the Treasury* (New York, 1846; reprint, New York: Lenox Hill, 1971), 2:399. Tracy's characterization was made in the aftermath of Fries's Rebellion, a movement in opposition to the Federalist agenda, particularly direct taxation, in which Pennsylvania Germans played a prominent role. South Carolina Federalist Robert Goodloe Harper recorded a similar assessment of the ethnic group in 1799. See Paul Douglas Newman, *Fries's Rebellion: The Enduring Struggle for the American Revolution* (Philadelphia: University of Pennsylvania Press, 2004), 152. On the importance of the Pennsylvania Germans to the Federalist Party in Pennsylvania, see Newman, *Fries's Rebellion,* 27–28, 192–99, and Edwin D. Eshleman and Robert S. Walker, *Congress—The Pennsylvania German Representatives, 1774–1974* (Lancaster, Pa.: Concorde Publishing, 1975), 26, 32, 36, 38–39. Speaker of the United States House of Representatives Frederick Augustus Conrad Muhlenberg, for example, was a Federalist.

66. Cazenove, *Cazenove Journal,* 34, 75.

67. Schöpf, *Travels in the Confederation,* 1:104.

68. Schöpf, *Travels in the Confederation,* 1:99. See also La Rochefoucauld Liancourt, *Travels Through the United States,* 1:68.

69. Cazenove, *Cazenove Journal,* 16–17, 34.

70. Schöpf, *Travels in the Confederation,* 1:105.

Chapter 3

1. On the association of certain houses and household furnishings with wealth and social standing, see, for example, Richard L. Bushman, *The Refinement of America: Persons, Houses, Cities* (New York: Alfred A. Knopf, 1992), 25, 74–78; Robert Blair St. George, "Artifacts of Regional Consciousness in the Connecticut River Valley," in *Material Life in America, 1600–1860,* ed. Robert Blair St. George (Boston: Northeastern University Press, 1988), 340, 342. On the high cost of renting a "large and convenient" brick house, see François Alexandre-Frédéric, duc de La Rochefoucauld Liancourt, *Travels Through the United States of North America, the Country of the Iroquois, and Upper Canada, in the Years 1795, 1796, and 1797; With an Authentic Account of Lower Canada* (London: R. Phillips, 1799), 1:71.

2. For German construction techniques and other distinctive

German traits such as the use of stoves and German-language date stones, see Philip E. Pendleton, *Oley Valley Heritage: The Colonial Years, 1700–1775* (Birdsboro, Pa.: Pennsylvania German Society; Oley, Pa.: Oley Valley Heritage Association, 1994), 63–65, 78–81; Cynthia Falk, "Symbols of Assimilation or Status? The Meanings of Eighteenth-Century Houses in Coventry Township, Chester County, Pennsylvania," *Winterthur Portfolio* 33, nos. 2/3 (Summer/Autumn 1998): 121–22; Gerald S. Lestz, introduction to *Lancaster County Architecture, 1700–1850* (Lancaster, Pa.: Historic Preservation Trust of Lancaster County, 1992), viii; *Lancaster County Architecture,* 43, 53, 54, 62, 63, 68, 69, 104.

3. Théophile Cazenove, *Cazenove Journal, 1794: A Record of the Journey of Theophile Cazenove Through New Jersey and Pennsylvania,* ed. Rayner Wickersham Kelsey (Haverford, Pa.: The Pennsylvania History Press, 1922), 76.

4. Salisbury Township Tax Records, 1750–1828, in Lancaster County, Pennsylvania, Tax Records, 1748–1855 (microfilm, Pennsylvania Historical and Museum Commission), Lancaster County Historical Society, Lancaster, Pa.; H. W. Kriebel, "The Ellmaker Family," *The Pennsylvania German* 10 (1909): 343. On the ownership of slaves among the elite residents of northern colonies, see Robert Blair St. George, "Artifacts of Regional Consciousness in the Connecticut River Valley," 341. On the preponderance of one-story log houses in late eighteenth-century Pennsylvania, see Falk, "Symbols of Assimilation or Status?" 128; Scott T. Swank, "The Architectural Landscape," in *Arts of the Pennsylvania Germans,* ed. Scott T. Swank et al. (New York: W. W. Norton for the Henry Francis du Pont Winterthur Museum, 1983), 24–27, tables 1–9. Of the eight townships and two borough wards covered by these sources, only in Lower Salford Township, Montgomery County, were the greatest number of houses not one-story log structures. For statistics on Cumberland County further west, see Nancy Van Dolsen, *Cumberland County: An Architectural Survey* (Carlisle, Pa.: Cumberland County Historical Society, 1990), 3, fig. 1. In all eleven townships Van Dolsen surveyed, the majority of houses were built of log. In all but three (Carlisle, Newton, and West Pennsboro) the average house was one or one-and-a-half stories.

5. In the decades surrounding the American Revolution, amid the rhetoric of freedom and liberty, acts of private manumission, particularly by individuals living outside the lower south, were not uncommon. In 1780, Pennsylvania became the first of five northern states to pass a gradual emancipation law. See Peter Kolchin, *American Slavery, 1619–1877* (New York: Hill and Wang, 1993), 77–79.

6. Salisbury Township Tax Records, 1750–1828; Probate Inventory for Peter Elmaker, Esq. (1798), Lancaster County Historical Society, Lancaster, Pa.; Edith L. Baldwin, "Old St. John's Pequea," *Historical Papers and Addresses of the Lancaster County Historical Society* 13 (1909): 144–45.

7. Probate Inventory for Peter Elmaker, Esq. (1798); Probate Inventory for Leonard Elmaker (1829), Lancaster County Historical Society, Lancaster, Pa.

8. Real Estate Advertisement, June 8, 1799, *Lancaster Journal* (microfilm, Lancaster County Historical Society, Lancaster, Pa.).

9. Real Estate Advertisement, June 8, 1799, *Lancaster*

Journal; 1815 Direct Tax for Salisbury Township, Lancaster County (photocopied and bound, Lancaster County Historical Society, Lancaster, Pa.).

10. Kevin M. Sweeney, "High Style Vernacular: Lifestyles of the Colonial Elite," in *Of Consuming Interests: The Style of Life in the Eighteenth Century,* ed. Cary Carson, Ronald Hoffman, and Peter J. Albert (Charlottesville: University Press of Virginia for the United States Capitol Historical Society, 1994), 5–9, 37; Bushman, *The Refinement of America,* 18–19; Lois Green Carr and Lorena S. Walsh, "Changing Lifestyles and Consumer Behavior in the Colonial Chesapeake," in *Of Consuming Interests,* 66–67; Margaretta M. Lovell, "'Such Furniture as Will Be Most Profitable': The Business of Cabinetmaking in Eighteenth-Century Newport," *Winterthur Portfolio* 26, no. 1 (Spring 1991): 30–32; Barbara G. Carson, *Ambitious Appetites: Dining, Behavior, and Consumption Patterns in Federal Washington* (Washington, D.C.: American Institute of Architects Press, 1990), 31, 36 63–66.

11. St. George, "Artifacts of Regional Consciousness," 338–39; Falk, "Symbols of Assimilation or Status?" 132–33. For period uses of the term "first class," see La Rochefoucauld Liancourt, *Travels Through the United States,* 2:26, 672, and *Four Letters on Interesting Subjects* (Philadelphia: Styner and Cist, 1776), 3. I wish to thank David Steinberg for alerting me to the latter source.

12. Examples of double-pile houses with distinct entry spaces built in Pennsylvania by people from various parts of the British Isles include Clivedon in Germantown, home of a lawyer of English Quaker descent; Mt. Pleasant in what is now Philadelphia's Fairmount Park, home of a Scottish sea captain; and Rock Ford in Lancaster, home of an Irish physician. See *Philadelphia: Three Centuries of American Art* (Philadelphia: Philadelphia Museum of Art, 1976), 80–83; Wayne Craven, *American Art: History and Culture* (Madison, Wis.: Brown and Benchmark, 1994), 84–85; Jerome H. Wood Jr., *Conestoga Crossroads: Lancaster, Pennsylvania, 1730–1790* (Harrisburg, Pa.: Pennsylvania Historical and Museum Commission, 1979), 178. German examples that will be discussed in this and following chapters include houses belonging to David Deshler, Philip Erpff, Henry Fisher, David Hottenstein, Johannes Lesher, Heinrich Melchior Muhlenberg, and Peter Wentz.

13. Cazenove, *Cazenove Journal,* 73–74.

14. Wood, *Conestoga Crossroads,* 178; Probate Inventory of Edward Hand (1802), transcribed and reproduced by Rock Ford Plantation, Lancaster, Pa.

15. David Hackett Fischer, *Albion's Seed: Four British Folkways in America* (New York: Oxford University Press, 1989), 477; Henry Glassie, "Eighteenth-Century Cultural Process in Delaware Valley Folk Building," *Winterthur Portfolio* 7 (1972): 37; Glassie, *Pattern in the Material Folk Culture of the Eastern United States* (Philadelphia: University of Pennsylvania Press, 1968), 49, 54; Scott T. Swank, "The Architectural Landscape," in *Arts of the Pennsylvania Germans,* 34; Dell Upton, "German and British Interaction in the Vernacular Architecture of the Virginia Uplands," manuscript, September 1977 (revised and expanded version of the lecture "British and German Interaction in the Blue Ridge," presented at the Blue Ridge Institute's Seminar on Blue Ridge Life and Culture, Ferrum

College, Ferrum, Va., September 24, 1977, now in Winterthur Library, Winterthur Museum, Garden and Library, Winterthur, Del.), 9. In "Eighteenth-Century Cultural Process in Delaware Valley Folk Building," Glassie does temper his view by stating that "the Georgian form is usually considered an English contribution to American domestic architecture, but while that notion connotes accurately the acculturative situation, English Georgian was part of an international Renaissance style. Distinctly Scottish and Germanic expressions of the style were built in Pennsylvania, and the fact that the basic Georgian form was known in seventeenth-century central Europe facilitated its acceptance by Continental settlers in the Mid-Atlantic region" (37).

16. Some of the most eminent Pennsylvanians did build closed-plan houses with unheated entries during the late decades of the seventeenth and first decades of the eighteenth century. These include the Slate Roof House (c. 1690), Fairhill (1712–17), Belaire (1714–19), and Stenton (1723–28). See Mark Reinberger and Elizabeth McLean, "Isaac Norris's Fairhill: Architecture, Landscape, and Quaker Ideals in a Philadelphia Colonial Country Seat," *Winterthur Portfolio* 32, no. 4 (Winter 1997): 247, 254, 260; Mark Reinberger, "Belmont: The Bourgeois Villa in Eighteenth Century Philadelphia," *ARRIS: Journal of the Southeast Chapter of the Society of Architectural Historians* 9 (1998): 14–15; Jack L. Lindsey et al., *Worldly Goods: The Arts of Early Pennsylvania, 1680–1758* (Philadelphia: Philadelphia Museum of Art, 1999), 81–86.

17. For a discussion of the importance of the passage, see Dell Upton, "Vernacular Domestic Architecture in Eighteenth-Century Virginia," in *Common Places: Readings in American Vernacular Architecture,* ed. Dell Upton and John Michael Vlach (Athens: University of Georgia Press, 1986), 320–23, and Mark R. Wenger, "The Central Passage in Virginia: Evolution of an Eighteenth-Century Living Space," in *Perspectives in Vernacular Architecture II,* ed. Camille Wells (Columbia: Curators of the University of Missouri, University of Missouri Press, 1986), 137–49.

18. This conclusion parallels that of scholars studying houses of people of British descent living in the Delaware Valley. See, for example, Jack Michel, "'In a Manner and Fashion Suitable to Their Degree': A Preliminary Investigation of the Material Culture of Early Rural Pennsylvania," *Working Papers from the Regional Economic History Research Center* 5, no. 1 (1981): 75, and Bernard Herman, *Architecture and Rural Life in Central Delaware, 1700–1900* (Knoxville: University of Tennessee Press, 1987), 14–41, especially 39.

19. Margaret Berwind Schiffer, *Survey of Chester County, Pennsylvania, Architecture: 17th, 18th and 19th Centuries* (Exton, Pa.: Schiffer Publishing, 1984), 42–43, 376; Steve Friesen, *A Modest Mennonite Home: The Story of the 1719 Hans Herr House, an Early Colonial Landmark* (Intercourse, Pa.: Good Books, 1990), 35, 41, 44–49; R. Martin Keen, "Community and Material Culture Among Lancaster Mennonites: Hans Hess from 1717 to 1733," *Pennsylvania Mennonite Heritage* (January 1990): 7, 9. Keen briefly discusses the Herr house on p. 13.

20. Robert A. Barakat, "The Herr and Zeller Houses," *Pennsylvania Folklife* 21, no. 4 (Summer 1972): 9, 19–20; 1798 Federal Direct Tax Records for Heidelberg Township, Dauphin County, Schedule A, Entry for Peter Zeller, National Archives, Washington, D.C. (microfilm, Center for Historic Architecture and Design, University of Delaware, Newark, Del.). The Zeller family presents an interesting case in discussing Pennsylvania German identity. According to genealogist Karen M. Green, Heinrich Zeller's ancestors were in fact French Huguenots who relocated to Manheim on the Rhine. Heinrich joined the "Palatine" immigration to New York in 1709 and from there traveled to Pennsylvania to settle (e-mail to author, April 29, 2006). The inclusion of people of French Huguenot descent among the Pennsylvania Germans was not limited to this case. See Don Yoder, "The Pennsylvania Germans: Three Centuries of Identity Crisis," in *America and the Germans: An Assessment of a Three-Hundred-Year History,* ed. Frank Trommler and Joseph McVeigh (Philadelphia: University of Pennsylvania Press, 1985), 1:43.

21. Contemporary buildings with a gambrel roof include Augustus Lutheran Church in Trappe, St. Michael's Lutheran Church in Philadelphia, and several buildings erected by Moravians. The house of Mennonite preacher Dielman Kolb, built in the 1740s in Lower Salford Township, Montgomery County, also had a gambrel roof.

22. Beatrice Garvan, *The Pennsylvania German Collection* (Philadelphia: Philadelphia Museum of Art, 1982), 6–7; Joseph Downs, *The House of the Miller at Millbach: The Architecture, Arts, and Crafts of the Pennsylvania Germans* (Philadelphia: Pennsylvania Museum of Art, 1929); 1798 Federal Direct Tax Records for Heidelberg Township, Dauphin County, Pennsylvania, Schedule A, Entry for Michael Miller, National Archives, Washington, D.C. (microfilm, Center for Historic Architecture and Design, University of Delaware, Newark, Del.).

23. For illustrations of the four first-floor rooms, see Albert T. Gamon, "Peter Wentz Farmstead," *Antiques* 72, no. 4 (October 1982): plates 4, 5, 6, 7, and 12. Images of two of the first floor-rooms can also be seen in Wendell Garrett, *American Colonial: Puritan Simplicity to Georgian Grace* (New York: Monacelli Press, 1995), 163, 165.

24. Gamon, "Peter Wentz Farmstead," 788–89.

25. Johann David Schöpf, *Travels in the Confederation, 1783–1784,* trans. and ed. Alfred J. Morrison (Philadelphia: William J. Campbell, 1911), 1:104; National Heritage Corporation, "Master Plan: Peter Wentz Farmstead, Volume 1: The Plan and Program" (January 1975), 37, 43, plate 7; National Heritage Corporation, "Master Plan: Peter Wentz Farmstead, Volume 2: Recommended Furnishings" (November 1973), 1; Gamon, "Peter Wentz Farmstead," 788–95; virtual tour, Peter Wentz Farmstead Historic Site Web site, http://historicsites.montcopa.org/historicsites/cwp/view,a,1440,q,24893.asp (accessed July 7, 2007).

26. National Heritage Corporation, "Master Plan: Peter Wentz Farmstead, Volume 2," 2.

27. Probate Inventory for Peter Wentz (1793), Montgomery County, Pennsylvania, transcription provided by Morgan McMillan at the Peter Wentz Farmstead; Roderic H. Blackburn and Ruth Piwonka, *Remembrance of Patria: Dutch Arts and Culture in Colonial America, 1609–1776* (Albany, N.Y.: Albany Institute of History and Art, 1988), 259–60; Susie Kilpatrick, "Textile Storage in Colonial America, 1680–1750" (paper presented at Annual Reports on Thesis Research, Winterthur Museum, Library and Garden, Winterthur, Del., May 29,

1998); Francis J. Puig, "The Early Furniture of the Mississippi River Valley," in *The Craftsman and the European Tradition, 1620–1820,* ed. Francis J. Puig and Michael Conforti (Hanover, N.H.: University Press of New England for the Minneapolis Institute of Arts, 1989), 157. Although the exact appearance of the Wentzes' *Schrank,* or clothes press, is not known, the form is illustrated in fig. 42 in a *Schrank* created in 1781 for David Hottenstein.

28. Probate Inventory for Peter Wentz (1793). In addition to the queensware in the corner cupboard, Peter Wentz also owned a dozen queensware plates that, given their position in the inventory listing, were presumably stored with the pewter. On the history of knives and forks, see Carson, *Ambitious Appetites,* 63–65.

29. See, for example, the house of ironmaster Johannes Lesher, illustrated in this work and discussed in Pendleton, *Oley Valley Heritage,* 76–79; the house of Lutheran minister Heinrich Melchior Muhlenberg included in this study and in John C. Shetler, "The Restoration of the Muhlenberg House: The Home of the Rev. Henry Melchior Muhlenberg," *Der Reggeboge: The Rainbow* 32, no. 2 (1998): 3–21; the house of Colonel John Hiester discussed in this work and in Falk, "Symbols of Assimilation or Status?" 114, fig. 2; 116; 117, fig. 4; and miller Peter Wentz's house included in this study and in Gamon, "Peter Wentz Farmstead," 788–95.

30. Falk, "Symbols of Assimilation or Status?" 119–22.

31. Scott T. Swank, "Henry Francis du Pont and Pennsylvania German Folk Art," in *Arts of the Pennsylvania Germans,* 84–91.

32. Probate Inventory for David Hottenstein (1802), Berks County, Berks County Courthouse, Reading, Pennsylvania.

33. Probate Inventory for David Hottenstein (1802); Garvan and Hummel, *The Pennsylvania Germans: A Celebration of Their Arts, 1683–1850* (Philadelphia: Philadelphia Museum of Art, 1982), 26–27, plates 6 and 180, entry 117. On the use of shells in the eighteenth century, see Margaretta M. Lovell, "Mrs. Sargent, Mr. Copley, and the Empirical Eye," *Winterthur Portfolio* 33, no. 1 (Spring 1998): 19.

34. Probate Inventory for David Hottenstein (1802).

35. Gabrielle M. Lanier, *The Delaware Valley in the Early Republic: Architecture, Landscape, and Regional Identity* (Baltimore: Johns Hopkins University Press, 2005), 64; Pendleton, *Oley Valley Heritage,* 63; Philip E. Pendleton, "Domestic Outbuildings," in *Guidebook for the Vernacular Architecture Forum Annual Conference: Architecture and Landscape of the Pennsylvania Germans, May 12–16, 2004, Harrisburg, Pennsylvania* (n.p.: Vernacular Architecture Forum, 2004), 51–52; Kenneth R. LeVan, "Building Construction and Materials of the Pennsylvania Germans," guidebook distributed at the meeting of the Vernacular Architecture Forum, Harrisburg, Pa., May 2004 (n.p.: LeVan, 2004), 4–7.

36. The lower level of roof framing was made up of large principal rafters, which rose from the top of the walls about halfway up toward the roof ridge; horizontal members, known as principal purlins, which ran parallel to the roof ridge and connected the principal rafters on one side of the building; hefty collar beams, connecting the principal rafters on opposite sides of the building; and braces, reinforcing the mortise and tenon joint between the principal rafters and collar beams. The smaller common rafters, rising all the way to the roof peak and connected to each other

with their own set of smaller collar beams, were erected on top of this substantial framed undergirding. See Pendleton, *Oley Valley Heritage,* 63–65; Chappell, "Acculturation in the Shenandoah Valley: Rhenish Houses of the Massanutten Settlement," in *Common Places,* 32–33. LeVan, "Building Construction and Materials of the Pennsylvania Germans," 36–37.

37. Homer Tope Rosenberger, *The Pennsylvania Germans, 1891–1965* (Lancaster: Pennsylvania German Society, 1966), 266; John K. Heyl, "The Building of the Troxell-Steckel House," *Proceedings of the Lehigh County Historical Society* 14 (1944): 112; Charles R. Roberts, "The Steckel House," *Proceedings: Lehigh County Historical Society* 13 (December 1942): 22–23; National Register of Historic Places Inventory–Nomination Form, Troxell-Steckel House, State Historic Preservation Office, Harrisburg, Pennsylvania.

38. Swank, "Henry Francis du Pont," 88; H. K. Landis, "Abbreviated Inscriptions in German Pennsylvania," *The Magazine Antiques* 32, no. 3 (September 1937): 122–23.

39. Numerous authors have made a similar argument concerning the introduction of Georgian architecture in other parts of what would become the United States. See, for example, Kevin M. Sweeney, "Mansion People: Kinship, Class, and Architecture in Western Massachusetts in the Mid-Eighteenth Century," *Winterthur Portfolio* 19, no. 4 (Winter 1984): 241, for Massachusetts; Upton, "Vernacular Domestic Architecture," 332, and Rhys Isaac, *The Transformation of Virginia, 1740–1790* (Chapel Hill: University of North Carolina Press, 1982), 37–39, for Virginia; Herman, *Architecture and Rural Life,* 39–41, for Delaware.

40. Doris D. Fanelli, "The Deshler-Morris House," *The Magazine Antiques* 124, no. 2 (August 1983): 284–89; Anna Coxe Toogood, *Historic Structure/Furnishings/Grounds Report, Deshler-Morris House, Bringhurst House, Historical Data Section, Independence National Historical Park, Pennsylvania* (Denver: Denver Service Center Branch of Historic Preservation, Mid-Atlantic/North Atlantic Team, National Park Service, United States Department of the Interior, [1980?]), especially 11–20, 59, 71; Stephanie Grauman Wolf, *Urban Village: Population, Community, and Family Structure in Germantown, Pennsylvania, 1683–1800* (Princeton: Princeton University Press, 1976), 13–14, 101–4.

41. Gottlieb Mittelberger, *Journey to Pennsylvania,* ed. and trans. Oscar Handlin and John Clive (Cambridge, Mass.: Harvard University Press, 1960), 49; La Rochefoucauld Liancourt, *Travels Through the United States,* 1:80; 2:672; Cazenove, *Cazenove Journal,* 62.

42. Benjamin Franklin, *Poor Richard Improved: Being an Almanack and Ephemeris of the Motions of the Sun and Moon . . . For the Year of Our Lord 1764, Being Bissextile, or Leap-year* (Philadelphia: B. Franklin and D. Hall, [1763]), n.p. For the use of the word "hut" in the context of colonial New England, see Robert Blair St. George, "'Set Thine House in Order': The Domestication of the Yeomanry in Seventeenth Century New England," in *Common Places,* 346, 359–60.

43. La Rochefoucauld Liancourt, *Travels Through the United States,* 1:59–60; Cazenove, *Cazenove Journal,* 16.

44. La Rochefoucauld Liancourt, *Travels Through the United*

States, 1:59–60; Cazenove, *Cazenove Journal,* 16.

45. United States Bureau of the Census, *Heads of Family at the First Census of the United States Taken in the Year 1790* (Washington, D.C.: Government Printing Office, 1907–8), 51.

46. Jacques-Pierre Brissot de Warville, *New Travels in the United States of America Performed in 1788* (Dublin: W. Corbet, 1792), 185–86.

47. Cazenove, *Cazenove Journal,* 73–74.

48. Franklin, *The Papers of Benjamin Franklin,* ed. Leonard W. Labaree (New Haven: Yale University Press, 1959–), 5:159; Cazenove, *Cazenove Journal,* 74; Probate Inventory for David Hottenstein (1802).

49. Brissot, *New Travels in the United States of America Performed in 1788,* 249–50, 256.

50. Edward Shippen to Richard Peters, December 9, 1766, Peters Family Papers, #499, Historical Society of Pennsylvania, Philadelphia, Pa.; Edward Shippen to George Craig, January 9, 1769 (not sent), Edward Shippen Letterbook, 1769, Library of the American Philosophical Society, Philadelphia, Pa.; Wood, *Conestoga Crossroads,* 52–53.

51. La Rochefoucauld Liancourt, *Travels Through the United States,* 1:76–77.

52. La Rochefoucauld Liancourt, *Travels Through the United States,* 1:77.

53. Henry Melchior Muhlenberg, *The Journals of Henry Melchior Muhlenberg,* trans. Theodore G. Tappert and John W. Doberstein (Philadelphia: Evangelical Lutheran Ministerium of Pennsylvania and Adjacent States and the Muhlenberg Press, 1942), 1:84; Cazenove, *Cazenove Journal,* 64; Brissot, *New Travels in the United States of America Performed in 1788,* 187. Brissot was perhaps incorrect in referring to William Richard's father as a "poor Scotchman" since, according to the Church of Jesus Christ of Latter-day Saints' Family Search Web site, Joseph Richardson hailed from Yorkshire, England.

54. Paul Douglas Newman, *Fries's Rebellion: The Enduring Struggle for the American Revolution* (Philadelphia: University of Pennsylvania Press, 2004), 73–77; *Annals of the Congress of the United States, Fourth Congress—Second Session: The Debates and Proceedings in the Congress of the United States* (Washington, D.C.: Gales and Seaton, 1849), 1898–99; *American State Papers: Documents, Legislative and Executive, of the Congress of the United States, Finance* (Washington, D.C.: Gales and Seaton, 1832), 1:440 (microfiche 7, Morris Library, University of Delaware, Newark, Del.).

55. *Annals of the Congress of the United States, Fourth Congress—Second Session,* 1887–88, 1904; *American State Papers, Finance,* 1:589–90 (microfiche 10, Morris Library, University of Delaware, Newark, Del.). For a general overview of the 1798 federal direct tax, see Lee Soltow, "America's First Progressive Tax," *National Tax Journal* 30, no. 1 (March 1977): 53–58.

56. Alexander Graydon, *Memoirs of a Life, Chiefly Passed in Pennsylvania, Within the Last Sixty Years; With Occasional Remarks Upon the General Occurrences, Character and Spirit of That Eventful Period* (Harrisburg, Pa.: John Wyeth, 1811), 358; [A Farmer], "Letter Addressed to Mr. Butler concerning 1798 Federal Direct Tax," *Oracle of Dauphin and Harrisburg Advertiser,* December 12, 1798 (microfilm,

State Library of Pennsylvania, Harrisburg, Pa.). Both Graydon's and the anonymous farmer's writings were partisan expressions of the Federalist position on the 1798 federal direct tax. See Newman, *Fries's Rebellion,* especially 102, 194.

57. *Annals of the Congress of the United States, Fourth Congress—Second Session,* 1870, 1877–78, 1880; *The Statutes at Large of Pennsylvania from 1682 to 1810* (Harrisburg, Pa.: Harrisburg Publishing, 1906), 11:65, 470; *American State Papers, Finance,* 1:427 (microfiche 7, Morris Library, University of Delaware, Newark, Del.); Graydon, *Memoirs of a Life,* 358; Brissot, *New Travels in the United States of America Performed in 1788,* 183.

58. *Annals of the Congress of the United States, Fourth Congress—Second Session,* 1880.

59. Cazenove, *Cazenove Journal,* 70; La Rochefoucauld Liancourt, *Travels Through the United States,* 2:383.

60. Mittelberger, *Journey to Pennsylvania,* 44. For a more detailed analysis of the expressions of status at funerals, see Ann Fairfax Withington, *Toward a More Perfect Union: Virtue and the Formation of American Republics* (New York: Oxford University Press, 1991), 127–28.

61. Joseph Scott, *The United States Gazetteer: Containing an Authentic Description of the Several States* (Philadelphia: F. and R. Bailey, 1795), n.p.; Thomas Cooper, *Some Information Respecting America,* 2nd ed. (London, 1795), 117; La Rochefoucauld Liancourt, *Travels Through the United States,* 1:23, 24; 2:58.

62. Cazenove, *Cazenove Journal,* 61–62; La Rochefoucauld Liancourt, *Travels Through the United States,* 1:23. In the 1922 translation of the Cazenove text, the editor included a question mark in brackets between the words "log" and "houses."

63. *Coleman's Re-print of William Penn's Original Proposal and Plan for the Founding and Building of Philadelphia in Pennsylvania, America* (London: James Coleman, 1881), 19; Henry Wansey, *An Excursion to the United States of North America, in the Summer of 1794* (Salisbury, England: J. Easton, 1798), 173; Cazenove, *Cazenove Journal,* 37, 70. The listing of buildings in Coleman's reprint is believed to date to 1720–30.

64. Brissot, *New Travels in the United States of America Performed in 1788,* 180; La Rochefoucauld Liancourt, *Travels Through the United States,* 1:63–64.

65. La Rochefoucauld Liancourt, *Travels Through the United States,* 1:70.

66. Benjamin Rush, "An Account of the Progress of Population, Agriculture, Manners, and Government in Pennsylvania," in *Essays: Literary, Moral, and Philosophical,* ed. Michael Meranze (Schenectady, N.Y.: Union College Press, 1988), 124–31; Jedidiah Morse, *The American Geography; or, A View of the Present Situation of the United States of America* (Elizabethtown, [N.J.]: Shepard Kollock, 1789), 313–18; Brissot, *New Travels in the United States of America Performed in 1788,* 330–38. For an interpretation of the essay, see Bernard L. Herman, "The Model Farmer and the Organization of the Countryside," in *Everyday Life in the Early Republic,* ed. Catherine E. Hutchins (Winterthur, Del.: Henry Francis du Pont Winterthur Museum, 1994), 35–59. A complete transcription of Brissot's version of the essay is included as an appendix to this work.

67. Rush, "An Account of the Progress," 124–25, 129.

68. Rush, "An Account of the Progress," 124–25, 129.

69. Rush, "An Account of the Progress," 125–26; La Rochefoucauld Liancourt, *Travels Through the United States,* 1:23.

70. Rush, "An Account of the Progress," 126–28, 129.

71. Scott, *The United States Gazetteer,* n.p. Doing fieldwork in the early 1970s, cultural geographer Richard Pillsbury confirmed at least some of the observations in period literature. He concluded, "The incipient pattern of dominating brick construction in Philadelphia and near suburbs and stone standing as the most important construction material of the adjacent counties of Bucks, Chester, and Montgomery is still present today" ("The Construction Materials of the Rural Folk Housing of the Pennsylvania Culture Region," *Pioneer America* 8, no. 2 [July 1976]: 100).

72. Billy G. Smith, *The 'Lower Sort': Philadelphia's Laboring People, 1750–1800* (Ithaca: Cornell University Press, 1990), 158–61; John Fransham, *The World in Miniature; or, The Entertaining Traveler* (London: John Torbuck, [1740?]), 2:93–94; Wansey, *An Excursion to the United States,* 173.

73. Jacob Duché, *Observation on a Variety of Subjects, Literary, Moral and Religious: In a Series of Original Letters, Written by a Gentleman of Foreign Extraction, who Resided Some Time in Philadelphia* (London: J. Deighton, 1791), 89.

74. Rush, "An Account of the Progress," 125.

75. Rush, "An Account of the Progress," 126–29.

76. Real Estate Advertisement, January 29, 1783, in Accessible Archives, *Pennsylvania Gazette,* CD-ROM edition, Folio 3 (1766–83) (Malvern, Pa.: Accessible Archives, 1995); Valeria Elizabeth Clymer Hill, *A Genealogy of the Hiester Family* (Lebanon, Pa.: Report Publishing, 1903), 25; La Rochefoucauld Liancourt, *Travels Through the United States,* 1:49–50; 1798 Federal Direct Tax Records for Middletown Township, Dauphin County, Schedule A, Entries for George Frey, National Archives, Washington, D.C. (microfilm, Center for Historic Architecture and Design, University of Delaware, Newark, Del.). Daniel Hiester's house is also discussed or illustrated in Hill, *A Genealogy of the Hiester Family,* 25; H. Winslow Fegley, *Farming, Always Farming: A Photographic Essay of the Rural Pennsylvania German Land and Life made by H. Winslow Fegley* (Birdsboro, Pa.: The Pennsylvania German Society), 92, fig. 79; and Brumbaugh, "Colonial Architecture of the Pennsylvania Germans," *Pennsylvania German Society Proceedings* 41 (1933): plate 92.

77. Probate Inventory for Philip Erpff (1803), Dauphin County Courthouse, Harrisburg, Pa. (microfilm E-1); Bergengren, "The Cycle of Transformations in the Houses of Schaefferstown" (Ph.D. diss., University of Pennsylvania, 1988), 87–88.

78. Probate Inventory for Philip Erpff (1803); Philip Erpff and Jacob Grubb, Rental Contract, March 3, 1800, Leon E. Lewis Jr. Collection, Lebanon County Historical Society, Lebanon, Pa., and Joseph Downs Collection of Manuscripts and Printed Ephemera, Winterthur Museum, Garden and Library, Winterthur, Del. (microfilm 11:A15).

Chapter 4

1. T. H. Breen, *The Marketplace of the Revolution: How Consumer Politics Shaped American Independence* (New York: Oxford University Press, 2004), 184; Ann Fairfax Withington, *Toward a More Perfect Union: Virtue and the Formation of American Republics* (New York: Oxford University Press, 1991), 96.

2. Just a sampling of the influences on Pennsylvania German religion suggests the wide diversity of doctrine adhered to by immigrants. Lutherans followed the teachings of Martin Luther as interpreted by Halle pietists such as August Hermann Francke. Members of German Reformed congregations adhered to the Heidelberg Catechism of 1563, which blended the theologies of Ulrich Zwingli, John Calvin, and other religious thinkers. Moravians traced their heritage to John Huss and the fifteenth-century *Unitas Fratrum.* Sectarian groups including Mennonites, Amish, and Dunkards (or Brethren) participated in diverse Anabaptist traditions. Followers of sixteenth-century Silesian nobleman Kasper Schwenkfeld von Ossig's teachings did away with all sacraments, including baptism. Still other people of German descent belonged to various, often short-lived, radical, hermitic and/or mystical faith communities. For an introduction to religious belief among Pennsylvania Germans, see Don Yoder, "Sects and Religious Movements of German Origin," in *Encyclopedia of the American Religious Experience: Studies of Traditions and Movements,* ed. Charles H. Lippy and Peter W. Williams (New York: Charles Scribner's Sons, 1988), 1:615–24; Milton J. Coalter Jr. and John M. Mulder, "Dutch and German Reformed Churches," in *Encyclopedia of the American Religious Experience,* 1:511–13; Charles H. Glatfelter, *Pastors and People: German Lutheran and Reformed Churches in the Pennsylvania Field, 1717–1793* (Breinigsville, Pa.: Pennsylvania German Society, 1980–81), 2:9–12, 64; Donald M. Herr, *Pewter in Pennsylvania German Churches* (Birdsboro, Pa.: Pennsylvania German Society, 1995), 11–12, 15, 20, 21–22, 23, 27–29; Beverly Prior Smaby, *The Transformation of Moravian Bethlehem* (Philadelphia: University of Pennsylvania Press, 1988), 3–6; Gillian Lindt Gollin, *Moravians in Two Worlds: A Study of Changing Communities* (New York: Columbia University Press, 1967), 4–5; William J. Murtagh, *Moravian Architecture and Town Planning: Bethlehem, Pennsylvania, and Other Eighteenth-Century American Settlements* (Chapel Hill: University of North Carolina Press, 1967), 4–5; Aaron Spencer Fogleman, *Hopeful Journeys: German Immigration, Settlement, and Political Culture in Colonial America, 1717–1775* (Philadelphia: University of Pennsylvania Press, 1996), 21–22; D. B. Eller, "Schwenkfelders," in *Dictionary of Christianity in America,* ed. Daniel Reid (Downers Grove, Ill.: InterVarsity Press, 1990), 1055–56. Fogleman notes 231 Catholics and 21 Jewish heads of household on Philadelphia ship lists and Pennsylvania and New York naturalization lists (*Hopeful Journeys,* 204n17). On the lack of German Catholic immigration, see Philip Otterness, *Becoming German: The 1709 Palatine Migration to New York* (Ithaca: Cornell University Press, 2004), 70.

3. Steven M. Nolt, *Foreigners in Their Own Land: Pennsylvania Germans in the Early Republic* (University Park: Pennsylvania State

University Press, 2002), 14–16; Otterness, *Becoming German,* 15; Fogleman, *Hopeful Journeys,* 111; David Walbert, *Garden Spot: Lancaster County, the Old Order Amish, and the Selling of Rural America* (Oxford: Oxford University Press, 2002), 20. Walbert states that "Church" Germans received their name "because they belonged to established churches, or because unlike Mennonites they built churches rather than worshipping in their homes." However, church folk did worship in dwelling houses during early years of settlement, and Pennsylvania Mennonites began building meetinghouses in the 1740s.

4. David Weaver-Zercher, *The Amish in the American Imagination* (Baltimore: Johns Hopkins University Press, 2001), 203n6; Walbert, *Garden Spot,* 20; Yoder, "Sects and Religious Movements," 615–21. In addition to the Anabaptist sects, eighteenth-century Schwenkfelders and Moravians were also pacifists. See Yoder, "Sects and Religious Movements," 622; Gollin, *Moravians in Two Worlds,* 5, 98.

5. Weaver-Zercher briefly discusses the importance of clothing in the use of the adjective "plain" (*The Amish in the American Imagination,* 203n6).

6. On the Amish, Mennonites, Moravians, and Ephrata residents, see Walbert, *Garden Spot;* John Hostetler, *Amish Society,* 4th ed. (Baltimore: Johns Hopkins University Press, 1993); Donald Kraybill, *The Riddle of Amish Culture,* rev. ed. (Baltimore: Johns Hopkins University Press, 2001); Steve Friesen, *A Modest Mennonite Home: The Story of the 1719 Hans Herr House, an Early Colonial Landmark* (Intercourse, Pa.: Good Books, 1990), 71; Henry Glassie, *Pattern in the Material Folk Culture of the Eastern United States* (Philadelphia: University of Pennsylvania Press, 1968), 62–64; Scott T. Swank, "Proxemic Patterns," in *Arts of the Pennsylvania Germans,* ed. Scott T. Swank et al. (New York: W. W. Norton for the Henry Francis du Pont Winterthur Museum, 1983), 35–38; Gollin, *Moravians in Two Worlds;* Fogleman, *Hopeful Journeys,* 100–126; Murtagh, *Moravian Architecture.* For works that deal specifically with Lutherans and Calvinists, see Glatfelter, *Pastors and People,* and A. G. Roeber, *Palatines, Liberty, and Property: German Lutherans in Colonial British America* (Baltimore: Johns Hopkins University Press, 1993). Roeber describes his book specifically as a response to previous "scholarly literature devoted to the 'folk' culture of the German speakers," which he feels "has tended to concentrate on the Plain Dutch" (ix). As an examination of the ecclesiastical pewter used by various denominations, Herr's book on church pewter breaks with the trend among material culture scholars of dealing with religious groups individually.

7. Henry Melchior Muhlenberg, *The Journals of Henry Melchior Muhlenberg,* trans. Theodore G. Tappert and John W. Doberstein (Philadelphia: Evangelical Lutheran Ministerium of Pennsylvania and Adjacent States and the Muhlenberg Press, 1942), 1:450; Ludwig Denig, *The Picture-Bible of Ludwig Denig: A Pennsylvania German Emblem Book,* trans. and ed. Don Yoder (New York: Hudson Hills Press for the Museum of American Folk Art and the Pennsylvania German Society, 1990), 1:129. For a previous interpretation of the conflicted relationship between refinement and virtue, see Richard L. Bushman, *The Refinement of America: Persons, Houses, Cities* (New York: Alfred A. Knopf, 1992), 60.

8. Murtagh, *Moravian Architecture,* 130; Fogleman, *Hopeful Journeys,* 111–12; Ralph Grayson Schwarz, *Bethlehem on the Lehigh* (Bethlehem: Bethlehem Area Foundation, n.d.), 17.

9. Morgan Edwards, *Baptists in Pennsylvania, Both British and German* (Philadelphia, 1770), as transcribed in Felix Reichman and Eugene E. Doll, *Ephrata as Seen by Contemporaries* (Allentown, Pa.: Schlechter's for the Pennsylvania German Folklore Society, 1953), 93.

10. Jeffrey Bach, *Voices of the Turtledoves: The Sacred World of Ephrata* (University Park: Pennsylvania State University Press, 2003), 31–35, 87–90, 93.

11. Fogleman, *Hopeful Journeys,* 107–13, 168–69; Vernon H. Nelson and Lothar Madeheim, "The Moravian Settlements of Pennsylvania in 1757: The Nicholas Garrison Views," *Pennsylvania Folklife* 19, no. 1 (Autumn 1969); Letter Addressed to Mr. Franklin, February 24, 1743, in Accessible Archives, *Pennsylvania Gazette,* CD-ROM edition, Folio 1 (1728–50) (Malvern, Pa.: Accessible Archives, 1991).

12. The nonfamilial living arrangements at these communities have been credited, at least partially, to the recognition of God's female characteristics. See Aaron Spencer Fogleman, "Jesus Is Female: The Moravian Challenge in the German Communities of British North America," *William and Mary Quarterly,* 3rd series, 60, no. 2 (April 2003): 295–332, especially 314, 324, 328, and Gollin, *Moravians in Two Worlds,* 93–100.

13. Jacques P. Rousselot de Surgy, *Histoire Naturelle et Politique de la Pennsylvanie* (Paris, 1768), as transcribed in Reichmann and Doll, *Ephrata as Seen by Contemporaries,* 89; Israel Acrelius, "A Visit by the Rev. Provost Israel Acrelius to the American Cloister at Bethlehem," in *A History of New Sweden; or, The Settlements on the River Delaware,* trans. William M. Reynolds (Philadelphia: Publication Fund of the Historical Society of Pennsylvania, 1876), 403.

14. Bach, *Voices of the Turtledoves,* 19, 115–38.

15. Ann Kirschner, "From Hebron to Saron: The Religious Transformation of an Ephrata Convent," *Winterthur Portfolio* 32, no. 1 (Spring 1997): 37–38, 45–49, 58–59; Conrad Weiser as quoted in Reichmann and Doll, *Ephrata as Seen by Contemporaries,* 35; Christopher Saur as quoted in Reichman and Doll, *Ephrata as Seen by Contemporaries,* 47.

16. Kirschner, "From Hebron to Saron," 49–50; Bach, *Voices of the Turtledoves,* 117, 133; Schöpf, *Travels in the Confederation,* as transcribed in Reichmann and Doll, *Ephrata as Seen by Contemporaries,* 137; "Zwei Briefe Aus Pennsylvanien—1784," as transcribed in Reichmann and Doll, *Ephrata as Seen by Contemporaries,* 124. Similar descriptions of the Ephrata buildings can be found in numerous other eighteenth-century accounts, including those in Reichmann and Doll, *Ephrata as Seen by Contemporaries,* 81, 99, 113, 117, 144, and 146.

17. Kirschner, "From Hebron to Saron," 40; 54, fig. 8; 56; 59; 60, fig. 13.

18. Bach, *Voices of the Turtledoves,* 87–89, 90; Israel Acrelius, "Visit by the Provost Magister, Israel Acrelius, to the Ephrata Cloister, Aug. 20, 1753," in *A History of New Sweden,* 382; *An Universal History, from the Earliest Account of Time to the Present* (London, 1764), as transcribed in Reichmann and Doll, *Ephrata as Seen by*

Contemporaries, 85; Pennsylvania Gazette, no. 303 (September 25, 1734), as transcribed in Reichmann and Doll, Ephrata as Seen by Contemporaries, 9.

19. Bach, Voices of the Turtledoves, 94; also see p. 88 on moderation of diet over time; Christopher Wiegner, The Spiritual Diary of Christopher Wiegner (1732–39), trans. and ed. Peter C. Erb (Pennsbury, Pa.: Society of the Descendants of the Schwenkfeldian Exiles, 1978), 110, 152 (original manuscript, Joseph Downs Collection of Manuscripts and Printed Ephemera, Doc. 1013, Winterthur Museum, Garden and Library, Winterthur, Del.); Jedidiah Morse, The American Geography; or, a View of the Present Situation of the United States of America (Elizabethtown, [N.J.]: Shepard Kollock, 1789), 324; François Alexandre-Frédéric, duc de La Rochefoucauld Liancourt, Travels Through the United States of North America, the Country of the Iroquois, and Upper Canada, in the Years 1795, 1796, and 1797; With an Authentic Account of Lower Canada (London: R. Phillips, 1799), 1:36–37; Kirschner, "From Hebron to Saron," 62.

20. Morrison H. Heckscher and Leslie Greene Bowman, American Rococo, 1750–1775: Elegance in Ornament (New York: Metropolitan Museum of Art), 60, plate 37; Schwarz, Bethlehem on the Lehigh, 14–15; F. J. Chastellux, Travels in North-America, in the Years 1780, 1781, and 1782 (London: G. G. J. and J. Robinson, 1787), 2:332–33; Muhlenberg, The Journals of Henry Melchior Muhlenberg, 1:158, 192.

21. Morse, The American Geography, 322, 323, 328; Théophile Cazenove, Cazenove Journal, 1794: A Record of the Journey of Theophile Cazenove Through New Jersey and Pennsylvania, ed. Rayner Wickersham Kelsey (Haverford, Pa.: The Pennsylvania History Press, 1922), 26; W[illiam] Winterbotham, An Historical, Geographical, Commercial, and Philosophical View of the American United States, and of the European Settlements in America and the West-Indies (London, 1795), 2:444; La Rochefoucauld Liancourt, Travels Through the United States, 2:406–7, 412–13; Isaac Weld Jr., Travels Through the States of North America and the Provinces of Canada During the Years 1795, 1796, and 1797 (London: John Stockdale, 1807), 2:357; Nazareth Hall Collection, Joseph Downs Collection of Manuscripts and Printed Ephemera, Col. 212, Winterthur Museum, Garden and Library, Winterthur, Del. Eighteenth-century students at Nazareth Hall are listed with their place of residence in Levin T. Reichel, A History of Nazareth Hall from 1755 to 1855 (Philadelphia: J. B. Lippincott, 1855), 49–54.

22. Acrelius, "A Visit by the Rev. Provost Israel Acrelius to the American Cloister at Bethlehem," in A History of New Sweden, 403; Thomas Anburey, Travels Through the Interior Parts of America (New York: Houghton Mifflin, 1923), 2:295; Weld, Travels Through the States of North America, 2:359. For more information on the Sun Inn, see Murtagh, Moravian Architecture, 79–82. On the Gemeinhaus, see Vernon H. Nelson, The Bethlehem Gemeinhaus: A National Historic Landmark (Bethlehem, Pa.: Oaks Printing, 1990), especially 10–11, 40, and Murtagh, Moravian Architecture, 25–30.

23. Donald L. Fennimore, "Metalwork," in Arts of the Pennsylvania Germans, ed. Scott T. Swank et al. (New York: W. W. Norton for the Henry Francis du Pont Winterthur Museum, 1983), 215–16; Wendy A. Cooper, An American Vision: Henry Francis du Pont's Winterthur

Museum (Washington, D.C. and Winterthur, Del.: National Gallery of Art and Winterthur Museum, Garden and Library, 2002), 129; Donald M. Herr, Pewter in Pennsylvania German Churches (Birdsboro, Pa.: Pennsylvania German Society, 1995), 132. Born in Saxony, Heyne had left the closed Moravian community of Bethlehem and was living in Lancaster when he made the candlesticks. It is believed that Heyne fashioned them for the Most Blessed Sacrament Church, a Catholic church in Bally, Berks County, rather than for a Moravian congregation.

24. Susan Garfinkel, "Quakers and High Chests: The Plainness Problem Reconsidered," in Quaker Aesthetics: Reflections on a Quaker Ethic in American Design and Consumption, ed. Emma Jones Lapsansky and Anne A. Verplanck (Philadelphia: University of Pennsylvania Press, 2003), 50–89. While I am specifically citing Susan Garfinkel's chapter, the entire volume provides an examination of objects as they relate to the religious beliefs of the Quakers.

25. Muhlenberg, The Journals of Henry Melchior Muhlenberg, 1:363, 369.

26. Muhlenberg, The Journals of Henry Melchior Muhlenberg, 1:214, 371.

27. Denig, The Picture-Bible of Ludwig Denig, 1:130–31; vol. 2, plate 9.

28. John Hunt, "John Hunt's Diary," Proceedings of the New Jersey Historical Society 52 (January 1935): 28–29 (entry for September—Ye 9th mo.—23, 1781); Morse, The American Geography, 325; Thomas Hughes, "Journal of Ensign Thomas Hughes," ed. Herbert H. Beck, Papers Read Before the Lancaster County Historical Society 58, no. 1 (1954): 17. Concerning the similar convictions of Dunkards, or members of the Church of the Brethren, see Stephen L. Longnecker, Piety and Tolerance: Pennsylvania German Religion, 1700–1850 (Metuchen, N.J.: Scarecrow Press, Inc. 1994), 67–69.

29. John L. Ruth, The Earth Is the Lord's: A Narrative History of the Lancaster Mennonite Conference (Scottdale, Pa.: Herald Press, 2001), 319, 647, 1257. Ruth cites the Groffdale document and provides a transcription of the original German in his footnotes. The document is now in the Groffdale Mennonite Church Collection, Lancaster Mennonite Historical Society. On the use of cotton cloth for clothing, see Adrienne E. Saint-Pierre, "Luther Edgerton's 'Cloathing Books': A Record of Men's Ready-to-Wear from the Early Nineteenth Century," in Textiles in Early New England: Design, Production, and Consumption, ed. Peter Benes (Boston: Boston University, 1999), 222.

30. Will of Maria Wenger (1773), Book X, vol. 2, p. 74 (microfilm, Lancaster County Historical Society, Lancaster, Pa.). Catherine L. West Emerson, "Clothing the Pennsylvania Mennonite Woman in the Eighteenth Century," Pennsylvania Mennonite Heritage (April 1997): 5n24, 19.

31. Friesen, A Modest Mennonite Home, 86; Ruth, The Earth Is the Lord's, 251; 1798 Federal Direct Tax Records for London Derry Township, Dauphin County, Schedule A, Entry for Henry Landis, National Archives, Washington, D.C. (microfilm, Center for Historic Architecture and Design, University of Delaware, Newark, Del.).

32. Ruth, The Earth Is the Lord's, 412–13.

33. James Hindman, "Map of Chester County," (1816), in Historical

Atlas of Chester County, Pennsylvania (West Chester: Chester County Planning Commission, 1971), 3.

34. John C. Wenger, *History of the Mennonites of the Franconia Conference* (Scottdale, Pa.: Mennonite Publishing House, 1938), 204–5, 207; Daniel K. Cassel, *History of the Mennonites* (Philadelphia: Daniel K. Cassel, 1888), 269; *Historical Atlas of Chester County Pennsylvania* (West Chester, Pa.: Chester County Printing Department for the Chester County Planning Commission, 1971), 3; Chester County Deed Book V2, p. 247, Chester County Archives, West Chester, Pa.; Carl Lounsbury, e-mail to author, July 12, 2000; Philip E. Pendleton, "Oley Valley Tour," in *Guidebook for the Vernacular Architecture Forum Annual Conference: Architecture and Landscape of the Pennsylvania Germans, May 12–16, 2004, Harrisburg, Pennsylvania* (n.p.: Vernacular Architecture Forum, 2004), 63–64. For the distinction between churches and meetinghouses in a New England context, see Kevin M. Sweeney, "Meetinghouses, Town Houses, and Churches: Changing Perceptions of Sacred and Secular Space in Southern New England, 1720–1850," *Winterthur Portfolio* 28, no. 1 (Spring 1993): 64. For a description of an auditory plan, see Sweeney, "Meetinghouses," 61.

35. Glatfelter, *Pastors and People,* 1:277, 324; 2:154–55.

36. Glatfelter, *Pastors and People,* 1:323–24; Jerry Clouse, "Religious Landscapes," in *Guidebook for the Vernacular Architecture Forum Annual Conference,* 111; Clarke Hess, "Religious Communities," in *Guidebook for the Vernacular Architecture Forum Annual Conference,* 125–26.

37. Glatfelter, *Pastors and People,* 1:379, 414; 2:154–55; William O. Fegely, "Augustus Lutheran Church, Trappe, PA: The Shrine of Lutheranism," rev. Herbert H. Michel (brochure, 1987), 4–9, 12; Nicholas Scull, *Map of the Improved Part of the Province of Pennsylvania* (Philadelphia, 1759); Carl Lounsbury, e-mail message to author, July 8, 2004.

38. Rush, "An Account of the Manners of the German Inhabitants of Pennsylvania," *Columbian Magazine,* January 1789, 27; Glatfelter, *Pastors and People,* 2:279, 280; Morse, *The American Geography,* 331; Winterbotham, *An Historical, Geographical, Commercial, and Philosophical View,* 2:413; Cazenove, *Cazenove Journal,* 73. Although it is difficult to discern whether Morse and his imitator, Winterbotham, were referring to the Lutheran or Reformed church in Philadelphia, the fact that Zion Lutheran was damaged by fire in 1794 makes the Reformed church the more likely target of their commentary. For a view of the Philadelphia Reformed Church, see Glatfelter, *Pastors and People,* 2:280. On the use of compass-headed windows in church buildings, see Dell Upton, *Holy Things and Profane: Anglican Parish Churches in Colonial Virginia* (Cambridge, Mass.: MIT Press; New York: Architectural History Foundation, 1986), 114–18.

39. William Russell Birch, *The City of Philadelphia, in the State of Pennsylvania, North America, as it Appeared in 1800, Consisting of Twenty-eight Plates* (Philadelphia: W. Birch, 1800), plate 7; Nelson and Madeheim, "The Moravian Settlements of Pennsylvania," 8, 10; Murtagh, *Moravian Architecture,* 105. Moravian choir buildings in Bethlehem and Lititz also had gambrel roofs. A nineteenth-century photograph of Zion (or Moselem) Lutheran, built in Richmond

Township, Berks County, in 1761, indicates it had a polygonal apse like Augustus Lutheran (Glatfelter, *Pastors and People,* 2:137). Perhaps the building's designers chose to copy this feature from the Trappe church or a common European prototype.

40. On Hottenstein, see Swank, "Henry Francis du Pont and Pennsylvania German Folk Art," in *Arts of the Pennsylvania Germans,* ed. Scott T. Swank et al. (New York: W. W. Norton for the Henry Francis du Pont Winterthur Museum, 1983), 87. On Erpff, see "St. Luke Evangelical Lutheran Church Parish Registers, 1763–1834" (typescript, St. Luke Evangelical Church, Schaefferstown, Pa.), viii, and P. C. Croll, *Ancient and Historic Landmarks in the Lebanon Valley* (Philadelphia: Lutheran Publishing Society, 1895), 117. On Elmaker, see F. Edward Wright, *Lancaster County, Pennsylvania: Church Records of the Eighteenth Century,* vol. 1 (Westminster, Md.: Family Line Publications, 1994), 85; *Register of Marriages and Baptisms Kept by Rev. Traugott Frederick Illing* (Harrisburg, Pa.: Harrisburg Publishing, 1891), 26, 27, 29; Glatfelter, *Pastors and People,* 1:66–67. On Wentz, see Glatfelter, *Pastors and People,* 1:384; Herr, *Pewter in Pennsylvania German Churches,* 15. George and Michael Müller are both buried at the Millbach Reformed Church (now St. Paul's United Church of Christ), which is adjacent to their house and mill. On George Müller's role in the congregation, see Glatfelter, *Pastors and People,* 1:334–35, and Lancaster County Deed Book N, p. 196 (microfilm, Lancaster County Historical Society, Lancaster, Pa.).

41. Lisa M. Minardi, "Of Massive Stones and Durable Materials: Architecture and Community in Eighteenth-Century Trappe, Pennsylvania" (M.A. thesis, Winterthur Program in Early American Culture, University of Delaware, 2006), 14–44.

42. Muhlenberg, *The Journals of Henry Melchior Muhlenberg,* 1:118, 121, 174.

43. Muhlenberg, *The Journals of Henry Melchior Muhlenberg,* 713; Minardi, "Of Massive Stones and Durable Materials," 45–78, especially 55–57, 64–67; John C. Shetler, "The Restoration of the Muhlenberg House: The Home of the Rev. Henry Melchior Muhlenberg," *Der Reggeboge: The Rainbow* 32, no. 2 (1998): 3–21.

44. Muhlenberg, *The Journals of Henry Melchior Muhlenberg,* 2:518; 3:109.

45. A. Hunter Rineer, *Churches and Cemeteries of Lancaster County, Pennsylvania* (Lancaster: Lancaster County Historical Society, 1993), 77–78, 353; Franklin Ellis and Samuel Evans, *History of Lancaster County, Pennsylvania* (Philadelphia: Everts and Peck, 1883), 742–43, as obtained from http://www.rootsweb.com/~pacahs/conestog.htm (accessed June 15, 2004).

46. Determining who among Conestoga Township's residents in 1798 was affiliated with one of the Mennonite congregations and who was Lutheran required me to use multiple types of sources, as none of the religious groups kept lists of congregants during the eighteenth century. Transcriptions of headstones played a key role, although many eighteenth-century Conestogans were either interred at family cemeteries rather than church cemeteries or their burials in church lots are no longer marked. However, the grave markers in church cemeteries provided a starting point for identifying religious affiliation. The River Corner Mennonite Church in Conestoga has an adjoining cemetery dating back to the eighteenth century, and

the site of the New Danville Mennonite Church includes a family cemetery that was expanded to serve the congregation when the land was deeded to the church. The union cemetery adjacent to the current Reformed Church contains burials going back to 1780. Worner Collection, Lancaster County Cemetery Inscriptions, vol. 16, ed. A. Hunter Rineer (Lancaster: Lancaster County Historical Society, 1983), secs. 214 and 216; Darvin L. Martin and Regina Christman Martin, *Let These Stones Speak: A Genealogical Guide to Lancaster County's Families Based on Cemetery Research,* vol. 1, Pequea Township, 3rd ed., CD-ROM (Brownstown, Pa.: Historic Impressions Press, 2004); Martin and Martin, *Let These Stones Speak: A Genealogical Guide to Lancaster County's Families Based on Cemetery Research,* vol. 2, Conestoga Township, CD-ROM (Brownstown, Pa.: Historic Impressions Press, 2003).

The identification of Mennonites was further aided by a 1777 tax list enumerating "nonassociators," or men between sixteen and fifty-three years of age who paid an extra tax of £3.10.0 rather than bear arms in the Revolutionary War, often for religious reasons ("1777 Assessment of the Nonassociators in Conestoga Township," Lancaster County, Pennsylvania, Tax Records, 1748–1855, Conestoga Township, 1751–1855 [microfilm, Pennsylvania Historical and Museum Commission, Pos. 7, Lancaster County Historical Society, Lancaster, Pa.]). For a transcription of the Pennsylvania Committee of Safety's *Resolutions Directing the Mode of Levying Taxes on Non-Associators in Pennsylvania* (August 19, 1775), see http://www.motherbedford.com/Articles.htm (accessed July 7, 2007). An original copy printed in Philadelphia by W. and T. Bradford is in the collection of the library of the York County Heritage Trust, York, Pennsylvania, in the Revolutionary War document collection. Because nonassociators were not always Mennonite, inclusion on the list was only one consideration in assigning Conestoga Township residents to that religious group. Householders who were nonassociators and who were buried in a Mennonite cemetery or had family members buried in a Mennonite cemetery were classified as Mennonite. Some Lutherans from Conestoga could be identified based on baptismal and communicant lists recorded in the pastoral accounts of Trinity Lutheran Church in Lancaster. Marriage records kept by Lutheran pastor John Jacob Strine beginning in 1815 proved less useful, as Strine performed ceremonies for both parishioners and nonparishioners, including many Mennonites (*Trinity Lutheran Church Records, Lancaster, Pennsylvania,* vol. 3 [1782–96], trans. and ed. Debra D. Smith and Frederick S. Weiser [Apollo, Pa.: Closson Press, 1998]; J. J. Strine, *Personal Marriage Records of Reverend J. J. Strine,* trans. and ed. Frederick S. Weiser and Debra D. Smith [Apollo, Pa.: Closson Press, 2001], v).

47. 1798 Federal Direct Tax Records for Conestoga Township, Lancaster County, Schedules A and B, National Archives, Washington, D.C. (microfilm, Lancaster County Historical Society, Lancaster, Pa.).

48. 1798 Federal Direct Tax Records for Conestoga Township, Lancaster County, Schedules A and B.

49. 1798 Federal Direct Tax Records for Conestoga Township, Lancaster County, Schedules A and B, Entries for Tobias Stayman and John Eshback, National Archives, Washington, D.C. (microfilm,

Lancaster County Historical Society, Lancaster, Pa.); *Trinity Lutheran Church Records,* 5, 258.

50. Will of Benedict Eshleman, Lancaster County Will Book D, vol. 1, p. 21 (microfilm #299D, Lancaster County Historical Society, Lancaster, Pa.); Lancaster County Deed Books CC, pp. 245, 248, 335, 338; SS, p. 112; D, vol. 3, p. 103 (microfilm, Lancaster County Historical Society, Lancaster, Pa.).

51. Betty Layton, e-mail to author, August 9, 2004.

52. Rineer, *Churches and Cemeteries,* 77; Lancaster County Deed Book SS, p. 117.

53. Probate Inventory for Benedict Eshleman (1780), Lancaster County Historical Society, Lancaster, Pa.; Will of Benedict Eshleman; 1798 Federal Direct Tax Records for Conestoga Township, Lancaster County, Schedules A and B, Entries for Mathias Miller, National Archives, Washington, D.C. (microfilm, Lancaster County Historical Society, Lancaster, Pa.).

54. Thomas Pownall, *A Topographical Description of the Dominions of the United States of America,* ed. Lois Mulkearn (Pittsburgh: University of Pittsburgh Press, 1949); Weld, *Travels Through the States of North America,* 2:361. I am grateful to Mark Turdo for supplying me with descriptions of Moravian clothing, which were compiled by Carol Hall, as well as a translation of the pamphlet *Die Herrnhuter Schwesternhaube in Zwei Jahrhunderten: Kirchliche Tracht der Herrnhuterinnen um 1750–1950 in Zwei Bildserien* [The Herrnhut Sisters' Cap Through Two Centuries: Churchly Dress of the Female Herrnhuter from 1750–1950 in Two Series of Pictures] (Herrnhut, Germany: Karl Siebörger, 1955).

55. Morse, *The American Geography,* 322. Morse was speaking specifically of Moravian women's clothing.

56. Bernard L. Herman, "Eighteenth-Century Quaker Houses in the Delaware Valley and the Aesthetics of Practice," in *Quaker Aesthetics,* 205, 211.

57. Simon Schama, *The Embarrassment of Riches: An Interpretation of Dutch Culture in the Golden Age* (New York: Knopf, 1987), 326–27. Schama's work provides great insight into the ambivalent nature of verbal attacks on luxury. He finds that in seventeenth-century Dutch culture, for example, religious exhortations against worldly expenditures had little effect: people still wore fine clothes and jewels and furnished their houses with fine art and furniture (298, 310, 320, 323).

58. G. C., *A Little Looking-Glass for the Times; or, A Brief Remembrancer for Pennsylvania Containing Some Serious Hints, Affectionately Addressed to People of Every Rank and Station in the Province: With an Appendix, by Way of Supplication to Almighty God* (Wilmington, Del.: James Adams, 1764), 9, 17, 19. See also Denig, *The Picture-Bible of Ludwig Denig,* 1:128.

59. Withington, *Toward a More Perfect Union,* 10–11, 96; Breen, *The Marketplace of the Revolution,* 195–200, 235–37, 265. Withington and Breen both argue that virtue and morality in the political realm were distinct from religious virtue (Withington, *Toward a More Perfect Union,* 36; Breen, *The Marketplace of the Revolution,* 209), but here I note that they were informed by the widespread religious sentiment of the day. The issue of luxury as it relates to religion and society generally is also noted in Gary B. Nash, *The Urban Crucible:*

The Northern Seaports and the Origins of the American Revolution, abridged ed. (Cambridge, Mass.: Harvard University Press, 1979), 127, 232; Rhys Isaac, *The Transformation of Virginia, 1740–1790* (Chapel Hill: University of North Carolina Press, 1982), 247–48; Edmund S. Morgan, "The Puritan Ethic and the American Revolution," in *In Search of Early America: The William and Mary Quarterly, 1943–1993* (Richmond, Va.: William Byrd Press for the Institute of Early American History and Culture, 1993), 78–79.

60. Benjamin Franklin, "Observations on the Increase of Mankind, Peopling of Countries, etc.," in *The Writings of Benjamin Franklin*, ed. Albert Henry Smith (New York: Macmillan, 1907), 3:69 (printed as it appeared appended to *Observations on the Late and Present Conduct of the French* by William Clarke [Boston, 1755]); Jacques-Pierre Brissot de Warville, *New Travels in the United States of America Performed in 1788* (Dublin: W. Corbet, 1792), 381–83.

61. Brissot, *New Travels in the United States of America Performed in 1788*, 317–18, 381.

62. Brissot, *New Travels in the United States of America Performed in 1788*, 383; La Rochefoucauld Liancourt, *Travels Through the United States*, 2:385, 673–74.

63. Abbott Lowell Cummings, "Inside the Massachusetts House," in *Common Places: Readings in American Vernacular Architecture*, ed. Dell Upton and John Michael Vlach (Athens: University of Georgia Press, 1986), 232.

64. Thomas Cooper, *Some Information Respecting America*, 2nd ed. (London, 1795), 49, 215, 224.

65. Alexander Hamilton, *Hamilton's Itinerarium, Being a Narrative of a Journey from Annapolis, Maryland Through Delaware, Pennsylvania, New York, New Jersey, Connecticut, Rhode Island, Massachusetts and New Hampshire from May to September, 1744* (Saint Louis, Mo.: William K. Bixby, 1907), 25; Jacob Duché, *Observation on a Variety of Subjects, Literary, Moral and Religious: In a Series of Original Letters, Written by a Gentleman of Foreign Extraction, who Resided Some Time in Philadelphia* (London: J. Deighton, 1791), 190.

66. Hamilton, *Hamilton's Itinerarium*, 25; Denig, *The Picture-Bible of Ludwig Denig*, 1:129; Muhlenberg, *The Journals of Henry Melchior Muhlenberg*, 1:314; 3:573.

67. Muhlenberg, *The Journals of Henry Melchior Muhlenberg*, 1:268, 450; 3:746.

68. Muhlenberg, *The Journals of Henry Melchior Muhlenberg*, 1:136, 450; for funerals, see 317–18.

69. Don Yoder, "The Book and Its Sources," in Denig, *The Picture-Bible of Ludwig Denig*, 1:79–81. Yoder provides a close analysis of another Denig tavern scene. He concludes that although there are similarities between the illustration and a print source, the subject matter and composition were largely Denig's creation. This differentiates this image—and probably the other tavern scenes as well—from many other illustrations in the "Picture-Bible," which were more closely based on previously printed works.

70. Muhlenberg, *The Journals of Henry Melchior Muhlenberg*, 1:316; Denig, *The Picture-Bible of Ludwig Denig*, 1:22–23, 128, 129.

71. La Rochefoucauld Liancourt, *Travels Through the United States*, 1:37; Muhlenberg, *The Journals of Henry Melchior*

Muhlenberg, 1:434.

72. Franklin, "Observations on the Increase of Mankind," 64; La Rochefoucauld Liancourt, *Travels Through the United States*, 2:674.

73. Brissot, *New Travels in the United States of America Performed in 1788*, 317; *Annals of the Congress of the United States, Fourth Congress—Second Session: The Debates and Proceedings in the Congress of the United States* (Washington, D.C.: Gales and Seaton, 1849), 1898–99; Cooper, *Some Information Respecting America*, 56–57.

74. La Rochefoucauld Liancourt, *Travels Through the United States*, 2:381; Cooper, *Some Information Respecting America*, 49.

75. La Rochefoucauld Liancourt, *Travels Through the United States*, 2:674; Henry Wansey, *An Excursion to the United States of North America, in the Summer of 1794* (Salisbury, England: J. Easton, 1798), xi.

76. La Rochefoucauld Liancourt, *Travels Through the United States*, 2:583–84.

77. Benjamin Franklin, *Political, Miscellaneous, and Philosophical Pieces* (London: J. Johnson, 1779), 13; Chastellux, *Travels in North-America*, 2:356, 363.

78. Chastellux, *Travels in North-America*, 2:357.

79. Chastellux, *Travels in North-America*, 2:357, 363.

80. La Rochefoucauld Liancourt, *Travels Through the United States*, 2:674. On the theory that knowledge is required to participate in genteel dining and related activities, see Carson, *Ambitious Appetites: Dining, Behavior, and Consumption Patterns in Federal Washington* (Washington, D.C.: American Institute of Architects Press, 1990), 16, 29, 59; Bushman, *The Refinement of America*, 73–78.

81. Withington, *Toward a More Perfect Union*, 16. Withington writes, "According to the accepted political theory of the day, articulated by Montesquieu, a relationship existed between the character (or *genius*) of a people and the government they could sustain. A people motivated by fear would have tyrannies; a people motivated by honor, monarchies; by virtue, republics."

82. Rush, "An Account of the Progress of Population, Agriculture, Manners, and Government in Pennsylvania," in *Essays: Literary, Moral, and Philosophical*, ed. Michael Meranze (Schenectady, N.Y.: Union College Press, 1988), 127–28. On Rush's religious background, see Michael Meranze's introduction, iii.

83. Johann David Schöpf, *Travels in the Confederation, 1783–1784*, trans. and ed. Alfred J. Morrison (Philadelphia: William J. Campbell, 1911), 1:134–35.

84. Muhlenberg, *The Journals of Henry Melchior Muhlenberg*, 1:269; La Rochefoucauld Liancourt, *Travels Through the United States*, 2:26.

85. Denig, *The Picture-Bible of Ludwig Denig*, 1:24; Will of Lewis Denig, Will Book D, p. 157–62, Franklin County Courthouse, Chambersburg, Pa.; Orphan's Court Records for Decedent Lewis Denig, D 99, Franklin County Courthouse; D. H. Davison, *Map of Franklin County, Pennsylvania* (1858); 1798 Federal Direct Tax Records for Chambersburg, Franklin Township, Franklin County, Schedule A, Entry for Ludwick Denig, National Archives, Washington, D.C. (microfilm, Center for Historic Architecture and Design, University of Delaware, Newark, Del.). For a house worth only $125,

see the entry for Josiah Crawford's property on Market Street in Chambersburg.

86. 1798 Federal Direct Tax Records for Rapho Township, Lancaster County, Schedule A, Entry for Isaac Wenger. Isaac Wenger, or more likely his father, Michael Wenger, was the owner of the Wenger house at the time it was built. Although their religious affiliation is not certain, Isaac was listed as a nonassociator in 1777 (microfilm, Pennsylvania Historical and Museum Commission, Lancaster County, Pennsylvania Tax Records, 1748–1855, Rapho Township, 1751–1825, Pos. 23, Lancaster County Historical Society, Lancaster, Pa.), and Michael's nephew Martin Wenger was a Mennonite deacon. Diane Wenger, e-mail message to author, June 22, 2004; Abigail Wenger, e-mail message to author, August 6, 2004; Daniel Wenger, e-mail message to author, October 11, 2004. Significant information on the Wenger family can be found on the DLW Database at RootsWeb.com.

87. Ruth, *The Earth Is the Lord's,* 294; *Lancaster County Architecture,* 54; Probate Inventory, Abraham Landis (1790), Lancaster County Historical Society, Lancaster, Pa.

88. Muhlenberg, *The Journals of Henry Melchior Muhlenberg,* 1:101, 280–81.

89. Michel-Guillaume Jean de Crèvecoeur, *Crèvecoeur's Eighteenth-Century Travels in Pennsylvania and New York,* trans. and ed. Percy G. Adams (Lexington: University of Kentucky Press, 1961), xviii–xx, 47.

90. I. Daniel Rupp, *History of Lancaster County, to which is Prefixed a Brief Sketch of the Early History of Pennsylvania* (1844; reprint, Spartanburg, S.C.: Reprint Company for the Pennsylvania Reprint Society and Southwest Pennsylvania Genealogical Services, 1984), 286–87; Friesen, *A Modest Mennonite Home,* 49–51; 1798 Federal Direct Tax Records for Lampeter Township, Lancaster County, Schedule A, Entries for the Miley Family, National Archives, Washington, D.C. (microfilm, Center for Historic Architecture and Design, University of Delaware, Newark, Del.).

91. Rupp, *History of Lancaster County,* 286–87.

92. Rupp, *History of Lancaster County,* plate between pp. 286 and 287; Ruth, *The Earth Is the Lord's,* 335–37, 417–19; Margaret C. Reynolds, "A Chronicle in Stone and Wood: The Magdalena House and the River Brethren," *Pennsylvania Mennonite Heritage* 16, no. 3 (July 1993): 2–10.

93. Clarke Hess, *Mennonite Arts* (Atglen, Pa.: Schiffer Publishing, 2002), 22.

94. Although Martin Mylin's birth date is not known, he is generally believed to have been thirty-six years old when he died in 1751 (Mylin family file, Lancaster County Historical Society).

95. Ruth, *The Earth Is the Lord's,* 252–54, 417–19, 428–29.

96. Herman, "Eighteenth-Century Quaker Houses," 189, 201, 211.

Chapter 5

1. Alexander Hamilton, *Hamilton's Itinerarium, Being a Narrative of a Journey from Annapolis, Maryland Through Delaware, Pennsylvania, New York, New Jersey, Connecticut, Rhode Island, Massachusetts and New Hampshire from May to September, 1744* (Saint Louis, Mo.:

William K. Bixby, 1907), 22.

2. François Alexandre-Frédéric, duc de La Rochefoucauld Liancourt, *Travels Through the United States of North America, the Country of the Iroquois, and Upper Canada, in the Years 1795, 1796, and 1797; With an Authentic Account of Lower Canada* (London: R. Phillips, 1799), 2:672.

3. Stuart Blumin, in describing the characteristics of the middling sort in eighteenth-century urban America, also found the nature of work to be especially important by the end of the century. Mechanics, or those who were engaged in manual labor, were limited in their social mobility. See Stuart M. Blumin, *The Emergence of the Middle Class: Social Experience in the American City, 1760–1900* (Cambridge: Cambridge University Press, 1989), 30–31.

4. See, for example, Théophile Cazenove, *Cazenove Journal, 1794: A Record of the Journey of Theophile Cazenove Through New Jersey and Pennsylvania,* ed. Rayner Wickersham Kelsey (Haverford, Pa.: The Pennsylvania History Press, 1922), 34–35, 46–47, 83–85; Johann David Schöpf, *Travels in the Confederation, 1783–1784,* trans. and ed. Alfred J. Morrison (Philadelphia: William J. Campbell, 1911), 1:103–6; and La Rochefoucauld Liancourt, *Travels Through the United States,* 2:391–92.

5. See, for example, Benjamin Rush, "An Account of the Manners of the German Inhabitants of Pennsylvania," *Columbian Magazine,* January 1789, 22–25; Jacques-Pierre Brissot de Warville, *New Travels in the United States of America Performed in 1788* (Dublin: W. Corbet, 1792), 334–35, 338. Specifically on the use of strong liquors, see Rush, "An Account of the Manners of the German Inhabitants of Pennsylvania," 24; Brissot, *New Travels in the United States of America Performed in 1788,* 338; Jedidiah Morse, *The American Geography; or, a View of the Present Situation of the United States of America* (Elizabethtown, [N.J.]: Shepard Kollock, 1789), 313.

6. R. Martin Keen, "Community and Material Culture Among Lancaster Mennonites: Hans Hess from 1717 to 1733," *Pennsylvania Mennonite Heritage* (January 1990): 5.

7. Max Weber, "The Origins of Ethnic Groups," in *Ethnicity,* ed. John Hutchinson and Anthony D. Smith (New York: Oxford University Press, 1996), 35; George DeVos, "Ethnic Pluralism," in *Ethnic Identity: Cultural Continuities and Change,* ed. George DeVos and Lola Romanucci-Ross (Palo Alto, Calif.: Mayfield Publishing, 1975), 16; Paul R. Brass, "Ethnic Groups and Ethnic Identity Formation," in *Ethnicity,* 86–89.

8. Jack L. Lindsey et al., *Worldly Goods: The Arts of Early Pennsylvania, 1680–1758* (Philadelphia: Philadelphia Museum of Art, 1999), 211; Donald M. Herr, *Pewter in Pennsylvania German Churches* (Birdsboro, Pa.: Pennsylvania German Society, 1995), 46–49. The inscription was printed with slight variation on the three pieces. On the flagon: "vor die re / formirte / gemeine de / kirch in pei / taunschip / anno 1757"; on the basin: "vor die reformirte gemeine der krch / in peicks town ship / 1757"; on the plate: "vor de reformirte gemeine de kirch in peicks taunschip chester county anno 1757."

9. Benno Forman, "German Influences in Pennsylvania Furniture," in *Arts of the Pennsylvania Germans,* ed. Scott T. Swank et al. (New York: W. W. Norton for the Henry Francis du Pont Winterthur Museum, 1983), 144–46; Esther S. Fraser, "Pennsylvania German

Dower Chests," part 1, *The Magazine Antiques* 11, no. 2 (February 1927), 121, and part 3, *The Magazine Antiques* 11, no. 6 (June 1927), 474–75. The trend of dual shop labels in German and English was noted in Philadelphia by Henry Wansey. He observed, "A great many Germans settled at Philadelphia; on the signs over their shop doors they have their names and trades expressed both in English and German text, viz. Alleyne Innis, Hat Maker. *Alleyne Innis, Huth Maker*" (*An Excursion to the United States of North America, in the Summer of 1794* [Salisbury, England: J. Easton, 1798], 173–74).

10. In his study of Peter Ranck, who was also a member of the so-called "Jonestown School" of cabinetmakers and decorators, Stephen Perkins finds that Ranck's customers, while predominantly German, also included people with English, Scots-Irish, and French surnames. Perkins notes that the Rancks were actually French Huguenots who fled to the Palatinate before traveling to America. Stephen James Perkins, "Command You Me from Play Every Minute of the Day" (M.A. thesis, Winterthur Program in Early American Culture, University of Delaware, 2001), 34, 54, appendix C.

11. See, for example, Stephanie Grauman Wolf, *Urban Village: Population, Community, and Family Structure in Germantown, Pennsylvania, 1683–1800* (Princeton: Princeton University Press, 1976), 127–153. Dell Upton had argued that most scholars adhere to "a view of ethnic values and ethnic practices as a static cultural system." Because those studying ethnic groups are conditioned to expect constancy, when they view change they turn to interpretations based on acculturation. See Dell Upton, "Ethnicity, Authenticity, and Invented Traditions," *Historical Archaeology* 30, no. 2 (1996): 1–2.

12. Elizabeth Johns, "Science, Art, and Literature in Federal America: Their Prospects in the Republic," in *Everyday Life in the Early Republic,* ed. Catherine E. Hutchins (Winterthur, Del.: Henry Francis du Pont Winterthur Museum, 1994), 348–50; Gary B. Nash, *The Urban Crucible: The Northern Seaports and the Origins of the American Revolution,* abridged ed. (Cambridge, Mass.: Harvard University Press, 1979), 246–47.

13. Thomas Cooper, *Some Information Respecting America,* 2nd ed. (London, 1795), 74; Alexander Graydon, *Memoirs of a Life, Chiefly Passed in Pennsylvania, Within the Last Sixty Years; With Occasional Remarks Upon the General Occurrences, Character and Spirit of That Eventful Period* (Harrisburg, Pa.: John Wyeth, 1811), 157–58.

14. Kevin M. Sweeney, "High-Style Vernacular: Lifestyles of the Colonial Elite," in *Of Consuming Interests: The Style of Life in the Eighteenth Century,* ed. Cary Carson, Ronald Hoffman, and Peter J. Albert (Charlottesville: University Press of Virginia for the United States Capitol Historical Society, 1994), 3–4; Richard L. Bushman, *The Refinement of America: Persons, Houses, Cities* (New York: Alfred A. Knopf, 1992), 103–22, especially 112. On New England, see Kevin M. Sweeney, "Furniture and the Domestic Environment in Wethersfield, Connecticut," in *Material Life in America, 1600–1860,* 266. On the Chesapeake, see Rhys Isaac, *The Transformation of Virginia, 1740–1790* (Chapel Hill: University of North Carolina Press, 1982), 73, and Lois Green Carr and Lorena S. Walsh, "Changing Lifestyles and Consumer Behavior in the Colonial Chesapeake," in *Of Consuming Interests,* 61, 65–66. On the Delaware Valley, see Bernard

Herman, *Architecture and Rural Life in Central Delaware, 1700–1900* (Knoxville: University of Tennessee Press, 1987), 39–41, and Jack Michel, "'In a Manner and Fashion Suitable to Their Degree': A Preliminary Investigation of the Material Culture of Early Rural Pennsylvania," *Working Papers from the Regional Economic History Research Center* 5, no. 1 (1981): 19, 22, 47, 51, 75.

15. Sweeney, "High-Style Vernacular," 5–8, 17–18, 21–22; Abbott Lowell Cummings, "Inside the Massachusetts House," in *Common Places: Readings in American Vernacular Architecture,* ed. Dell Upton and John Michael Vlach (Athens: University of Georgia Press, 1986), 225; Margaretta M. Lovell, "'Such Furniture as Will Be Most Profitable': The Business of Cabinetmaking in Eighteenth-Century Newport," *Winterthur Portfolio* 26, no. 1 (Spring 1991): 30; Carr and Walsh, "Changing Lifestyles and Consumer Behavior," 65–67; Cary Carson, "The Consumer Revolution in Colonial British America: Why Demand?" in *Of Consuming Interests,* 497; Bushman, *The Refinement of America,* 18–19.

16. *South Carolina Gazette,* July 8, 1771, as quoted in Arlene Palmer Schwind, "Pennsylvania German Glass," in *Arts of the Pennsylvania Germans,* 203. On the promotion of domestic manufacturing, including glass making, in the 1760s, see T. H. Breen, *The Marketplace of Revolution: How Consumer Politics Shaped American Independence* (New York: Oxford University Press, 2004), 212–13, 242.

17. Jacques-Pierre Brissot de Warville, *New Travels in the United States of America Performed in 1788* (Dublin: W. Corbet, 1792), 338; Cazenove, *Cazenove Journal,* 74. From the passage in Brissot, it is difficult to tell whether the author intended his comments to refer to Gotthilf Henry Ernest Muhlenberg, the first president of Franklin College in Lancaster, or to his brother Frederick Augustus Conrad Muhlenberg, the first speaker of the United States House of Representatives.

18. Benjamin Franklin, *Observations on Smoky Chimneys, Their Causes and Cure; With Considerations on Fuel and Stoves* (London: I. and J. Taylor, 1793), 48–49; Cazenove, *Cazenove Journal,* 83. On the entry-kitchen house as the predominant German house type, see Edward Chappell, "Germans and Swiss," in *America's Architectural Roots: Ethnic Groups that Built America,* ed. Dell Upton (Washington, D.C.: Preservation Press, 1986), 68, and Beatrice Garvan and Charles Hummel, *The Pennsylvania Germans: A Celebration of Their Arts, 1683–1850* (Philadelphia: Philadelphia Museum of Art, 1982), 145.

19. Philip E. Pendleton, *Oley Valley Heritage: The Colonial Years, 1700–1775* (Birdsboro, Pa.: Pennsylvania German Society; Oley, Pa.: Oley Valley Heritage Association, 1994), 76–79; Pendleton, "Oley Valley Tour," in *Guidebook for the Vernacular Architecture Forum Annual Conference: Architecture and Landscape of the Pennsylvania Germans, May 12–16, 2004, Harrisburg, Pennsylvania* (n.p.: Vernacular Architecture Forum, 2004), 76–79.

20. Charles Bergengren, "Pennsylvania German House Forms," in *Guidebook for the Vernacular Architecture Forum Annual Conference,* 32–35; Hagenbuch, Building Contract, Joseph Downs Collection of Manuscripts and Printed Ephemera, Doc. 250, Winterthur Museum, Garden and Library, Winterthur, Del. In his work on the antecedents to Pennsylvania German houses, William Woys Weaver includes a

remark by twentieth-century European scholar Richard Weiss, "*Ohne Ofen, keine Stube, ohne Stube, keine Häuslichkeit* [No stove, no *Stube*; no *Stube*, no home]." It appears that this adage did not hold true in an American context ("The Pennsylvania German House: European Antecedents and New World Forms," *Winterthur Portfolio* 21, no. 4 [Winter 1986]: 257).

21. Both Gabrielle Lanier and Charles Bergengren have used the term "creolized" to describe buildings of this type. See Gabrielle M. Lanier, *The Delaware Valley in the Early Republic: Architecture, Landscape, and Regional Identity* (Baltimore: Johns Hopkins University Press, 2005), 35–36, 65; Bergengren, "House Forms," 23, 32, 35, 38.

22. Dell Hymes, "Preface," in *Pidginization and Creolization of Languages,* ed. Dell Hymes (Cambridge: Cambridge University Press, 1971), 3; David Decamp, "Introduction: The Study of Pidgin and Creole Languages," in *Pidginization and Creolization of Languages,* 15–16; Mervyn C. Alleyne, "Acculturation and the Cultural Matrix of Creolization," in *Piginization and Creolization of Languages,* 169; Jay D. Edwards, "French," in *Architectural Roots: Ethnic Groups that Built America,* ed. Dell Upton (Washington, D.C.: Preservation Press, 1986), 62; Jay D. Edwards, "Architectural Creolization: The Meaning of Colonial Architecture," in *Architectural Anthropology,* ed. Mari-Jose Amerlinck (Westport, Conn.: Greenwood Publishing, 2001); Bergengren, "House Forms," 23.

23. Ira Berlin, "From Creole to African: Atlantic Creoles and the Origins of African-American Society in Mainland North America," *William and Mary Quarterly,* 3rd series, 53, no. 2 (April 1996): 253–54.

24. Robert F. Ensminger, *The Pennsylvania Barn: Its Origin, Evolution, and Distribution in North America* (Baltimore: Johns Hopkins University Press, 1992), 10, 15–16, 89, 109, 128–29, 144–46.

25. Ensminger, *The Pennsylvania Barn,* 107–8.

26. This is a markedly different interpretation from the one offered in the exhibition catalogue *American Rococo.* Commenting on Stiegel's use of the Rococo style, its authors conclude, "Clearly, he did so in an effort to attract the Philadelphia gentry to a type of stove previously intended for Pennsylvanians of German origin" (Morrison H. Heckscher and Leslie Greene Bowman, *American Rococo, 1750–1775: Elegance in Ornament* [New York: Metropolitan Museum of Art], 227). Reading between the lines, it appears that the authors considered all gentlefolk to be English in background.

27. Georg Caspar Erasmus, *Seulen-Buch Oder Bründlicher Bericht von der Fünff Ordnungen der Architectur-Kunst wie solche von Marco Vitruvio, Jacobo Barrozzio, Hans Blumen C. und Andern* (Nürnberg, 1688); Henry Glassie, *Folk Housing in Middle Virginia* (Knoxville: University of Tennessee Press, 1975), 88–89; Bushman, *The Refinement of America,* 101.

28. Cynthia Falk, "Symbols of Assimilation or Status? The Meanings of Eighteenth-Century Houses in Coventry Township, Chester County, Pennsylvania," *Winterthur Portfolio* 33, nos. 2/3 (Summer/Autumn 1998): 128–30, 132–33.

29. Mark Reinberger, "Belmont: The Bourgeois Villa in Eighteenth Century Philadelphia," *ARRIS: Journal of the Southeast Chapter of the Society of Architectural Historians* 9 (1998): 23, 25, 28, 29.

30. Peter Ranck Account Book, 1794–1817, Joseph Downs Collection of Manuscripts and Printed Ephemera, Doc. 708, Winterthur Museum, Garden and Library, Winterthur, Del.; Abraham Overholt and Peter Ranck, *The Accounts of Two Pennsylvania German Furniture Makers: Abraham Overholt, Bucks County, 1790–1833, and Peter Ranck, Lebanon County, 1794–1817,* trans. and ed. Alan G. Keyser, Larry M. Neff, and Frederick S. Weiser (Breinigsville, Pa.: Pennsylvania German Society, 1978), 45, 47, 71, 131; Forman, "German Influences in Pennsylvania Furniture," 59; Perkins, "Command You Me from Play," 17–18, 55–56.

31. On the commoditization of all things Amish, see David Walbert, *Garden Spot: Lancaster County, the Old Order Amish, and the Selling of Rural America* (Oxford: Oxford University Press, 2002), 13, 29, 32, 67–100 113–14, and David Weaver-Zercher, *The Amish in the American Imagination* (Baltimore: Johns Hopkins University Press, 2001), 82–121. In the post–World War II period, Weaver-Zercher aptly describes the emphasis on the Amish as part of the "simple life industry" (86).

32. See www.dutchwonderland.com (accessed June 9, 2005) and http://www.discoverlancaster.com/ (accessed January 8, 2007).

33. Beatrice Garvan, *The Pennsylvania German Collection* (Philadelphia: Philadelphia Museum of Art, 1982), ix.

34. Garvan, *The Pennsylvania German Collection,* xi–xiii; quotation from p. xiii.

35. Jacob Duché, *Caspipina's Letters; Containing Observations on a Variety of Subjects* (Bath, 1774; reprint, London: R. Crutt Well, 1777), as transcribed in Felix Reichman and Eugene A. Doll, *Ephrata as Seen by Contemporaries* (Allentown, Pa.: Schlechter's for the Pennsylvania German Folklore Society, 1953), 99.

36. The subject of identity has recently gained significant attention in the museum field. See Jay Rounds, "Doing Identity Work in Museums," *Curator* 49, no. 2 (April 2006): 133–50, and John H. Falk, "An Identity-Centered Approach to Understanding Museum Learning," *Curator* 49, no. 2 (April 2006): 151–66.

Appendix A

1. Benjamin Rush, *An Account of the Manners of the German Inhabitants of Pennsylvania Written in 1789, by Benjamin Rush, M.D. Notes Added by Prof. I. Daniel Rupp* (Philadelphia: Samuel P. Town, 1875).

Appendix B

1. Jacques-Pierre Brissot de Warville, *New Travels in the United States of America Performed in 1788* (Dublin: W. Corbet, 1792). I viewed editions of this text at the Winterthur Library, Cornell, and the Library of Congress. The Library of Congress edition can be accessed online at American Memory. For a modern translation of the French text, see Jacques-Pierre Brissot de Warville, *New Travels in the United States of America, 1788,* ed. Durand Echeverria, trans. Mara Soceanu Vamos and Durand Echeverria (Cambridge, Mass.: Harvard University Press, 1964).

Index

Page numbers in *italics* indicate illustrations.

Pennsylvania German History and Culture Series, Number 9

Publications of the Pennsylvania German Society, Volume 42